Take Another Step With Jesus:
Devotional Messages for the Growing Christian

Lynn (Jordan) Adams
Edited by: Lisa Lickel

Printed in the United States of America
ISBN - 13: 978-1470127398
ISBN – 10: 1470127393

This book is dedicated first to God.
Father, You have given me messages for encouraging Your people to know You better. May this work accomplish all that You desire, for the glory of Your Name.
I also want to recognize my husband Bart, without whose support I never would have completed the project. I thank my parents, and friends Lois, Lori, Mark, and many others who have encouraged me along the way and carried me in prayer.

Lynn Adams lives in northern Michigan with her husband, Rev. Bart Adams, and two children. She left a career as a school psychologist to be a stay-at-home Mom. She is involved in ministry to children, youth, women, and people who are grieving. She is active in school and community activities. Lynn also serves as helpmate to her husband in leading missions trips, marriage retreats, and small group Bible study.
Contact her at: llynnadams@gmail.com

Contents

Introduction

In late 2004 I felt led of the Spirit to encourage women in our church to come alongside those who were newer to Christianity and help them walk in faith (based on Titus 2:4). I suggested that several of us write out lessons God had taught us and ways that he had worked in our lives, as a testimony to others. I offered to write up a couple of these messages as an example while others were thinking of what to share. Always the sophisticated type, I hung a file folder on the bulletin board and put a few copies of each week's message inside for young women seeking to grow in their Christian walk. Three other women each wrote a couple of devotionals, but it became clear that this was God's call for me more than for them. Once started, I just kept writing these messages week after week. They were well-received and seven years later I am still writing weekly devotional messages to encourage people (both men and women) to grow closer to the Savior.

During these years, I have learned a lesson, like Joshua. Just before Moses died, God appointed Joshua as the new leader of Israel. God used him to lead the people across the Jordan River at flood stage and to defeat Jericho. Joshua knew what he was supposed to do – conquer the Promised Land and wipe out the wicked people groups that lived there. He knew God was with them, so he went forward. After the victory at Jericho he turned toward the smaller town of Ai. He sent only part of his army against them, but they were soundly defeated. Joshua did not know that Achan had sinned, and was thus blocking God's blessing. He apparently did not seek God's help and direction for attacking Ai as he had for routing Jericho. Joshua learned that he needed to be in continual communication with Almighty God, who would then lead him step by step, day by day.

I have learned the same is true with writing devotionals. Even though I know God wants me to write them each week, I cannot run ahead of him and decide what to say or how to say it. I need to wait for him to show me what to say. I usually email these devotional messages on Saturday evening. Some weeks God will tell me on Sunday or Monday what to say for the following week.

Sometimes he shows me in my personal worship time during the week. There are times, however, when it is Saturday evening and I still don't know what to write. Early on I used to try to write something on my own, something from Scripture that I thought people might need to hear. It never worked well and I could not get the message to flow. I eventually learned to say, "Lord, if you don't give me a clear message, I am not going to write anything this week. I will only say that which you give me to say." Week after week, year after year he has given me messages of exhortation for his people. Through those weeks he has taught me to listen to his Spirit and to wait on him. As God said to Jeremiah, so he has said to my spirit, "Write in a book all the words I have spoken to you" (Jeremiah 30:2). It is my prayer that these thoughts will encourage you to know and love him more. Take another step with Jesus, growing and blossoming in the new life he has made available to you. The messages are loosely divided into seasons, according to the time period in which they were written.

Each of the following devotionals speaks to the new life believers learn to live. I invite you to grab a cup of tea or coffee, and find a quiet place for fifteen minutes. Have your Bible ready and an attitude of wonder and respect as you enter the presence of the Lord, who welcomes you.

Spring

Spring is a time of hope, a season of change. Those of us in cold climates rejoice when the days get longer and the snow melts away. The wonder of spring, however, is not just the absence of winter's cold. Even before the last piles of snow fade away, bright green grass and tender daffodils force their way through the muted browns and grays that fall left behind. Bare branches remind us that something is missing. The beauty of spring is new or renewed life. Tiny buds form on branches. Hardy flower stems push up through the thawing earth. New stalks of green grass advance and conquer the brown. The animal kingdom abounds with young. Spring is the season of new life, and it is wonderful.

Every life needs to experience a spiritual springtime. Sinners by birth, we are dying even as we live. When an individual comes to know Jesus, a beautiful transformation begins. Christian life is not just the absence of bad habits, any more than spring is just the absence of snow. Rather, Jesus changes a life so completely that it is like a new birth. Each person who becomes a child of God becomes a new creation (2 Corinthians 5:17). This teaching is reiterated throughout the New Testament (see Acts 5:30, Romans 6:4, Ephesians 4:24, Colossians 3:10, 1 Peter 1:3). The process takes time and effort. Becoming more and more like Jesus, our perfect example, is something we as believers strive toward until the day we die. God works to help us change our attitudes, our values and priorities, our perspectives, bringing them into line with his own.

Read God's Word

"Faith will not grow unless you read the Word." When I first heard my Dad make this statement, I thought he was overstating things. Now I am not so sure. Let's consider the spiritual discipline of reading the Bible. The Bible is a collection of books, in which God reveals himself to humans. It is the very Word of God, given to individuals to write down, so that we may know God. Through it we learn what God expects, what pleases and displeases him, and how he views the world he created. How many of us read our Bibles regularly?

Since the Bible is a collection of books, spanning several hundred years and several genres of literature, it may be difficult to decide where to begin reading. One strategy is to start at the beginning and read to the end as you would with a novel. It is helpful, though, to understand that the Bible is not written chronologically. Some events are referred to multiple times by different authors, from different perspectives. The first section of the Bible, The Old Testament, starts with an account of how God created the world, and describes his interaction with various people over a period of several hundred years. There is particular emphasis on the nation of Israel. The Old Testament teaches about sin (choices that are in direct disobedience to God) and the need for a perfect sacrifice. It includes prophesies about the Savior who would come – all of which were fulfilled in the life of Jesus.

Another method for reading the Bible is to just let it fall open and read whatever you see. It is possible to find nuggets of truth and encouragement this way, but the reader misses the opportunity to see the big picture of God's revelation in the book as a whole. In order to know God as fully as a human can know the Almighty, All-Powerful Creator, we need to study all that he has given us in His Word. New believers are often encouraged to start reading in the New Testament, which comprises approximately the last one-third of the Bible. The first four books of the New Testament (known as the Gospels of Matthew, Mark, Luke, and John) share accounts of Jesus' life on earth. They describe his teaching and his miracles, his death on the cross and his resurrection. Jesus instructed people about how God wanted them to live. The rest of the New Testament describes the development of the Christian church and instructions on living a godly life. To develop a mature faith, believers must seek to understand who God is and how he relates to his creation. One effective way to accomplish this is through reading and studying His Word.

As with everything, God looks at a person's heart and the motivation, rather than just the action. If you are motivated by a desire to know him, rather than by somebody telling you to read the Bible, God will bless you and help you to grow in relationship with him. As you read, he will help specific passages to catch your attention, helping you to understand a little more of what God is like. He longs for people to have hearts that long to know him and honor him.

In order to know God, we must read the whole book that he has given us. Through reading about people and their choices (both good and bad), we understand more of God's character and how he relates to people. We see his faithfulness in spite of people, and it helps our faith to grow. Faith is what sustains us in the hard times – which are guaranteed to come to all of us. Knowing how God has come through for individuals since the dawn of time will help you to hold onto faith that he will also come through for you.

I encourage you, before you start each day, to ask the Holy Spirit to help you understand as you read God's Word. This is your spiritual food. When you miss a day (as we all do some times), or a week, or a month, just pick up where you left off and start reading again. I have found that I am far more likely to focus on what I am reading and remember it later if I write down a sentence or two about the passage. I may write a question I have, or part of a verse that caught my attention, or what I can learn from that chapter.

Friend, it is my prayer that each of us be able to say with Job, "I have treasured the words of [God's] mouth more than my daily bread" (Job 23:12).

The God Who Heals Me

If you have not read the book of Ruth lately, I encourage you to read this short Bible book. It is a narrative about loyalty and about how God brings sweet from bitter experiences. Naomi and her two daughters-in-law, Orpah, and Ruth planned on longer marriages, with children and grandchildren to bring laughter. Yet, within ten years all three were widows. It was a very dark time in their lives. Naomi changed her name to Mara, which means bitter, saying, "I went away full, but the Lord has brought me back empty."

Can you relate to these hurting women? Have your castles and dreams turned to ashes? Maybe your health, your marriage, or your career is not as great as you had hoped it would be. Maybe pain and disillusionment make the future look bleak. Maybe in the recesses of your mind you have changed you name to *bitter*, or *broken*, or *worthless*.

Let us shift our focus from names for ourselves to names for our Lord. Nathan Stone, in *Names Of God*[1] refers to the experience of the Israelites in the desert (Exodus 15). Great rejoicing after the deliverance through the Red Sea turned to grumbling and complaining when they needed water. They eventually found water at Marah but it was so bitter as to be undrinkable. God told Moses to cast a branch into the water and the water became sweet. God used this miracle to reveal a new part of his character to the people, expressed in the name, Jehovah-rophe, which means "God heals."

Take courage, believer. God is not dead. He is not powerless, nor has he stopped caring for you. As you grieve over the pain of unmet expectations, let go of your own dreams for your life and embrace his dreams. In the second half of the book of Ruth, God brings new love, new family, new joy and hope and purpose. Ruth, a foreigner from Moab, actually becomes the great grandmother of David – Israel's greatest king. She is even in the lineage of Jesus! God's plans for her were much bigger and richer than she ever dreamed.

Friend, God has great plans for your life too, but I think I can safely guarantee that they do not perfectly match the plans you have made. An all-powerful God with infinite wisdom is better at planning your life than you are – so let him. He said, "For my thoughts are not your thoughts, neither are your ways my ways," declares the Lord. "As the heavens are higher than the earth, so are my ways higher than your ways, and my thoughts than your thoughts" (Is. 55:8-9). Hold on to him by choosing to have faith in the hard times. Pray, believing that God hears, God cares, and God will help you. He alone can bring good from terrible circumstances.

Am I a "Judas"?

I – AM – THAT . . . . villain!?" In reading the story of Easter and Good Friday I often wonder about Judas. What was he thinking? He spent many months, probably a couple of years, walking day after day alongside the Son of God. He saw the power and goodness of God Incarnate! How could he sell Jesus for pittance? In my self-righteousness I want to believe that I would never do that, but I have.

As a young, single, professional I was sincere in my desire to serve God and live as a witness for him. I was trying to learn to know God better and to encourage others to do the same. One day at work I lost my temper with an elementary school principal. He had failed to attend a scheduled meeting, and then questioned my conclusions. Rather than patiently explaining, I snapped at him for missing the meeting and left in a huff. Right or wrong, he was my supervisor and I should have shown him respect, but instead I was short and unprofessional toward him. Neither that principal, nor the office secretary saw a good representation of Jesus in my life. God definitely would have been better off without me on his team that day. Even though I had been walking close to the Savior, I betrayed him. Have you done the same? Perhaps you started to walk with Christ but kept it hidden from friends, even laughed at those 'Jesus freaks.' Rather than receiving 30 pieces of silver you were rewarded with acceptance in the crowd – but it's not so different from Judas, is it?

Representing Christ is a heavy responsibility. People make decisions about what God is like, and about whether to seek him, based on our example. What happens when we "blow it"? Perhaps at work or a sporting event or with extended family members you, like me, have betrayed the God you claim to represent. The crucial question is "What do we do afterward?" When a Christian dishonors God's reputation, the first step is to repent. I need to start by praying, "Father, please forgive me for I have sinned. Please do not let that person reject you because of what he/she has seen in me today." Then I must humble myself and take steps toward reconciliation. That does not mean taking all the blame for the confrontation, but rather, taking ownership of my own wrong actions and attitudes. When I called that principal the following day, I apologized for not acting in a way that would honor God. It was a tough phone call to make, but I needed to be sure my actions did not diminish this man's view of God.

We often see Judas as the most unforgiveable character in the Easter story. They all should have known better, but Judas knew Jesus better than the other "bad guys." If anyone was without excuse, it was Judas. How painful it is then, to admit that he and I have a lot in common. I too have betrayed the Savior. I have represented him as a lucky charm rather than as a life-changer. I have shown people an unattractive picture of what it means to be a child of God. The only question left is, what will I do now? Judas hanged himself, but he didn't have to. Jesus offered forgiveness. He offers the same to you and to me. If we don't accept it, Satan wins.

Friend, let us determine today to shine the light of Jesus brightly. When we have betrayed him, let us humble ourselves and seek forgiveness from the people before whom we have fallen. Truthfully, seeing that humble, repentant spirit may be a louder, clearer call to Christ than anything else a Christian could do or say. To God be all the glory. May you be blessed as you seek to draw near to him.

A Capstone

In February 2010, I, along with five others, had the privilege of traveling to Ireland to spend a week with missionary friends. In the cities and countryside, many old churches and cathedrals are falling apart. It is illegal to tear these buildings down, so they are left to deteriorate over time. In many cases the roof was destroyed in battle, but the walls, minus doors or gates, still stand. Today the walls serve no purpose, engulfed and upstaged by newer buildings.

Newgrange is a remarkable ancient site, estimated to be 5,000 years old. Its builders placed mammoth boulders in overlapping layers to form a cave of sorts, with short tunnels in roughly the shape of a cross. Decorative symbols were carved on some of the stones. The huge slabs of rock were transported to this site, and to others like it in the area. Researchers believe, with 300 workers, it would have taken at least 20 years to build the structure. The entrance and main passageway is 19 meters long. From the center, looking up about 6 meters, visitors can see the huge boulders, with each layer overlapping to leave a smaller opening at the top. The very top stone, the capstone, is estimated to weigh roughly 6 tons. Grass covers the exterior of the mound. Because of the placement of the capstone, and the grooves cut into the top side of each boulder, the interior is completely water tight. There is no evidence of water inside over the past 5,000 years. Apparently one of the uses was as a burial site for cremated remains. Historians are not sure what other uses it may have had.

In Ireland, as in America, the outward appearance of many people is decidedly Christian. They are polite, kind, helpful, and may even go to church. However, just like the roofless skeletal remains of ancient churches, humans with no internal connection to the Savior are not a part of Christ, who serves as the head of his church. No matter how good a person may seem to us, Jesus clearly tells us that the only way to draw near to God is through him (John 14:6).

A church is far more than a building. The people of God make up his church. Jesus is the capstone of Christianity. The capstone is the finishing piece, the One who makes the process complete. In the book of Acts, Peter spoke of Jesus, saying he is "The stone you builders rejected, which has become the capstone. Salvation is found in no one else, for there is no other name under heaven given to men by which we must be saved" (4:11-12). The capstone helps to shield everything under it from destructive forces. The Christian church is an organism (not an organization) made up of individuals who have come to God through Jesus Christ.

Friend, is Jesus your capstone today? Have you asked him to forgive your sins and be Lord over all of your life? Under his Lordship there is protection from the enemy. Although the attacks still come, we abide in peace and hope because of the promises of our Savior. We have victory over fear, despair, addictions, and loneliness as we walk every day connected to the All-Powerful One. May we, his church, be a beautiful shining light of holiness in the world around us, so that others may come to know him as Lord and Savior.

The Holy Spirit as a Power Tool

Several months after Hurricane Katrina devastated the south in August 2005, I was part of a rebuilding team sent to Mississippi. Although we were shocked at the extent of the devastation, we heard testimony of so many answers to prayer that we couldn't help but be encouraged. It is great to know that no matter how big the storm, God is in control!

Judges 6:14-16 says, "The Lord turned to him and said, 'Go in the strength you have and save Israel out of Midian's hand. Am I not sending you?' 'But Lord,' Gideon asked, 'how can I save Israel? My clan is the weakest in Manasseh, and I am the least in my family.' The Lord answered, "I will be with you, and you will strike down all the Midianites together.'" In this passage, God commissioned Gideon as a rebuilder of a splintered nation. He was a follower, not a leader, and planning to stay that way. That was how many of us felt about going to Mississippi. There was rebuilding and/or repair work happening on every street for miles around. Different volunteers came from different places week after week. Thousands of willing volunteers were doing work they may or may not have been qualified to do - without ever meeting the people who worked on these buildings before them. Somehow, our great big God would take the flawed little pieces from a few dozen people and make a home. Logically, it should have been an uncoordinated mess, yet God brought it together for the glory of his Name.

Although we had opportunity to spend a considerable amount of time in the community helping with homes, our primary project was building an addition to the church (replacing the modular destroyed by Katrina). There is nothing like using hand tools to help a person appreciate power tools. When my arm was too tired to drive any more nails through plywood into studs, God shared the following thought with me. As Christians we strive and struggle to do right and live according to Scripture. We fall often. It is like trying to drive a 16 penny nail into a 2"x 6" plate using an 8 oz. hammer. It is a very difficult and discouraging process. My nails just kept popping back out of the wood. I made progress, but it was painfully slow. This is like trying to live the Christian life without the power of the Holy Spirit.

One of the most beautiful gifts the Lord gives his children is the opportunity to be filled with the Holy Spirit. For some this is a quick, definite experience. For many others it is a process that takes place over a period of time. Being filled with the Holy Spirit is like using a nail gun to do the same job you were doing with a little hammer. It enables us to use his power rather than our own. What a relief. It requires skill and practice to learn to listen to his voice. Spirit-filled Christians still make errors, but the work is so much more efficient and less frustrating.

Friend, if you find yourself exhausted from trying to live out your faith in your own strength, I invite you to begin asking God to fill you with his Spirit. It is his desire for each of us to live in constant communion with the One who comforts, counsels, and convicts. As he helped Gideon, so he will help us, if we ask.

Steps Leading Nowhere

For many weeks after returning home from Mississippi, I couldn't stop thinking about the massive destruction we had seen. One picture kept flashing through my mind. Where homes used to stand, all that remained were steps. Without any "before" pictures, we could only guess what the buildings had looked like and what kinds of families lived there. They were left with stone or concrete steps leading nowhere.

After the death of Joshua, the Israelites did not stay true to their God, so he repeatedly allowed them to be oppressed by their enemies in order to get them to turn back to him. When they cried out to God in repentance, he would raise up a judge to lead them to deliverance. Then the whole cycle would repeat. Throughout this time when many hearts were not fully devoted to the Lord, some still talked about God as if they knew him, but they did not. For example, a mother learned that her son had stolen silver from her. When he returned it she said, "I solemnly consecrate my silver to the Lord for my son to make a carved image and a cast idol" (Judges 17:3). God had clearly stated in the second commandment that his people were not to make "An idol in the form of anything in heaven above or on the earth beneath or in the waters below. You shall not bow down to them or worship them; for I, the Lord your God am a jealous God . . ." (Exodus 20:4,5). Yet, this woman and her son made an idol of silver they said was consecrated to the Lord. They set it up in their home and the man appointed one of his sons as a priest. Later, a Levite came to live with them and they hired him to be their family priest using their shrine, ephod, and idols. The man said, "Now I know that the Lord will be good to me, since this Levite has become my priest" (17:13). These people were in total opposition to God's commands, yet they still talked like they knew him and served him.

What does all this have to do with what we saw in Mississippi? The steps looked like they would lead somewhere, but they didn't. The words sounded like they represented a relationship, but they didn't. Both are empty and meaningless. Most of us who attend church somewhat regularly talk about God (at least when we are with church people). Talk is cheap. Talking about God, attending church, even praying and reading my Bible does not make me a Christian. All those things are like steps that lead us to a destination. They are good and useful and important, but they are not the focal point. The issue is a personal, intimate relationship with the Savior. It means total surrender of my will, allowing him to direct every part of my life. It takes time and repeated commitment to learn to live this way, but until I make that surrender, Jesus is not Lord of my life. When I commit to live my life to honor God, then church attendance, regular prayer, and Bible reading become steps that lead to somewhere beautiful – a personal friendship with Jesus my Savior.

Jesus, our Savior, made an incredible sacrifice on our behalf. Let us not cheapen it with lip service. Talking like a Christian without truly knowing Christ is like steps leading nowhere. It is more of a hindrance than a help to the kingdom. Giving him so little might be excusable if he had only suffered a hangnail for you. But the perfect Son of God suffered hanging from nails for you. Jesus found fault with people who "honor me with their lips, but their hearts are far from me." Knowing the right words to say (one of the steps mentioned above) will not get you into heaven. He told us that many who claim to be his followers (another step) will not be allowed into the Kingdom (Matthew 25:41-46).

Friend, it is my earnest prayer that you will take steps today and every day to know Jesus better and to learn to love him more.

Seeking Approval

"I am so glad you are my sister-in-law. You are an inspiration, and I am a better person because of you." These words were an unexpected blessing to my heart, but I am troubled by my reaction. I responded in kind with encouraging words of my own, but I walked away kicking myself. I wish I had said, "Thank you so much, but anything good you see in me is really God's love shining through. I am glad it is a blessing to you, but it's not me." Why didn't I think of saying that? Why did I keep the accolades for myself, rather than reflecting them back to the One from whom all good things come?

Samuel (who had been dedicated to God at birth) was a leader and judge for the people of Israel for most of his life. As an old man he spoke to the people, making sure the air between them was clear. He asked that anyone who felt Samuel had wronged him speak up in order that he might make it right. The people insisted that Samuel had not been unjust, or stolen, or accepted bribes. Samuel called the Lord as witness and the people also acknowledged God as witness that they held nothing against him (1 Samuel 12:2b-5). Samuel was a man of integrity. Both his words and his actions over several decades defined who he was as a leader and as a person. He spoke and acted as a representative of his God, which was evident to those around him.

The apostle Paul instructed believers, "And whatever you do, whether in word or deed, do it all in the name of the Lord Jesus, giving thanks to God the Father through him" (Colossians 3:17). Whatever we do, whatever we say, should bring glory to our Father in heaven. Just as our struggles with temper, criticism, foul language, etc. must be surrendered to him, so too must the things we do well. Any good that others see in us (kindness, generosity, musical talent, compassion, leadership, or whatever) is only the fruit of the Holy Spirit beginning to grow. Therefore, all accolades and applause should be immediately redirected to the One responsible for those good things. Such an attitude should also be evident in the way we honor or applaud others.

The Bible teaches strongly and repeatedly against the sin of pride. Jesus said that those who do their religious deeds (such as public prayer) to be seen by men have received all the reward they will ever get (Matthew 6:5). How sad, to do good things only to be seen by others, and receive the fleeting approval of men rather than the reward of hearing the Father say "Well done." Friends, let us invite the Holy Spirit to examine our lives and hearts, showing us areas where we are not reflecting the light of Christ as we should. Let everything we do and say bring glory to our Lord Jesus Christ.

In The Wilderness

I once had opportunity to visit the pediatric/cardiac intensive care unit at the University of Michigan Hospital with friends whose baby needed an operation. In that place, tiny babies born with undeveloped arteries or missing chambers of their hearts would undergo major surgery while their parents paced the floor. A baby with life-threatening medical problems is one of many wilderness experiences that people face. Have you been in the wilderness? Have circumstances of life left you feeling lost and alone, disoriented, thirsty, afraid you won't be rescued? Maybe you are there today, facing relational heartache, weariness, financial strain, uncertain purpose, broken dreams. But a wilderness experience can help you learn to let go of everything else and hold on desperately to the Savior. That is faith.

David, one of the greatest heroes of the Bible, knew all about life in the wilderness. Samuel had anointed David as the next king of Israel, as God directed. Now, years later, he was living in the wilderness, running from Saul, eating dirt, and wondering about the promise. Many of the Psalms are prayers or journal entries written by David in the wilderness. Several of the worship songs we sing today come directly out of those verses. Sometimes he asked God, "How much longer?" Sometimes he cried out for rescue, or for the punishment of his enemies. Sometimes he thanked God for peace and direction and hope. No matter where he started, he ended focusing on God rather than on himself. When you are in the wilderness of life, you may or may not write songs, but do you deliberately shift your focus from the problem to the One who is Lord and Master over everything? That, my friends, is the only source of peace, of hope, and of rest.

Moses, in Exodus 33:13-15, said that if God would not go with them, then he would rather stay in the wilderness than seek paradise without God. He understood that there is no such thing as paradise outside of the presence of the Father. If you are in the wilderness today, I ask you, I charge you, to seek his face with every ounce of strength you possess. If you are not in the wilderness today, pray for those who are and earnestly seek God to build you up so that you will be prepared to withstand your trial in the wilderness that inevitably comes. If you know him, you will find comfort which you can in turn use to comfort someone else (2 Corinthians 1:3-4).

Jonathan's Legacy

In the book of 1 Samuel we find several references to a young man named Jonathan. Although the son of Israel's first king is a fairly minor character in the storyline, he plays a very significant role. Jonathan led a successful military campaign and earned the respect of the whole army (Chapter 14). Military prowess, however, is not Jonathan's claim to fame. He is most remembered as David's best friend. Jonathan was a loyal, one-of-a-kind, do-anything-for-you, kind of friend. What a legacy to leave! Any one of us would be blessed to have such a friend. There are others in Scripture whose legacy is based primarily on one specific characteristic – Abraham's persistent faith, Job's patient trust in God, Thomas' doubt, Solomon's wisdom, Jonah's disobedience. Often a person may not even be conscious that a particular action or attribute will end up defining his life. I am sure that was true of Jonathan.

What description best fits your life? When people in your work place, your community, your sphere of friends and acquaintances think of you, what characteristic comes to mind? Are you the clown who makes everybody laugh? Maybe you are the angry, foul-mouthed parent. Are you the critic who has something negative to say about everyone? Or perhaps you're the generous person who is ready to help others. Are you the whirlwind who is too busy for family and friends? Maybe you are unreliable – quick to say you will do something, but inconsistent in following through. Would people say that you are so wrapped up in your own problems that you never think to ask what is happening in someone else's life?

What defines your life? While we should not be enslaved by fears of what others might think of us, a wise person is attentive to his/her own reputation. The way others perceive me tells me about attitudes and actions I may not recognize in myself. Knowing who I am is a good start.

The follow-up question is this: What do I want to be known for? Jonathan chose to be a friend who was loyal and honest – becoming one of the richest blessings in David's life. Personally I want to be remembered by the fruit of the Spirit shining through my life – love, joy, peace, patience, kindness, goodness, faithfulness, gentleness, and self-control (Galatians 5:22,23). I have a long path learning to submit to the Spirit, but that is my goal. What about you? Do you want to be known as a joy-filled person? A generous person? A person at peace no matter what is happening around you? Do you want to be an encourager or a prayer warrior? A businessman of integrity? A loyal friend, like Jonathan? You can determine what kind of influence you will have on others. Choose wisely, but be careful not to just portray an image. Unfortunately, the reputation that Christians have for being hypocrites has too often been accurate. Insincerity is an insult to God and to others. Let each of us choose to be the kind of person that brings honor to God and blessing to people. Your influence on others, while important, is secondary to pleasing God. Leave a legacy of a life lived to honor God. May God bless you as you become all that he wants you to be.

No Half-hearted Obedience

God wants, expects, and demands total obedience from his children. He is not a slipshod, give 70% kind of God. Imagine if he had made three parts of the water cycle, but no way for it to return to the air and come down as precipitation. What if he had made our amazing lungs and most of our respiratory system, but no way to expel the poisonous carbon dioxide? What if the sacrifice Jesus made on the cross only covered some of our sins? Those committed unintentionally, without malice aforethought, could be forgiven, but every deliberately unkind thought or action would be held against us? Clearly our 100% Savior deserves 100% surrender and obedience.

After the Israelites had settled in the Promised Land, King Saul was given instructions to go to battle against the Amalekites and completely destroy them (I Samuel 15:3). He and his soldiers won the battle and destroyed the enemy – mostly. They spared the king and some of the livestock. When Samuel came to confront him, Saul claimed twice that he had done what he was told to do. He blamed the soldiers for keeping the animals, but claimed they were for sacrificing (1 Samuel 13-21). But Samuel replied, "Does the Lord delight in burnt offerings and sacrifices as much as in obeying the voice of the Lord? To obey is better than sacrifice, and to heed is better than the fat of rams. For rebellion is like the sin of divination, and arrogance like the evil of idolatry. Because you have rejected the word of the Lord he has rejected you as king" (1 Samuel 15:22-22).

Friend, what has God called you to do? Maybe you heard him speak to your heart at a camp meeting or retreat or in a service several years ago. Have you followed through with the work he called you to do? He has given you gifts, experiences, and opportunities to be used in his kingdom. He is not interested in partial obedience. Just going to church, giving offerings occasionally as the basket goes by, or your cast-offs to your local charity center, and being kind to those who are kind to you is no better than what Saul offered. God rejected Saul. Christianity is not about doing mostly the right things most of the time. It is about seeking to really know and love God, living a life of obedience and faith in direct proportion to the gratitude you feel toward Christ for what he has done for you. Serve where you are with all your ability as though everything you do, you do for him, because you love him. May the words of the Psalmist be the prayer of your heart and of mine, "Teach me Your way, O Lord and I will walk in Your truth; give me an undivided heart, that I may fear Your Name. (Ps. 86:11). May we never offer to him partial obedience.

Victory Over the Enemy

The only nightmares I can remember having as a child were about fire. Our house was burning or sometimes it was Grandma's house. In the worst version, the devil was in the house setting things on fire and looking for my family as we crouched in a corner of my basement bedroom. My fear of the devil and hell translated subconsciously into a fear of fire, including fire trucks and even sirens. Every night for at least a year I piled my favorite things on top of my dresser (strategically placed under the small window). Dresser drawers were pulled open like stair steps so if the house caught on fire, my sister and I could grab the younger kids, run up those dresser drawer steps, grab a metal pipe (kept there just in case) and break the window so we could get out. Fortunately this plan never had to be executed. The nightmares and the fear of fire faded with time. Looking back I am surprised at the intensity of the fear I felt.

Most children (and many adults) deal with fear of some kind. From real possibilities like fire or getting lost or falling, to more obscure fears like monsters in the closet, fears plague us from time to time. Although most of the things we fear never come to pass, there is a real monster, an enemy, who is out to destroy us. He is after our loved ones, our neighbors, anyone he can get. In battle, a good soldier learns to know his enemy in order to be prepared to fight him. Scriptures help us to know about the enemy we face so that we won't fall victim to his schemes. The devil is the tempter, who tempted Jesus in the desert for forty days (Matthew 4 and Luke 4). The devil is the father of all lies (John 8:44). The devil lays traps for us (2 Timothy 2:26). "Your enemy the devil prowls around like a roaring lion looking for someone to devour" (1 Peter 5:8). "He who does what is sinful is of the devil, because the devil has been sinning from the beginning. The reason the Son of God appeared was to destroy the devil's work" (1 John 3:8).

Our enemy is strong, but the good news is that our God is infinitely stronger. He has all power. Nothing is too hard for him (Jeremiah 32:17). He will never leave us nor forsake us (Hebrews 5:5). Everything good comes from him (James 1:17). He is truth and he always keeps his promises. Praise his Holy Name! For those of us who have a personal relationship with God, there is no reason to fear the devil. I am very thankful for that truth.

God created human beings for relationship. Through Jesus' death on the cross, every person has the opportunity to repent and have his/her sins forgiven. To be forgiven means to be accepted as a chosen, adopted child of God. As his children, we spend time with our Father through prayer, reading His Word, and singing songs of praise. We learn to think about him all through the day, and to center our decisions and values and attitudes on that which we believe would please him. That is what it means to live in personal relationship with God through Jesus Christ. It is the most fulfilling relationship possible for a human being to have.

As we walk in friendship with God our Father, he shows us how to gain the victory over our enemy. The only way to stand victorious against the attacks of the evil one is through the mighty power of Jesus' Name. He gave us permission to ask in his Name for that which we need, so when you pray against the attacks of the enemy, pray in Jesus' Name. Jesus already defeated the enemy and he stands ready to help you. "Resist the devil and he will flee from you" (James 4:7). "Put on the full armor of God so that you can take your stand against the devil's schemes" (Ephesians 6:11). Seek to draw ever-nearer to the Lord who saves, and intercede continually in prayer for those whom our enemy is claiming as his own. Dear Friend, let us live every day in sweet relationship with Jesus. Let us praise God for his power, and let us fight boldly on our knees for lost souls who have believed the devil's lies.

Keep Your Eye on the Master

My husband Bart is an administrative pastor. One of the greatest joys of marriage for me is being a helpmate to him in ministry. When we facilitate marriage retreats, participants are encouraged to focus on the long view rather than just on the current struggles. This is a good reminder for all of us. Strife and conflict and struggles come into each life. Whether your struggle today is with people (family, co-workers, neighbors) or with a difficult situation (finances, employment, illness, loneliness, etc.), I encourage you to keep focused on the long view. God will lead you through each problem in the way that brings him glory. "Know therefore that the Lord your God is God; he is the faithful God, keeping his covenant of love to a thousand generations of those who love him and keep his commands" (Deuteronomy 7:9).

God is better at focusing on the long-term goal than we are. Palm Sunday marked the beginning of the last week of Jesus' life on earth before his crucifixion. Jews were flooding into Jerusalem to celebrate Passover Week. The disciples and other followers had an impromptu parade, honoring Jesus as king. Within just a matter of days, however, Jesus was betrayed and arrested. How quickly the cheers turned to jeers! Although Jesus deserved greater kingly honor than any human parade could give, God chose to think long-term. There is a song that says, "He grew the tree that he knew would be used to make the old rugged cross. Nothing took his life. With love he gave it. He was crucified on a tree that he created. With great love for man, God stayed with his plan, and he grew the tree so that we might go free."[2]

As God saw our need for a Savior, he was prepared with a plan to meet that need before he created the earth. He weighed the cost before he ever said, "Let there be light!" and decided a relationship with you and with me was worth the horrendous price. That same God still looks down through time beyond our big problems and sees how he is working out all the details for his glory. Friend, I encourage you today to keep your eyes set on the Savior and all he has promised you. He will never leave you nor forsake you. His long-term plans are always good.

God's Power in our Darkest Days

In the beautiful, terrible Easter story, sandwiched between the heart-breaking descriptions of Jesus' betrayal and fake trial and torturous death, are glimpses of Almighty God. The soldiers and officials came to arrest Jesus in the garden. "Jesus, knowing all that was going to happen to him, went out and asked them, 'Who is it you want?' 'Jesus of Nazareth' they replied. 'I am He' Jesus said. . . When Jesus said, 'I am he,' they drew back and fell to the ground" (John 18:4-6). The servant of the high priest had his ear cut off and Jesus restored it (Luke 22:51). During the crucifixion darkness came over the all the land for three hours in the middle of the day (Matthew 27:45 and Mark 15:38). At the moment Jesus died, the curtain of the temple was torn in two from top to bottom (Matthew 27:51, Mark. 15:38, Luke 23:44). The earth shook and the rocks split. The tombs broke open and the bodies of many holy people who had died were raised to life. They came out of the tombs, and after Jesus' resurrection they went into the holy city and appeared to many people (Matthew 27:52-53). "After the Sabbath, at dawn on the first day of the week . . . There was a violent earthquake, for an angel of the Lord came down from heaven and, going to the tomb, rolled back the stone and sat on it" (Matthew 28:1-2). Of course, the greatest display of God's power was in Jesus' resurrection, bringing the free gift of salvation to all who believe and accept the gift.

Good Friday was the darkest day in human history. It was a day of despair, the death of hope. Still, in the midst of that weekend-long nightmare, God made himself known. As we read the gospel accounts we can clearly see his hand at work, prodding, comforting, listening, encouraging, sorrowing.

Although you did not personally experience that horrendous Friday, chances are you have known some dark days. Perhaps a lost job or serious medical condition has left your financial situation in desperate straits. Perhaps the pain of a broken relationship with a child or a parent or close friend, or regret over words that can never be taken back, keeps a dark cloud over your head day after day. Maybe it is broken dreams or broken promises that leave you feeling hopeless. Whatever the reason for your heartache, please do not despair. As God was present on that dark day long ago, so he is present in your problem today. I encourage you to look for his hand in the details. As you see him at work, both your hope and your faith will grow.

Don't Lose Sight of the Goal

God, through Moses, had instructed the people of Israel to conquer the Promised Land, completely ridding the land of its inhabitants (Deuteronomy 20:16-18). That was their goal when they crossed the Jordan River. God had told them that he would not drive out all the people groups at once, because there were not enough Hebrews to populate the land and it would be overrun by wild animals (Deuteronomy 7:22). In the book of Joshua the people fought and conquered thirty-one kings and began to settle in their territories (Joshua 12). They had climbed the first couple of rungs on the ladder toward their goal by the time that Joshua died. Even after these victories, the opening chapter of Judges indicates that there were still many of the native peoples left in the land. Over time the Israelites got comfortable living near these pagans. Fighting battles is hard, exhausting, dangerous work. It was easier to postpone any further fighting and just settle down. As they conscripted some of the people into forced labor, they got to know them and even intermarried with them. In so doing, they lost sight

25

of the goal, and the pagan inhabitants of the land proved to be their undoing. The Israelites' constant and continuous disobedience to God led to their eventual capture and disbursement, just as God said it would.

Four hundred years later Jesus came to earth with a clear goal – to die for sins, making it possible for individuals to learn to walk in relationship with Holy God and with one another. Good Friday and Easter Sunday had been the goal since the beginning of creation. While on earth, Jesus developed friendships and a following. He enjoyed a sense of camaraderie with his disciples, and was able to influence many people to turn to God. Still, he never lost sight of the goal. When Peter tried to redirect the plan that so that Jesus would not die, Jesus responded strongly, "Get behind me, Satan! You are a stumbling block to me; you do not have in mind the things of God, but the things of men" (Matthew 16:23). Jesus was resolutely determined to reach the goal, even at immeasurable cost to himself.

The Israelites had a goal, but failed to reach it. Jesus had a goal and he reached it flawlessly. What about us? What is the goal of the Christian? It is to become more and more like Jesus, being continually filled by the Holy Spirit. As with the Israelites, so with us, God does not demand immediate victory over all the strongholds of sin before or when a person comes to faith. Rather, he works through the Holy Spirit to chip away at areas of our lives that need to be surrendered to him – temper, honesty in business dealings, language, habits, attitudes, service, level of devotion, etc. Step by step he helps us climb toward the goal. The problem is that we get tired of having to work so hard. We begin to get comfortable on a particular rung and decide to rest. Soon we settle into a routine (go to church, talk the talk, pray before meals, put some money in the plate) and we stop yearning/reaching for the goal. We ignore the prompting of the Holy Spirit urging us onward. But you cannot stay in one place spiritually for long. When you stop striving, you start sliding. Somewhat like climbing a descending escalator. When you stop moving up you immediately begin to lose ground.

Israel stopped fighting, and dropped their focus from the goal. God eventually refused to help them drive out any more of the enemy (Judges 2:3). These people groups were left to test the

Israelites and see whether they would obey God's commands (Judges 3). The Israelites disobeyed and within a few generations they were heavily involved in idol worship. Jesus, in contrast, persevered all the way to his goal. If he had not, we would be utterly without hope. His success makes it possible for us to reach our goal, following his example. Are you persevering? Are you making strides toward holiness (which means set apart for God's glory) or have you grown comfortable in a rut? Can you hear the Holy Spirit calling you to come higher, closer to God, or has your heart grown cold to his voice? I urge you to seek the Holy Spirit in humility asking him to lead you all the way to the goal. May each of us move ever closer to the One who came to give his life for us. May God's dreams and goals for each of our lives be fulfilled.

Caring for Newborns

In April 2010, A Houston man was taking out his trash when he found a newborn baby girl inside an abandoned dryer at his apartment complex. Sadly, this is not an isolated case, but rather an all-too-common problem. Even in a political and social climate where babies are not seen as a blessing, the prevalence of abandoned infants is recognized as such a terrible tragedy that many states have passed laws allowing people to drop off newborn babies at specified sites without fear of prosecution. Those babies are then made available for legal adoption, so that those precious infants can receive the care they need to survive and thrive.

The same month that abandoned baby was found in Texas, dozens of people committed or re-committed their lives to Christ during the Stand Strength events at our church. Jesus described this experience as being "born again" (John 3:3f). Like newborn babies, new believers need care and training and support. All of us who walk with the Lord are to disciple new believers. Jesus commanded his followers to make disciples (Matthew 28:19). To make a disciple involves walking alongside a person, showing him how to live out his faith and how to grow closer to God. One hour per week in a worship service is not enough, any more than one hour of care a week is adequate for a new baby. Sunday School classes and small group Bible studies are useful tools. Books, music, and video messages can help. However, as with newborn babies, one-to-one contact is absolutely essential for healthy growth in the spiritual realm. The process of disciple-making is not about teaching a set of rules for behavior – it is all about relationships. The purpose is to help newer believers learn to walk day by day in a personal relationship with God, and to develop healthy relationships with other members of his family.

Jesus spent three years showing his disciples how to walk with the Father through life day by day. Disciple-making is an intentional process that takes place over a period of months or years. Without that care and support, new believers - like abandoned babies – cannot thrive and may not even remain in the faith. We cannot afford to disobey this directive from our Lord. Let us not abandon even one of those who have been reborn into the family of Christ.

Debris Removal

For many months after Hurricane Katrina, FEMA contractors were hard at work removing debris. The debris trucks ran all day every day, hauling loads to landfills. Like the mess left by a hurricane, the storms of life leave debris in their wake. Storms like broken relationships, a terminal diagnoses, loss of job, betrayal by a friend, damaged reputation, or death of a loved one, all leave debris in our lives. After such a storm, debris may be evident in the form of bitterness, lack of faith, ungratefulness, wrong priorities, or a complaining spirit. These things don't help us, and they might hurt us. Just like the debris trucks working tirelessly to remove all the useless stuff left by the hurricane, God is trying to remove the debris from our hearts. In Mississippi, property owners were instructed to put all of their debris into one pile. FEMA workers would remove one pile, (seemingly of any size). God is waiting for us to be willing to allow him to remove the debris in our hearts. He will not just come in and take it. We need to put it in the pile and ask him to remove it. It may take time, but he will clear it out, if we let him.

Too often, however, we refuse to even admit that there is debris in our lives. Hurricane debris in Mississippi was evident to the eyes – it lined the curbs. Spiritual debris is evident to the ears – it comes out in our speech for all to hear. Jesus said, "For out of the overflow of the heart the mouth speaks" (Matthew 12:34). Others hear it, even if I refuse to acknowledge it and ask God to remove it. This is about as wise as leaving debris spread all over the yard and pretending it isn't there. The first step in moving forward is clean up. I encourage each of us to prayerfully ask the Lord if there is debris in our lives, left from past storms, and if so, to remove it. The cleanup effort along the Gulf Coast has taken years. Some of us have had spiritual debris in our lives for decades. Let's allow God to remove it, and heal those places in our hearts. Let's start today. Your loving Savior longs to make you whole. (See Romans 12:9-13:14.)

His Blood is Enough

The book of Numbers records an enormous number of animal sacrifices the Israelites were required to make every year. Sacrificed animals were slaughtered by the priests on behalf of individuals, families, or the whole community. Some of these sacrifices were offered in repentance of sin, some as an expression of thanks to God, and others as a sign of faith and putting God first. Numbers chapters 28 and 29 list these requirements:

- The daily burnt offering was 2 lambs, a year old, offered every morning and evening along with grain and drink offerings.
- Every Sabbath day two additional lambs were to be sacrificed along with grain and drink offerings.
- On the first of each month, in addition to the daily offering, the priests were to sacrifice two bulls, one ram, and seven lambs, along with their grain and drink offerings, and one goat for a sin offering.
- Then there were additional sacrifices for special annual celebrations: Passover, Feast of Weeks, and Day of Atonement. Each required 2 bulls, 1 ram, 7 lambs with their grain and drink offerings, with 1 goat for sin offering, in addition to the daily burnt offering.
- The Feast of Tabernacles brought specific sacrificial requirements for eight days.

- o Day 1: 13 young bulls, 2 rams, 14 lambs with grain and drink offerings, 1 goat for sin offering, in addition to daily burnt offering.
- o Day 2: required all the same offerings, except only 12 young bulls. The number of bulls decreased by one each day until Day 7 when seven bulls were sacrificed.
- o On Day 8, 1 bull, 1 ram, and 7 lambs were offered in addition to 1 goat, and the daily burnt offering.

All of this was in addition to special sacrifices made for dedication ceremonies, freewill or fellowship offerings, and those given in fulfillment of a vow. There were also regulations for sin offerings (chapter 15).

That is a lot of animals to sacrifice. I don't know how many years the Israelites faithfully followed these instructions, but it was at least decades, perhaps centuries. The Jewish calendar is based on lunar cycles with each new moon signifying the start of a new month. Over the years it has been standardized somewhat. There are 13 months, all of which have 29 or 30 days. Three of those months may have either 29 or 30 days in a given year. So, today there are 382-385 days in a calendar year. The first month is in the spring, correlating with Passover.

Using the low end (382) as an estimate of how many days were in a year during the time of Moses' leadership, that would be 764 animals sacrificed in daily burnt offerings. 41 or 42 weeks would mean at least 82 Sabbath offerings. There were 13 Monthly offerings, with eleven animals sacrificed at each one, totaling 143. Three of the annual Festivals each required eleven animals. The Feast of Tabernacles required 199 animals over the course of 8 days. So a bare minimum of 1,221 animals were sacrificed every year. The actual numbers were probably much higher, with the extra offerings for dedication of the tabernacle and temple, freewill offerings, and more. For example, when King Solomon dedicated the new Temple, he sacrificed 22,000 cattle, and 120,000 sheep and goats for just a single occasion (2 Kings 8:63). The magnitude of this process is mind-boggling and somewhat gruesome.

All of that slaughter still was not enough. "The law is only a shadow of the good things that are coming – not the realities themselves. For this reason it can never, by the same sacrifices repeated endlessly year after year, make perfect those who draw near to worship . . . But those sacrifices are an annual reminder of sins, because it is impossible for the blood of bulls and goats to take away sins. Therefore, when Christ came into the world, he said: 'Sacrifice and offering you did not desire, but a body you prepared for me; with burnt offerings and sin offerings you were not pleased. Then I said, "Here I am – it is written about me in the scroll – I have come to do your will, O God"' (Hebrews 10:1-7).

The writer of Hebrews clearly pointed out all that sacrifice and bloodshed never actually accomplished its purpose. The slaying of animals did not take away the sins of humans. It was only a way of seeking God's favor – since he is the One who can forgive sins – and an illustration of the need for sacrificial payment. His plan from the beginning was to provide a perfect Lamb, whose sacrifice would take away sins. For, "Without the shedding of blood there is no forgiveness" (Hebrews 9:22). The combined blood of all those thousands of animals was not enough to buy back our souls. But the 5 quarts (approx.) of precious, holy, perfect blood from Jesus Christ was enough to bring forgiveness to all humanity for all time. No other offering will ever be enough to buy a person's salvation. Neither animal sacrifices nor good works of any kind are adequate. Even all the good works of someone like Mother Theresa would not be enough to get herself into heaven. Our sins must be covered by the blood. Then, as an act of overflowing love, devotion, and gratitude, good deeds should flow from our lives.

"For all have sinned and fall short of the glory of God and are justified freely by his grace through the redemption that came by Christ Jesus" (Romans 3:23-24). Friend, all of us have sinned. The only forgiveness is found in Jesus. Have you come in repentance to receive that free gift? If you have not, I pray that you will. If you have already come, is your life a beautiful gift of devotion to God? Is it a gift of love and service and gratitude that brings joy to him?

Choose Life

As Moses neared the end of his life, he reminded the Israelites of all God's instructions. He told them clearly that obedience to God would bring abundant blessings, but disobedience would bring terrible curses. Then he said, "See, I set before you today life

31

and prosperity, death and destruction . . . This day I call heaven and earth as witnesses against you that I have set before you life and death, blessings and curses. Now choose life, so that you and your children may live and that you may love the Lord your God, listen to his voice, and hold fast to him. For the Lord is your life and he will give you many years in the land he swore to give to your fathers, Abraham, Isaac and Jacob" (Deuteronomy 30:15,19, 20). Two chapters later, in giving final instructions to Joshua, the next leader, Moses said, "Take to heart all the words I have solemnly declared to you this day, so that you may command your children to obey carefully all the words of this law. They are not just idle words for you – they are your life. By them you will live long in the land you are crossing the Jordan to possess" (Deuteronomy 32:45-47). Moses encouraged the people to choose life. He said that the Lord and his Word are life for the people of God. Hundreds of years later, Jesus ("The Word of God" according to John 1:1) said, "I am the way and the truth and the life. No one comes to the Father except through me" (John 14:6).

Although we are not the children of Israel, and the Promised Land of Canaan was not for us, the choice given by Moses still applies to you and to me. Each of us must choose between the ways that lead to death (disobedience to God's laws) or the way that leads to life eternal – which is Jesus Christ. What does it mean to choose life? First, it means to choose Jesus as the King of your life, Lord and Master of all you do and all you are and all you have. This is by far the most important decision an individual can make.

But after choosing Jesus and beginning to live in him, there are countless other opportunities to choose life. Here are just a few examples of people who are choosing life:

- A woman still building friendships and telling nurses about her love for Jesus at the age of 104
- Another woman refusing to give in to fears about the possibility of having a leg amputated, just going on living and looking for ways to help others
- A widow moving on after the death of her husband, into a new and completely foreign type of ministry

- A man continuing to serve others and to find reasons to thank God even in the face of a lost job, and few promising prospects
- A single mom doggedly choosing to believe that God is good and he will take care of her in the shadow of insurmountable financial pressures
- Weary grandmothers ministering to many people through cards of encouragement, as they deal with their own health struggles
- A young husband and wife choosing to trust God and find joy in each new day, ten years into a losing battle against his cancer

So friend, as in the days of old, today each person faces a choice. In the words of Moses, I urge you today to "Choose Life." Live every day to the fullest. God has a plan and a purpose for you today. I encourage you to live in Christ, for he is your life. May our lives bring him joy and honor.

Buried Treasure

As the Israelites prepared to take the city of Jericho, Joshua gave them instructions from the Lord. "The city and all that is in it are to be devoted to the Lord. Only Rahab the prostitute and all who are with her in her house shall be spared, because she hid the spies we sent. But keep away from the devoted things, so that you will not bring about your own destruction by taking any of them. Otherwise you will make the camp of Israel liable to destruction and bring trouble on it. All the silver and gold and the articles of bronze and iron are sacred to the Lord and must go into his treasury" (Joshua 6:17-19). A man named Achan disobeyed, and took some treasure for himself, burying it in the dirt inside his tent. As a result of this secret sin, God did not bless the army when they went out against the city of Ai. Thirty-six soldiers were killed. When Achan's sin was discovered, it cost him and his family their lives as well. (Joshua 7.) To take and bury something that is to be devoted to the Lord is no small matter. Sometimes God commanded that portions of the plunder be devoted to him by being placed in the temple treasury. Other times it was to be completely destroyed. Devoted meant wholly committed, so that God alone would determine how it would be used.

Centuries later, Jesus told a parable about a man who buried a talent - in this case, money - that was to be wholly committed in a different way. The master had given his servants leeway in deciding how to use or invest what they were given in order to multiply it. The money, however, still belonged wholly to the master (Matthew 25:14-30). The man who did not use the talent he was given, but instead buried it in the ground, came under severe judgment. The talent was taken away and given to a more faithful – the first recorded use of the concept of "use it or lose it."

In each of these stories the treasure that had been buried was dug up and justice was done. The greatest treasure devoted to God that was ever buried was his one and only Son, but he did not stay buried either. He rose again and lives forevermore as our Savior. Let us treasure him above all else, and let us be devoted, wholly committed, to honoring him with our lives

High Places

After leaving Egypt, the Hebrews lived as nomads in the wilderness for more than 40 years. God, through Moses, gave instructions for building a portable tabernacle, to which the people would bring their sacrifices, rather than offering them in the open field (Leviticus 17:5). When the people of Israel moved into the Promised Land, the people living there worshipped idols on hills and mountains, called high places (Numbers 33:52, Deuteronomy 12:2). These were supposed to be destroyed as the different nations were conquered (Deut. 33:29). God told the people that he would choose a city as a dwelling for his Name, and that would be the place for sacrifices (Deut. 12:11). In the intervening years, before the temple was built, the Israelites offered their sacrifices on the high places (1 Kings 3:2). Even King Solomon, who built the beautiful temple of God, offered sacrifices and burned incense at the high places (1 Kings 3:3). After the temple was built, the high places were not removed. They continued to be used, in disobedience to the Lord. During the reign of Solomon's son Rehoboam, the people had set up "high places, sacred stones and Asherah poles on every high hill and under every spreading tree"

(1 Kings 14:23). For decades afterward, even during the reigns of kings who followed God, those high places were not removed, and the people continued to offer sacrifices there (see 1 Kings 15:14, 22:43, and 2 Kings 12:3, 14:4, 15:4, and 15:35). They were finally removed during the reign of Hezekiah.

Friend, you and I have decided to follow God and live our lives to please him. I wonder though, have we, like the kings of old, allowed the high places to remain in our lives? Are we offering sacrifices of our time, money, and energy, to old habits that are ungodly? Do addictions still have a grip on us? Perhaps some type of entertainment on TV, or the computer, or the radio is pulling our hearts and minds further from God. Maybe it is foul language or an uncontrolled temper. It is not the particular activity so much as the attitude of the heart that really matters. God has clearly told us that he is a jealous God (Exodus 20:5). He will not share first place in our affections with anything or anyone or any activity. Those high places must be removed if we are ever to enjoy close fellowship with our Savior. May our hearts echo the prayer of the Psalmist, "Teach me your way, O Lord, and I will walk in your truth; give me an undivided heart, that I may fear your name" (Ps. 86:11).

God Sees Our Motives

David was probably the most celebrated military man in the Old Testament, yet he was surrounded by valiant warriors whose names are all but forgotten. 1 Chronicles chapter 11 lists more than three dozen of David's Mighty Men and shares some of their notable accomplishments. For example, Jashobeam "Raised his spear against three hundred men, whom he killed in one encounter." "Benaiah son of Jehoida was a valiant fighter from Kabzeel, who performed great exploits. He struck down two of Moab's best men. He also went down into a pit on a snowy day and killed a lion" (1 Chronicles 11:11,22). These men and many others were very important to David.

In addition to military leaders, there were many others who served alongside David. After the ark was brought to Jerusalem, King David "Appointed some of the Levites to minister before the ark of the Lord, to make petition, to give thanks, and to praise the Lord, the God of Israel" (1 Chronicles 16:4).

Friend, what have you been called to do in God's kingdom? Are you in a visible position of leadership, or serving in obscurity? Cleaning the church, folding bulletins, mowing the lawn, sending cards of encouragement, intercessory prayer, making meals, teaching preschoolers, and many other jobs within the church body go almost unnoticed. As with David's mighty men, every single person is known to God. He sees what you do and the motivation of your heart as you do it. "And whatever you do, whether in word or deed, do it all in the name of the Lord Jesus, giving thanks to God the Father through him" (Colossians 3:17). "Whatever you do, do it all for the glory of God" (1 Corinthians 10:31b). "If anyone speaks, he should do it as one speaking the very words of God. If anyone serves, he should do it with the strength God provides, so that in all things God may be praised through Jesus Christ. To him be the glory and the power for ever and ever. Amen" (1 Peter 4:11). I encourage you to honor God and give him your very best, whether you ever receive commendation from men or not. Just as David's men fought bravely, but he received the credit for the victory, so each of us should diligently strive to live a life to glorify God.

A Strong Anchor

On March 10, 2011 a horrific tsunami, spawned by a massive earthquake, wrought unprecedented tragedy in Japan. More than 20,000 people were left dead or missing. Rescue workers searching for survivors were repeatedly delayed because of subsequent tsunami warnings. How do we grasp numbers like that? The estimated population of the county where I live is 26,000 people. The number of dead and missing in Japan would be equivalent to having my entire county wiped out. We have to ask ourselves, "Is my faith strong enough to withstand a blow like that?" Are we, like Job, rooted deeply enough in God that we would still cling to him in the face of such terrible loss? (See Job 1:21, 2:10.) Before the storms of life come, we should be intentionally deepening our faith and knowledge of God.

Worship starts with loving God. No matter what rituals we might engage in, we are not worshipping unless we are expressing a deep and sincere love for God. Singing beautifully, reciting prayers or Scripture verses, standing /kneeling/sitting, even taking communion . . . all of these can be a part of worship or just an empty routine depending upon the condition of our hearts. Jesus told us that the most important commandment is to love God with all that we are.

Early in a life of faith, we thank God for all he has done. We discover that our blessings are too numerous to count. May we never cease to thank him for the grace and mercy he has shown in forgiving our sins. We are thankful for health, for family, for regular income, for a place to live, for a church family, etc. This thankfulness is a part of worship, but it is conditional, and somewhat self-focused. There is a much deeper level of love and praise that goes far beyond what God has done and worships him for who he is. We should be learning to know him better and more deeply day by day throughout the Christian life. The more we discover who God is, the more we love him, and the richer our worship becomes. As we read Scripture, we seek to know more of God and how he has made himself known. We discover that God is all-powerful, all-knowing, unchanging, eternal and so much more.

It is highly unlikely that a tsunami will wipe out our entire county, but loss and tragedy take many forms and eventually strike most everyone. How firmly are you anchored in Jesus your Lord? What would it take to push you to despair? My prayer is that each one of us will continually be growing deeper in relationship with God, learning to know him more and more fully.

Walking in the Dark

On a warm August day, a young family set out to drive to town. The tires on the little car were badly worn, but replacements were not in the budget for another week. Uncharacteristically, the mother was behind the wheel. Their two-year-old daughter was in the back, while the baby sat on her daddy's lap in the passenger seat. Suddenly a tire blew. As the young wife struggled to maintain control of the car, a second tire blew. The Buick rolled before coming to rest upright, straddling the ditch. The driver (the only person wearing a seatbelt) found herself alone in the car. She soon located her young daughter, with a small cut on one leg, crying in the field nearby. Repeated calls for her husband brought no response. The young father, still holding his 8-month-old child, was underneath the car. Carefully, he inched his way into the clear, burning his arms on the tailpipe, but never losing his grasp on his daughter. Soon, the family was reunited, with no serious injuries to anyone. Law officers at the scene could not believe the family walked away from the wreck. Somehow, miraculously, my Daddy held me tightly through the entire ordeal and God spared our lives. This story is a reminder of the way God carries and protects his children.

When the second generation of Israelites who had come out of Egypt prepared to enter the Promised Land, they faced trials and enemies and the great unknown (without the comfort of parents and grandparents to lead and advise them). Moses said, "Do not be terrified; do not be afraid of them. The Lord your God, who is going before you, will fight for you, as he did for you in the desert. There you saw how the Lord your God carried you, as a father carries his son, all the way you went until you reached this place" (Deuteronomy 1:31). Even before they set out for the Jordan River to prepare to enter the land, God said, "This very day I will begin to put the terror and fear of you on all the nations under heaven. They will hear reports of you and will tremble and be in anguish because of you" (Deut. 2:25).

Like the people of Israel, all of us have times in our lives when we are tempted to fear - times when we don't understand the path God has chosen for our lives. When the road is dark the enemy will try to tell us that life would be easier going a different way. He will suggest that God cannot be trusted and does not have our best interests in mind. In the dark valley is the time to hold on in faith, choosing to believe that God knows best and he will lead us through in his perfect timing. Walking with Jesus - or being carried by him - makes even the most miserable circumstance bearable. If you are walking in a dark valley today, I want to share these encouraging lyrics:

Where are You taking me – why are we turning here?
This road is strange to me – this path is not so clear.

Must be the place where my doubt turns to faith,
When I close my eyes and take your hand

> I'd rather walk in the dark with Jesus than to walk in the light on my own. I'd rather go through the valley of the shadow with Him than to dance on the mountains alone.
>
> I'd rather follow wherever he leads me than to go where none before me has gone. I'd rather walk in the dark with my Jesus than to walk in the light on my own.

There will be shadows – but I won't be shaken
'Cause You've never forsaken a vow
You've never failed me before this I know
And, Jesus, You won't fail me now"[3]

I have seen this truth in my own life in various ways over the years. At one point, walking in the dark with Jesus meant trying to be content in my singleness rather than getting into a relationship of which he was not the center. After college it meant saying "no" to a job offer in which he was not leading (and then waiting months before another offer came along). When my kids were very young and I was exhausted, it meant encouraging my husband to lead his first missions trip rather than whining that parenting alone was miserable.

What does it mean for you? Are you walking in the dark, wondering where in the world God is leading and why it has to be so long and hard? Be comforted, friend. God your Father carries you in his arms to the place he has chosen (remember Deut. 1:31). He is already at work in the circumstances of your life, working out all the details for your good and his glory.

Generational Faithfulness

Faithfulness is not just something God does sometimes. It is a part of his unchanging character. For example, he promised Abraham his descendants would inherit the land of Canaan, that is why it was called the Promised Land. God was not only faithful to lead the Israelites into the land of Canaan, but faithfully kept his promise to send a Savior to provide forgiveness of sins. God is absolutely faithful to keep his promises and do just as he said he would do. Unfortunately, the same cannot be said for us. Consider one of the most tragic verses in all of Scripture, "After that whole generation had been gathered to their fathers, another generation grew up, who knew neither the Lord, nor what he had done for Israel" (Judges 2:10). How can this be? How could all that knowledge of the Lord and his great deeds be lost in a few generations? Whose responsibility was it to teach the young ones? Obviously, it was primarily the job of the parents, but other members of the community were also responsible. In fact, anyone who had experienced God's working could have and should have told others about it. God had divided the waters so the people could pass through on dry land – twice! He provided manna from heaven and water from rocks. He kept clothing and sandals from wearing out. He displayed great faithfulness. In that time and culture, information was passed down by word of mouth. There were no formal schools. Children were taught their way of life by parents, extended family, and the whole community.

After this verse in Judges 2:10, the rest of the book and most of the rest of the Old Testament shows a painful pattern of people trying to do things their own way, falling into captivity, and then crying out to God for help. Somehow some of them knew that God was the one that could help them. Some people must have passed down some information about God. In every generation there were some who sincerely tried to please God with their lives. These faithful few who taught others made a huge difference in the life of the nation.

What can we learn from this sad passage of Scripture? No matter who I am, it is my personal responsibility to share with others who God is and what he has done. This includes not only my own children and grandchildren, but other children, youth, adults, and seniors – everyone I know. It is right and important to teach Bible stories and facts and principles, but we must also share about our personal relationship with Jesus Christ our Savior. We need to be telling others about all the ways God has been faithful to us. This will encourage and strengthen their faith as well as our own. We don't just want our children and friends to cry out to God for help after they get into trouble. We want them to experience the peace, hope, joy, and purpose that come from walking in step with

Jesus day by day through seeking to know him, love him and please him.

Bigger Than My Fear

I am not generally a person who is ruled by fears, at least not consciously. However, every time Bart goes away on a trip, especially a missions trip overseas, the same fear raises its ugly head. The relentless question, "What if he never comes home?" attacks me again and again. Each time God and I pray through it and I place my husband in God's hands, trusting him to care for Bart as only he can. In March 2011, for whatever reason, the experience was different. All week I sensed the Spirit challenging my spirit – "Don't pray for a safe return. Pray for a mighty working of the Holy Spirit to the glory of God!" God was calling me to pray for something far bigger than protection. Of course, this sent my thoughts reeling through some of the ramifications of what life would be like if God had better plans for Bart than continued life on this earth. Through the daily tears, God gradually gave me the strength to say with Jesus, "Not my will but Thy will be done." I didn't like it. It was not nearly as comfortable as praying, "please bring the team home safely" but then again, is a safe return the best ultimate result of a missions trip? If that is the extent of our expectation, why even go?

Brothers and Sisters, God wants to do far, far more in and through his people than just to return them home unharmed! He has visions and plans far beyond what we can imagine – plans to bring people to Jesus and glory to his Name, here at home and abroad. My prayers, even when I pray for his will to be done, have often been far too small. Through that painful week of soul searching, God brought me to realize that in my deepest heart of hearts, more deeply rooted than the fear of raising my kids alone, is my unshakable faith that God is good.

If you look beyond your fears, what is it that you truly, in the deepest part of who you are, desire more than just safety and comfort? Do we truly long to see God's will being done "On earth as it is in heaven"? Will you give him the freedom to break you and transform you by the renewing of your mind (Romans 12:2) or will you just sit on the comfortable, familiar sidelines as he works mightily in other lives? He is calling people to a much deeper level spiritually than most of us have ever known. He wants to take us far beyond the best that we can envision, into the beautifully scary places we cannot imagine. He is calling us to move far beyond our prayers for comfort and safety and health, into praying for a miraculous moving of His Spirit that will shake our church, our lives, our families, our community. He stands with outstretched hand inviting us to come closer and pray bigger than for those in our own circles. Your response to his invitation will determine the extent to which he will work in and through your life.

Making God Jealous

Remember what it feels like to be jealous? Probably all of us have felt jealous of what someone else received – attention, promotion, toys, or whatever. For me, jealousy was a miserable, self-inflicted emotion based on self-absorption. Some of you have experienced a far more powerful jealousy resulting not from selfishness, but from the unfaithfulness of a spouse. What does the Bible mean when it says "God is a jealous God"? "Do not worship any other god, for the Lord, whose name is Jealous, is a jealous God" (Exodus 34:14, see also Ex. 20:5, Deuteronomy 4:24; Joshua 24:19, Nahum 1:2.) Jealousy happens what someone else receives what I deserve or think I deserve. In my case it is the sinful nature coming through. In God's case, he alone is worthy of our greatest love, affection, attention, effort, etc. God's jealousy is, therefore, rightly and righteously aroused when we give to someone or something else that which rightfully belongs to him.

My mom explained it in terms of human relationships. There are many people in my life whom I care about, I think about, and I spend time with. I am interested in what is happening in their lives. As sincere as I am in my love for them, none of those relationships compares to the love I have for my husband. He is a far greater priority in my heart and my life than any of those other relationships. In the same way, our love for God and devotion to him should supersede every other interest or relationship we have.

The people of Israel aroused God's jealousy by following after the idols of surrounding nations. In fact, he often referred to their unfaithfulness as committing adultery. Those of you who have endured the heart-wrenching betrayal of unfaithfulness understand this feeling. Therefore, God refused to help them conquer the rest of their enemies (Judges 2:3). Repeatedly throughout their history they provoked him to jealousy and repeatedly he disciplined them, allowing them to reap the consequences of what they had sowed. He even allowed them to be carried into captivity by enemy armies.

There are many things in the lives of American believers which arouse God's jealousy. Although not the severity of unfaithfulness, many of our daily activities may arouse a degree of holy jealousy as we put other things before God. Maybe God is jealous of the overtime hours you work, or your preoccupation with food, or the time you spend researching and planning for your next vacation or toy. Do you arouse his jealousy by running to a friend rather than to him when you have a problem and need somebody to talk to? Maybe God is jealous of your technology devices or the time, attention, and affection that you give to family rather than to him. I encourage you to take the time to examine your own life and ask the Spirit to highlight that which arouses your God to jealousy. Consider what steps you might take to re-order your life and priorities so that nothing, absolutely nothing, will compete with God for first place in your life.

Aim Higher

Consider the statement below and decide whether you agree. "The quest of the modern Christian is likely to be for peace of mind and spiritual joy, with a good degree of material prosperity thrown in as an external proof of the divine favor."[4] For one who is young in the faith, still battered by the world's way of thinking, "peace of mind and spiritual joy" sound like very great pursuits. It takes time and effort and several falls before most of us learn to walk with the Savior, holding on to the joy and peace he offers in the midst of our struggles. To be blessed, then, with material comforts in addition to spiritual blessings, probably is the expectation for many American Christians today. The next question that naturally follows is: Is the quest for spiritual joy and peace, and physical comforts, the ultimate goal of a life of faith? Or is there more?

I am discovering that the answer is a resounding "yes!" In my own walk of faith, I finally learned to be content and at peace most of the time and to encourage others to grow. I was comfortable on that plateau, but the Holy Spirit began to call me further. He challenged me to develop a mindset that is aware of God and praising God all day every day. It is taking time, but I am learning. He is calling me to a deeper level of faith and relationship. The same truth applies in your life. Wherever you are in your own walk of faith, the Spirit is calling you to climb higher and to know God better.

One Sabbath day Jesus encountered a man with a shriveled hand at the synagogue. He tried to get the people there to have mercy and to see that it was lawful and right to do good on the Sabbath, but they refused to even answer him. "He looked around at them in anger and, deeply distressed at their stubborn hearts, said to the man, 'Stretch out your hand.' He stretched it out and his hand was completely restored" (Mark. 3:5). "Angry and deeply distressed" is not how we usually see Jesus pictured. What was it that distressed him (The KJV says "grieved")? It was their stubborn hearts. Jesus wanted to demonstrate compassion, but their stubborn heart wouldn't hear. Friends, if we sense the calling of the Spirit, and our stubborn hearts refuse to respond, are we incurring God's anger? Is he distressed or grieved by us? Doing that which displeases him is never a good choice. He is calling each of us to a greater depth of relationship than we have ever known. He beckons us to come further, deeper, higher. And he waits for our response. Today, if you hear his voice, I implore you to respond in obedient surrender. One of the greatest tragedies in the Christian life is to have a personal encounter with the Holy One and yet remain unchanged. Grieve not the Master

Pray Together

In 1993 I was finishing my first year of professional employment and would be receiving pay checks all through the summer even though school was out. I decided God wanted me to make good use of the time, so I spent the summer in the impoverished city of Camden, NJ working in a day camp program called Urban Promise. For the first couple of weeks we had temperatures over 100 degrees and humidity near 100%. Far from home, living in a house with 23 strangers, padlocked bars on the windows, and no air-conditioning . . . was clearly a recipe for frayed nerves and short tempers. Several teams in other parts of the city experienced conflicts between members. We decided early on that the only way to avoid those conflicts was to pray together daily. I learned that summer that it is nearly impossible to harbor hard feelings toward someone while you sit knee-to-knee praying for God to bless him or her. Not only that, there is something very touching about hearing someone pray for you. There is no more powerful way to bond believers together than joining in prayer.

The Bible talks a lot about prayer. Jesus, our example, spent time alone in prayer, talking and listening to his Father. God's Word teaches us to praise God, to pray for others (both believers and unbelievers), and to draw near to God through prayer. It is good for us to pray with and for our fellow believers. Near the end of his life, Samuel said to the people of Israel, "As for me, far be it from me that I should sin against the Lord by failing to pray for you" (I Samuel 12:23). Have you ever considered it a sin to fail to pray faithfully for others? We usually see that as optional, or something for those really spiritual people to do. Not so. All of us are to lift our brothers and sisters up in prayer faithfully, even as Jesus prayed for his disciples and also for us (John 17:6-24).

I firmly believe that real, earnest prayer is the hardest spiritual discipline to cultivate. Our enemy would rather have us do anything than pray. That is because there is far more power in prayer than in reading or singing or even telling people about Jesus. God has power far beyond our wildest imagination, but it can only be accessed through earnest prayer. He wants to work in our lives and in our families. One of the most powerful and effective things Christian parents can do is to pray with and for their children every day. When we model and teach children to pray God's blessings on one another, and pray for His help in various situations, it creates a deep bond. Making prayer a foundation of your family is far from a natural part of parenting. It is hard work. Of course it is. Doing battle with the enemy has always been hard work. I want to encourage you to develop the habit of prayer. Spending time talking and listening to the Savior brings a delighted smile to the face of God and unleashes blessings untold.

Giving God Thanks, Publicly

Periodically in our Sunday services we invite people in the congregation to share about what God has been doing and saying in their lives. I always look forward to hearing those praise reports. Scriptures encourage us repeatedly to share with others what God has done for us. Among the prescribed offerings the Israelites were invited to bring to the Lord was a Fellowship Offering, an expression of thankfulness (Leviticus 7:11, 12). Throughout the Psalms we are encouraged to give praise to the Lord for who he is and all he has done. 1 Chronicles 16:24 (repeated in Psalm 96:3), tells us "Declare his glory among the nations, his marvelous deeds among all peoples."

Friends, we need to give thanks publically to God for all he has done for us. That is the most powerful kind of testimony a believer can give. Unbelievers may argue with your theology, but they cannot argue with the difference God has made in your life. "My mouth is filled with your praise, declaring your splendor all day long" (Psalm 71:8).

I remember as a child hearing people thank God for speaking to them through his Word and for leading them through all kinds of problems from expensive car repairs to physical healing to restored relationships. Hearing those reports strengthened my own faith and helped me to learn about how God works in the day to day details of life. I encourage you, whenever you have opportunity, to give praise to the God who has saved you and continues to bless you abundantly. Such opportunities may arise not only in a public service, but also informal gatherings with friends, family, or co-workers. Always be ready to talk about Jesus.

The Ultimate Family Reunion

Family Reunions bring great joy, but also sorrow. One sorrow is the heartache of saying good-bye so soon after coming together. Another is strained relationships. Then there are absences. On such occasions we look forward to the next time everyone is together, and hope those who are missing this year will be with us. At those times, also, we grieve the loss of those who will never be with us again in this life.

Reunions are hard to coordinate, but such a blessing to attend. There is coming a day when the ultimate reunion will kick off with a bang! A whole crowd of us will arrive at once, transported by Jesus himself up through the clouds and into his glory. Oh what a day that will be! Those believers who have gone before us will be waiting. All the loved ones we miss so much; spouses, parents, children, and friends who were a part of the Family of God will come together in a reunion that will last for eternity.

Thinking about that eternal reunion in heaven brings a sense of hope and joy and peace as we anticipate being together with loved ones we haven't seen in too long, and the opportunity to meet our heroes of the faith. Those meetings will indeed be wonderful. They will not, however, be the highlight of the reunion. As intensely as we long to be reunited with loved ones, the central focus of heaven is, and always will be, Almighty God. One of my favorite hymns includes this verse:

> Friends will be there I have loved long ago. Joy like a river around me will flow. Yet, just a smile from my Savior I know, will through the ages be glory for me. O that will be glory for me, Glory for me, Glory for me! When by His grace I shall look on His face, that will be glory, be glory for me![5]

Friend, I hope the words of this song ring true in your heart. As you seek to know Christ, and him crucified, you will live the abundant life he has planned for you and delight in him. As we anticipate the ultimate family reunion, and the joy of seeing our Savior, let us continue to invite everyone we know. Time is running out for lost souls to RSVP.

Defining Success

I want to express my gratitude and a word of encouragement to all believers who are working in God's Kingdom, as pastors, teachers, custodians, and so many other areas. Ministry can be very discouraging at times. You faithfully work and prepare materials for a class or presentation, only to have two people show up. You have earnestly prayed and tried to witness to a lost friend or family member, but your words seem to fall on deaf ears. You seek the direction of the Holy Spirit in selecting worship music or a message for Sunday morning, but your efforts are met with complaints and criticism rather than gratitude. You faithfully open your home for a small group Bible study week after week, but members are sporadic in their attendance. Maybe you have poured hours of time and love and counsel into the life of a floundering believer, only to have her return to her life of sin. Likely if you work in children's ministry, you have prayed for workers and asked people to join the team, but you are continually filling in gaps because there are too few volunteers to do the work. Whatever area of ministry you serve in, it is likely you experience frustration at times. Even believers tend to judge success by visible results. The most successful pastors, missionaries, and ministries are often seen as those who appear to have influenced the most people. The Bible does teach that those who are true believers will produce fruit that is recognizable (Matthew 7:20). Still, we need to remember that God is the only one who really knows what results our actions will eventually yield. He is the judge of success.

Let's remember to pursue God's definition of success, rather than man's definition. Each one of us is required to give him our best. The results are God's responsibility, not ours. The Apostle Paul noted, "I planted the seed, Apollos watered it, but God made it grow" (1 Corinthians 3:6). Friend, if you are doing what God has told you to do, with your best effort and best attitude, you are a success, even if you don't see many positive results. "But thanks be to God! He gives us the victory through our Lord Jesus Christ. Therefore, my dear brothers, stand firm. Let nothing move you. Always give yourselves fully to the work of the Lord, because you know that your labor in the Lord is not in vain" (1 Cor. 15:57-58). Continue to give God your best. Carry on in the work he has called you to do. If you are living in obedience to his plans for your life, you are a success. You will one day hear him say, "Well done, good and faithful servant." (Mt. 25:21). God has work for you to do. According to the parable in Matthew 25, those who do not use the talents they have been given will not be welcomed by the Master. For those who claim to know God, that is a very clear definition of failure. Let's seek his approving smile

God's Dreams are Bigger

In the Easter story, it took only four days for the crowds to shift from shouting "Hosanna!" to shouting "Crucify Him!" The people, even the disciples, expected Jesus to set himself up as a political leader and free them from the rule of Rome. God's purpose for Jesus' life on earth was so much bigger! People wanted him to get a few a paragraphs in the history books. God planned to use him to change all of human history.

God does have bigger and better plans for your life than you do. However, I believe Scripture teaches that there is a window of opportunity. In Judges 2:1-5 Joshua led the people into the land, and helped them begin the conquest. Then he died and the people somehow lost the vision. They failed to drive out all of the people groups living in the land. Therefore, God said, "I will no longer drive them out" (Judges 2:5 NLT). They had been given instructions. They started well. Then they fizzled out. The window of opportunity closed. God refused to give the help they would have needed to complete the task. The same type of situation is recorded in Numbers 14:20-25, and 14:39-45. After the spies brought back a negative report, the people were afraid to enter the Promised Land. When they found out the consequences of their disobedience (40 more years in the wilderness) they belatedly tried to obey. The window of opportunity had slammed shut on their fingers and they were soundly defeated.

God usually reveals only the next step rather than his long-term plans. It is all about obedience. We are to do what God says when he says it. We must respond when he calls. If we miss the opportunity God is calling us to, we will miss out on the richness and blessings he wants to give. Jesus lived on this earth from day to day doing whatever God gave him to do. When God said it was time to die, Jesus obeyed. His work was nearly completed.

Friend, I urge you, do not delay. If God is calling you to do something (surrender your life fully to him, be baptized, tithe regularly, or move into a new area of ministry, or whatever else he may be saying), now is the time. Jesus loved us so much he endured cruel torture and crucifixion in our place. He said "If you love me, you will obey what I command." (John 14:15). How much do I love him?

Be Still and Listen

When Moses was near the end of his life, God appointed Joshua to become the next leader of the Israelites. Right from the start God showed that he was with Joshua as he had been with Moses, so the people followed him. I always enjoy reading the story of the Israelites marching around Jericho, and trying to picture what a strange sight they must have been. It is a beautiful illustration of how obedience is far more powerful than all of man's strength. Notice Joshua 6:10. "Do not shout; do not even talk," Joshua commanded. "Not a single word from any of you until I tell you to shout. Then shout!" Pondering the significance of this command, I try to imagine the atmosphere among the Israelites as they walked. Without this little part of the instructions, I envision a rather stiff walk the first day with nervous laughter, telling one another how foolish they feel. By the second or third day, however, I imagine people are sharing gossip, talking about the antics of the kids, or the winner of last night's camel races, or the newest health problem in the family - just your basic social chit chat.

Now imagine the people walking in silence. The nervousness and uncertainty lead to questions about what God is doing. Day after day, they walk and meditate on what God is going to do, perhaps drawing courage by mentally reviewing the many ways God has worked on their behalf in the past. By the seventh day, I imagine a real sense of awe and anticipation that God is going to do something big.

In my mind, when the walls fall, the two groups react very differently. The first hypothetical group is kind of wandering along marking time. When the walls fall they kind of look at each other questioning, "Did you see what I just saw?" The second group, mentally prepared and filled with anticipation, reacts with, "Yes! I knew God was going to do something amazing!"

How does this apply to you and to me? The most obvious application that I see is in the way we gather for Sunday morning worship services. Often, we greet one another and fill the minutes with social chit chat right up until the service begins. There is nothing wrong with social chit chat, but there is a time and a place. I am convinced that the sanctuary on Sunday morning is neither the time nor the place. I am as guilty as anyone. When I focus on people I want to talk to, and make a mental list of those who are missing, it might take two or three songs before I even start to think about God - if I ever do. True worship means I stop thinking about me and start thinking about God. Are we really worshiping him on Sunday morning? Is it any wonder we don't often hear him speak powerfully to our spirits? Imagine what the atmosphere would be like if we gathered in silence. Perhaps a quiet welcome at the door, and then each one passes into the sanctuary and quietly takes a seat. The moments before the service starts are filled with prayer, meditation, and preparation of our hearts. Think of the sense of anticipation that would bring if each of us was convinced that God had something important to say to us, and we were ready to hear it. Even more important than trying to be a friendly, loving, welcoming church family, let us be deliberate about making sure the Holy Spirit is welcome.

Such a Time As This

Single father, single mother, foster mother, adoptive mother, biological mother, grandmother acting as mother, full-time babysitter, mother of toddlers and preschoolers, mother of teens, mother of adult children with or without families of their own . . . be encouraged! God is with you. He loves you. He has plans to use you and to bless you.

In the book of Esther a date had been set for annihilation of all the Jews. Mordecai implored Queen Esther (whom he had raised as his own daughter) to intercede with the king on behalf of her people. In his plea he makes this profound statement: "Do not think that because you are in the king's house you alone of all the Jews will escape. For if you remain silent at this time, relief and deliverance for the Jews will arise from another place, but you and your father's family will perish. And who knows but that you have come to royal position for such a time as this?" (Esther 4:13,14). Esther did not desire or seek the position of queen, but God placed her there for his glory.

Whether you are parenting today by choice (having planned your family) or by default (filling in for a biological parent), you have been placed in the life of this child by God's will for just such a time as this. He chose you. I am quite confident that the job is harder, more draining, and more costly than you ever imagined. Likely you are not the perfect housekeeper, the perfect role model, the perfect cook, the perfect disciplinarian. Satan, our enemy, will try to knock you down and beat you up over these issues. Remember, conviction comes from the Holy Spirit to lead us to change. Condemnation comes from Satan to keep us from changing. God called you to be one thing in the life of this child - the perfect reflection of his love. Whether this child is tiny or full grown, he is watching how knowing Jesus affects your life.

In the book, *The Power of a Praying Parent*, Stormie Omartian says, "The battle for our children's lives is waged on our knees. When we don't pray, it's like sitting on the sidelines watching our children in a war zone getting shot at from every angle. When we do pray, we're in the battle alongside them, appropriating God's power on their behalf."[6]

Please pray for the children you love. Pray every day. Pray silently. Pray out loud in their hearing. Pray together over struggles they face. God has called you to this role of parenting. If you refuse, he can raise up someone else, but he chose you. Please do the best you can. As you seek to know him better through his Word and through prayer, you will learn to love him more and will become a more perfect reflection of his love. "Let us not become weary in doing good, for at the proper time we will reap a harvest if we do not give up" (Galatians 6:9). "His divine power has given us everything we need for life and godliness through our knowledge of him who called us by his own glory and goodness" (2 Peter 1:3). God has asked me to give you this message: Be encouraged! Keep up the good work – someone's eternity may depend on it.

Lead Well

The Hebrew people frequently grumbled on their journey through the wilderness. Like them, we are often quick to complain when life does not go the way we had hoped. Although all of the people complained at times, their leaders seemed to contribute to the problem rather than encouraging faith in God. In Numbers 13, tribal leaders scouted out the Promised Land. Ten of the twelve brought back a negative report, focusing on the big giants rather than on their big God. Because of their words the people chose not to enter Canaan and it cost them 40 additional years in the wilderness. It cost those tribal leaders even more. "Then the ten scouts who had incited a rebellion against the Lord by spreading discouraging reports about the land were struck dead with a plague before the Lord" (Numbers 14:36-37). In Numbers 15 three men named Korah, Dathan, and Abiram "incited a rebellion against Moses involving 250 other prominent leaders, all members of the assembly." They complained against the leader God had chosen and tried to take over control. In the end, God showed that Moses was his chosen leader and those responsible for the rebellion suffered God's wrath. "The earth opened up and swallowed the men, along with their households and the followers who were standing with them, and everything they owned . . ." A couple of verses later, "Then fire blazed forth from the Lord and burned up the 250 men."

These leaders paid with their lives for their failure to lead the people the way God wanted. Leadership, is an invitation for others to follow my lead and do as I do. It is a tremendous, frightening responsibility and privilege. That is why the apostle Paul lists such high standards for those who would serve as deacons and overseers (1 Timothy 3). James warns "Dear brothers and sisters, not many of you should become teachers in the church, for we who teach will be judged by God with greater strictness. We all make many mistakes, but those who control their tongues can also control themselves in every other way" (James 3:1-2).

It seems that every time the people complained and/or leaders rebelled, Moses' response was to fall on his face to plead with God for his help and his mercy. All of us could learn from his example. Rather than lashing out or becoming defensive, we should take it to God.

One final example is found in Numbers 20. The people were complaining again. Moses went to God, who told him to speak to a large rock and water would flow out. He gathered the people around the rock. "Listen you rebels!" he shouted, "Must we bring you water from this rock?" (Numbers 20:10). His disobedience seems minor, striking the rock rather than speaking to it, but he also took some of the credit, using the pronoun "we." As a result, Moses was not allowed to enter the Promised Land. The punishment seems harsh after all the whining and rebellion he had endured. Still, he was the leader and therefore a model for the people. Scripture teaches that leaders and teachers will be held to a higher standard. He was.

This is a sobering passage. Those who are leaders are challenged to seek God and obey all the time. Each of us is to respect, support, and pray for the leaders God has placed over us. Although leadership brings major responsibility, failure to lead when God calls brings judgment. If/when God calls you to lead, walk in holiness before him.

Reluctant Leaders

In the previous passage we looked at the twelve spies sent into the Promised Land, and the results of the report that they brought back. Ten of the spies discouraged the people from marching into the land God had promised to give them. The spies paid with their lives for discouraging the people. The people, for choosing fear over faith, were sentenced to an additional 40 years in the wilderness (read Numbers 14:22-23). Not one of the adults who were 20 years or older, with the exception of Caleb and Joshua, was allowed to enter the Promised Land. That whole generation of leaders died off. Think about what that meant for those who were left. That was a culture in which age brought honor, and the oldest men were the leaders of their families and communities. Losing all of them in a 40 year span meant that members of the next generation were thrust into positions of leadership, probably before they felt ready. In his wisdom, God used Moses to provide the stability of leadership that was needed. What was it like for those relatively young men to stand in leadership? How many were reluctant to lead, either out of fear or out of a desire to focus on their own lives rather than on the needs of the people?

What other reluctant leaders do we see in the Scriptures? Moses is a classic example. When God called him to lead Israel, Moses literally said, "O Lord, please send someone else to do it" (Exodus 4:13). God was angered by this. Moses humbly obeyed and God blessed him like no other leader in all of Scripture. In fact, Deuteronomy 34:10f tells us that there has never been another prophet in Israel like Moses, who spoke with God face to face.

Another reluctant leader was Barak in Judges 4. Because of his hesitancy to lead the people into battle as God instructed, the honor for the victory went to a woman. Just two chapters later God called Gideon to lead. He too was reluctant but God patiently assured Gideon, "I will be with you" (6:16). God brought about great victory for Israel through Gideon. Jonah was not only reluctant to share the call to repentance with the people of Ninevah, he flat out refused (Jonah 1:3). God found ways to persuade Jonah to obey. Thousands of people were spared, but Jonah apparently did not receive a blessing because of his attitude.

Solomon was not necessarily reluctant to lead Israel as king, but he told God, "I am only a little child and do not know how to carry out my duties" (I Kings 3:7). He was asking for big help with a big job. Because of his heart attitude, God blessed him and answered his prayer.

Did you notice that God did not take "no" for an answer when he called these people to leadership? He used each one. Some received great blessing, some received very little. I believe that the degree to which each one's life was enriched was directly proportional to the degree to which he surrendered to God. Friend, is God calling you to a greater level of leadership? If he is, I urge you to submit to him. Nothing excuses disobedience, not age, lack of experience, past mistakes, or lack of qualifications. God will do what he wants done. He chooses to use ordinary people. He wants to use you as a part of his perfect plan. Forget all the rationale, and say with Isaiah, "Here am I. Send me" (Isaiah 6:8). The richest people in all the world are those whose hearts are at peace with God because they have fully surrendered their lives to him. Does that describe your life?

Unexpected Difficulties

Once upon a time, a beautiful Killdeer built her nest upon a gravel rooftop. It was the perfect location - peaceful, safe from predators, yet not too high for teaching her young to fly. With a nest full of eggs, her future looked bright and promising.

Then came the church roof project. People, tools, noise, and commotion invaded her peaceful home. Closer and closer they came. This poor mama saw all of her good planning begin to crumble. Soon, the only rocks left on the entire roof were those which made up her nest. Valiantly she faced her foes and protected her eggs. She squawked more and more loudly every time a worker came too close. God gave a threatened killdeer the instinct to mimic a broken wing to draw a predator away from the nest, or the instinct to puff its tail to frighten larger foes away. Roof workers watched this poor mama try again and again to keep them away from her eggs. Eventually, after postponing work on that corner as long as possible, workers carefully moved her nest and eggs off the roof.

Can you relate to this poor mama? Maybe the plans you had laid out for your life are crumbling . . . your steady job, your fulfilling relationships, your good health, your solid bank account, your security. Or, perhaps, in spite of your dreams, the nest has not yet been built - much less filled with eggs. Maybe years of hoping or trying or planning have not led to security in a career, or in a family, on in financial stability, or health. Do you, like the mama killdeer, want to protest loudly? Do you put on an air of pretense? Are you tempted to give up and abandon your responsibilities (like another bird nesting on the roof did)?

Although the roof crew had compassion for the birds, they displaced the killdeer - for reasons the birds might never understand. The Bible tells us that God cares about all of his creation, including the birds. Jesus, who knows the Father better than anyone, said, "Are not two sparrows sold for a penny? Yet not one of them will fall to the ground apart from the will of your Father. And even the very hairs of your head are all numbered. So don't be afraid; you are worth more than many sparrows" (Matthew 10:29-31).

Friend, I do not know why God in his wisdom has allowed this difficult time in your life. I do know, however, that he loves you and will carry you through. I do not know how the mama killdeer adjusted to the upheaval and relocation forced upon her. Only you can determine how you will react when unexpected problems are forced upon you. I encourage you to hold tightly to the Father who loves you. He will see you through. Remember

"God has said, 'Never will I leave you; never will I forsake you.' So we say with confidence, 'The Lord is my helper; I will not be afraid. What can man do to me?'" (Hebrews 13:5b, 6). Be encouraged, my friend. God will see you through.

Cost Vs. Comfort

Each year on the last weekend of May we remember the men and women who served in our armed forces, and honor those who never came home. Memorial Day was originally established immediately following the Civil War to honor those who lost their lives in battle – and gradually grew more encompassing – although the south preferred their separate day. Nobody likes war or wants to fight in one, but from earliest times men have believed that some ideals were worth fighting for, and some were evil enough to be worth fighting against. Faithful soldiers leave the comforts of home and family. They willingly submit to someone else's authority. From the bitter cold of Siberia where my Grandpa fought in WWI, to the beach at Normandy where my uncles landed many years later . . . from the horrible jungles of Vietnam that left so many nightmares and scars, to the blinding sandstorms of Desert Storm, wars have been fought and lives have been lost. Conditions in which soldiers live and fight have always been difficult, even in the wars fought here on our own soil. Brave soldiers endure conditions far worse than most of us can comprehend.

These thoughts bring troubling questions: Why is it that soldiers fighting for a cause assume uncomfortable living conditions as a part of the cost, but soldiers fighting for the cross complain about every little discomfort? How much time, energy, and money do we Christians spend just trying to make ourselves comfortable? Do we pray as much for lost souls as we do for our own comfort and freedom from pain?

The apostle Paul urged Timothy, "Endure hardship with us like a good soldier of Christ Jesus" (2 Timothy 2:3). As soldiers in the battle of the ages, we too are called to sacrifice our very lives. Look at Galatians 2:20, "I have been crucified with Christ and I no longer live, but Christ lives in me. The life I live in the body, I live by faith in the Son of God, who loved me and gave himself for me." What will it mean to really allow Christ to live through every aspect of your life?

A uniformed soldier is easily and clearly identifiable to the civilians in the area. Are you, as a part of God's army, clearly recognized as such by your family, friends, and co-workers? As we remember those who laid down their lives for our freedom, let us in turn allow our lives to be controlled by our God and Savior.

Medals and Crowns

Our government gives special honor and recognition to those who have gone above and beyond the call of duty. The Medal of Honor is the highest award for valor which our government bestows. The Distinguished Service Cross (Army), the Navy Cross (Navy and Marine Corps), and the Air Force Cross are awarded for "extreme gallantry and risk of life in combat with an armed enemy force." The Silver Star and the Bronze Star are also military decorations awarded for heroism. Finally, the Purple Heart (the oldest symbol and award still given out today) is awarded by the President to those who have been wounded or killed in military action. Generally these awards are given long after the heroic action occurs. Still, there are countless service men and women who serve faithfully and do their jobs very well who never receive public recognition.

In the army of the Lord, Scriptures tell us there is a crown to be given to God's faithful servants. "Everyone who competes in the games goes into strict training. They do it to get a crown that will not last; but we do it to get a crown that will last forever" (1 Corinthians 9:25). "Now there is in store for me the crown of righteousness, which the Lord, the righteous Judge, will award to me on that day – and not only to me, but also to all who have longed for his appearing" (2 Timothy 4:8). "Be faithful, even to the point of death, and I will give you the crown of life" (Revelation 2:10b). There are several mentions of rewards given in heaven based on our conduct while on earth (see Proverbs 19:17, Jeremiah 17:10, Matthew 5:12 and 16:27). Even if you will never be awarded a military Medal of Honor, you can still receive the greatest honor possible for any human being – the voice of God saying "Well done, good and faithful servant."

A good soldier, wholly committed to his country, does not base his decision to act on the probability of receiving a medal, but rather on doing his best. A true believer lives to honor his Lord, not to get a crown. In the end all those wonderful military medals are just pieces of metal with ribbon. No recipient takes his or hers to heaven. The crowns we will be awarded in heaven will be beautiful beyond our imaginations, yet they too will seem small compared to the glory of being in the presence of Almighty God. Even the heavenly beings "lay their crowns before the throne and say: 'You are worthy, our Lord and God, to receive glory and honor and power, for you created all things, and by your will they were created and have their being'" (Rev. 4:10).

I encourage you, brothers and sisters, "Do your best to present yourself to God as one approved, a workman who does not need to be ashamed and who correctly handles the word of truth" (2 Timothy 2:15). Even as we honor those who serve our nation, may we live to Honor the One who created it.

Every Believer

Too many times I have heard Christians say that visiting people is primarily the job of the pastor. Does this phrase, "It wouldn't really help for me to go see this person who is struggling, because people want to see the pastor" sound familiar? I have concluded that such a statement is a cop-out because it is unbiblical. Matthew 26:41-45 says, "Then he will say to those on his left, 'Depart from me, you who are cursed, into the eternal fire prepared for the devil and his angels. For I was hungry and you gave me nothing to eat, I was thirsty and you gave me nothing to drink, I was a stranger and you did not invite me in, I needed clothes and you did not clothe me, I was sick and in prison and you did not look after me." Did you notice he does not say, "You never asked the pastor to go visit me?" A person is found lacking because he did not go himself. The passage is a stern caution for each of us who claims to be a believer in Jesus Christ.

In kindergarten my younger brother learned that some teachers yell at students. When it happened for the first time, he hid under the table and refused to come out. We had just moved to Midland that summer and I was in my new third grade class when a lady I had never seen before came to the door and asked for me. She was my brother's teacher and wanted me to come and get him out. I went with her to the kindergarten room. I did not yell at him to come out. Rather, I crawled under the table and hugged him. In my vast 8-year-old wisdom I explained that teachers do that sometimes, and we have to just ignore them. I stayed with him until he was ready to come out.

When someone is hurting (whether in the church or outside of it) they often long for someone to crawl under the table and be close to them. They long for someone to care enough to come and visit, preferably someone they know. Then again, some prefer to be left alone to heal and/or process. It depends upon the person. Our role is to be attentive and available, offering a helping hand. You don't have to say anything profound. As a matter of fact, please don't. Many people have said that the most hurtful things said to them were comments by believers. Saying things like, "Well he is in a better place now" or "This is for the good", while well-meaning, can sound very callous to a heart that is raw. It is usually far better to say, "I'm sorry. I care. I am praying." Jesus said those who refused to minister to the hurting ones were refusing to minister to him. Would he expect you to come with profound theological comfort? Of course not. He was talking about showing love and friendship and compassion.

If you have never lived in a parsonage, you probably have no idea how many times pastors get called to go and visit people. Some are people from the church. Some are people from the community. Some are the third cousin of an ex-in-law, twice removed. Pastors willingly go and try to minister. They will continue to do that, even as they would to Jesus. Every one of us who claims to be a Christian should be seeking to minister to those who are desperately hurting all around us. Each of us knows someone who needs that love. Each of us is invited, expected, yea commanded, to give it. We are literally surrounded by hurting, lonely, desperate people. Let each of us reach out and love someone else as Christ first loved us.

God's Desire for You

What does the God who created you, wish for you? What are his dreams for you? Yes, he desires for us to be obedient, loving children, but I am not asking what he wants you to become; I am asking, what does he long to do for you? There are numerous Scripture passages that show us God's desire to pour out abundant blessings upon his children.

Deuteronomy 7:13-14 "He will love you and bless you and increase your numbers. He will bless the fruit of your womb, the crops of your land – your grain, new wine and oil – the calves of your herds and the lambs of your flocks in the land that he swore to your forefathers to give you. You will be blessed more than any other people; none of your men or women will be childless, nor any of your livestock without young. Is this how life would have been without sin? Is this what God dreamed of when he created us?

Deut. 5:29 "Oh that their hearts would be inclined to fear me and keep all my commands always, so that it might go well with them and their children forever!

Jeremiah 29:11 "For I know the plans I have for you," declares the Lord, "plans to prosper you and not to harm you, plans to give you hope and a future."

Isaiah 30:18 "Yet the Lord longs to be gracious to you; he rises to show you compassion. For the Lord is a God of justice. Blessed are all who wait for him!

Matthew 7:9 "Which of you, if his son asks for bread, will give him a stone? Or if he asks for a fish, will give him a snake? If you, then, though you are evil, know how to give good gifts to your children, how much more will your Father in heaven give good gifts to those who ask him!"

Most of us, like people in the Bible, ask God for things much smaller than what he longs to give us. It is easy to see him as the perfect, righteous Creator who puts up with us because he is stuck with us. I think he should be frustrated with my failures and roll his eyes when he looks at me. These passages portray God as our loving Father. I think there are at least three reasons why we don't receive these abundant blessings from him; 1) Sometimes he withholds gifts he longs to give because of our disobedience; 2) At other times, I believe he withholds them because we are not yet mature enough to receive them without shifting our faith and confidence from the Giver to the Gift; 3) Finally, James 4 says, "You do not have because you do not ask God. When you ask you do not receive, because you ask with wrong motives, that you may spend what you get on your pleasures." I want to encourage you to expand your understanding of who God is and also of his great heart for you. He longs to make himself known.

Kinsmen Redeemer

Late one Saturday evening I was not yet sure what God wanted me to write for that week's devotional message, even though I had been asking him for days. That night the kids asked me to stay upstairs with them while they were falling asleep. I used that quiet time to seek the Lord, who said, "Come to me, all you who are weary and burdened, and I will give you rest" (Matthew 11:28). As I sat there trying to picture him, based on Isaiah's description, and started to praise him, my loving Father gave me a picture. He reminded me of Boaz who was a kinsmen redeemer for Ruth.

In the quietness of those moments God helped me to see myself, weary and burdened, lying at his feet. Jesus, my kinsman-redeemer spread the garment of his grace over me. He flooded my heart with the peace of his presence, reminding me of his glorious salvation. I was totally renewed and revived.

Beloved, Jesus your Savior wants to spread his garment over you and warm you with his grace and his love. Make time today to be at rest, to be encouraged and strengthened as he reminds you he loves you enough to die for you. May you receive the gift of rest he longs to give.

Learning to Pray

The most powerful and effective teaching I have received on prayer came from my young children. First, focus prayer on giving thanks. Little children's prayers are often composed of long lists of things they are thankful for. "Thank you, Jesus for this day. Thank you for Daddy and Mommy. Thank you for my bed and my toys," etc. In contrast, most adults I know throw in a couple of thank-you's along with a long list of requests. We have our focus on what we want him to do, with too little focus on what he has already done. My five-year-old daughter often thanked Jesus for dying on the cross for our sins. She thanked him for that far more often than I ever did, even though I understood his sacrifice better (or so I thought). This is to my shame. She taught me to pray.

Second, my children showed me what a genuine desire to pray looks like. At mealtime, my son wouldn't eat until he prayed. No matter how many times the food had been blessed by others, he wanted to say a prayer too, giving his own thanks. Not only that, but he would often pray again before eating a second helping. In contrast, many adults and older children just go through the routine without ever really focusing our attention on our Provider. When given an opportunity to pray aloud, many of us just quietly wait for someone else to do it, rather than insisting on adding our own voice in praise even when invited to do so.

Third, a child's prayer is informal and conversational, without concern for using the right words. One night in our church's midweek kids' program we had a store for the final night. Kids could spend points they had earned through attendance and Scripture memorization. Earlier in the day my four-year-old daughter told me she knew just what she was going to buy at the store, "a truck for Hunter to show him Jesus' love." Hunter (age 3) was eagerly awaiting this gift, but it never came. His sister ended up spending all of her points on things for herself. I didn't hear my son react to that until bedtime prayers, when he said, "Thank you Jesus for Daddy and Mommy. Thank you that Sissy didn't get me a truck at the 'Venture club store, only stuff for her." I don't think he was really giving thanks for this. He thought all sentences in prayer started with "Thanks." He was just discussing with Jesus something from the day that made an impression on him. It was a conversational prayer between a three-year-old and his Jesus. It was priceless!

Like children, let us truly give thanks. Let us be eager to pray. Let us try to pray conversationally, as with a dear friend. God Bless you as you pursue him.

Seek the Giver

Friends of ours had two cats that would come into the bedroom well before sunrise every morning. They didn't come searching for attention or affection which some animals want from their humans. No, these cats came demanding to be fed. They would pounce, meow, even nip at toes until someone got up to feed them. They were only interested in the gift, not in the giver. It was kind of an "I-want-what-I-want-when-I-want-it" attitude. Does this sound like the way many of us approach God?

Biblical encounters with the Almighty often resulted in fainting in terror. Both Isaiah and Ezekiel saw visions of the Holy One seated on his throne, with indescribable creatures constantly declaring "Holy, Holy, Holy is the Lord God Almighty!" How many of us are more like the cats than like the prophets? How many of us start talking and listing our wants without ever bothering to "Be still and know that I am God"? If we could experience his awesome presence, sheer awe of him would reduce us to silence. If we learn to seek God with an attitude of longing and worship, the relationship will be rich and fulfilling. I encourage you to seek to know him more personally. Focus on who he is, not just on what you want him to do for you. The gift of the Savior means so much more when you know the Giver personally. Spend some time studying the accounts in Isaiah chapter 6, Ezekiel chapter 1, and Revelation 1:12-18. Make time to be still and know the One who is God (Psalm 46:10).

Remember the Cross

Memorial, by definition, means commemorative, "serving to help people remember some person or event."[7] On Memorial Day we honor the memory of those who have given all for this great country. We set aside a day to help us remember their service and honor their sacrifices. We also give thanks for those who have served and those who are serving currently, and we thank God for the many ways he has blessed this country.

We see reminders and examples of memorials in Scripture. "Then Samuel took a stone and set it up between Mizpah and Shen. He named it "Ebenezer," saying, 'Thus far has the Lord helped us'" (1 Samuel 7:12). "Jacob took the stone he had placed under his head and set it up as a pillar and poured oil on top of it. He called that place Bethel . . . Then Jacob made a vow . . ." (Genesis 28:19). During what is now known as "The Last Supper" Jesus "took bread, gave thanks and broke it, and gave it to them, saying, 'This is my body given for you; do this in remembrance of me'" (Luke 22:19). As Joshua led the people into the Promised Land, God provided yet another miraculous crossing on dry ground. "When the whole nation had finished crossing the Jordan, the Lord said to Joshua, 'Choose twelve men from among the people, one from each tribe, and tell them to take up twelve stones from the middle of the Jordan from right where the priests stood and to carry them over with you and put them down at the place where you stay tonight'" (Joshua 4:1-3). So Joshua gave them instructions, telling the chosen twelve that these stones were "to serve as a sign among you. In the future when your children ask you, 'What do these stones mean?' tell them that the flow of the Jordan was cut off before the ark of the covenant of the Lord. When it crossed the Jordan, the waters of the Jordan were cut off. These stones are to be a memorial to the people of Israel forever" (Joshua 4:6, 7).

Song-writer Jennie E. Hussey wrote *Lead Me to Calvary* in 1921. Look at the words of the chorus: "Lest I forget Gethsemane, Lest I forget Thine agony, Lest I forget Thy love for me, Lead me to Calvary."[8] God forbid that we should ever forget. There are many types of reminders, from physical markers, to worship songs, to written notes, to pictures and jewelry. Any of these can be an effective memorial. What you do to remember is not as important as whether you do something, and why you do it.

Each Memorial Day, as you visit the cemetery and notice graves marked with crosses, take time to be still and remember those who fought for our country. Then, take time to remember The One who hung on the cross to give us life.

No Lucky Charm

While teaching kids a new game, I saw one little boy hold the dice in his hands and whisper over them with closed eyes. He was praying for the numbers he wanted to roll. Kids are still learning about God's power and how it works. Many adults who should know better, are no better. I had a friend who refused church, but called every time her family was in crisis, asking me to pray for God's help. I did pray with her and for her many times, but eventually I had to explain to her that God had no interest in being her magic wand, to be prayerfully waved when she was in trouble.

God's people, like those described above, have tried to use him as a lucky charm. The Israelites were losing their battle against the Philistines, who killed 4,000 the first day. As the Israelite army regrouped, they wondered why God wasn't helping them. Rather than going to him in humility and pleading for help, they "brought the ark of the covenant of the Lord Almighty, who is enthroned between the cherubim" (1 Samuel 4:4). The ark represented God's presence continually with his people. He made it his throne, which is why nobody except a priest was supposed to come near it, and then only in prescribed ways at prescribed times. When the ark entered the camp the Israelites cheered (but didn't seek the Lord) and the loud noise was heard in the Philistine camp. The Philistines remembered God's great display of power in Egypt and they were afraid. They determined to fight as hard as they could. In the battle that followed, 30,000 Israelite soldiers were killed and the ark was captured. What a terrible day it was for Israel. The victorious Philistines carried the ark of the Lord's covenant home with them, but every city where they placed it began to suffer afflictions because God's hand was heavy upon them. They eventually sent the ark back to Israel. The people in the first town it came to celebrated and sacrificed offerings to the Lord, but some still treated the ark (and the God of the ark) irreverently. Seventy of them died at the celebration (1 Samuel 6:19).

God's great desire is for people to know him. In fact, there are at least 87 references in Scripture where God says "They will know that I am the Lord" or a similar statement. He says this not only in reference to his chosen people, but also about other nations. God longs to be known by all. God delights in blessing his people, but a far greater longing of his heart is for individual people to live in personal relationship with him.

Let us not act like those without judge or Lord in 1 Samuel 4-6, when they didn't even think to seek God's approval for battle. If they asked, "Do you want us to fight the Philistines now? Where? Who should lead our army?" there is no record of it. Let us learn from the example of the people of Israel. Living in personal relationship with God means asking him to lead us, and then following. Sometimes we decide what to do (take this job, buy this house, enter into this relationship) and then ask God to bless what we are doing. This is upside down, as if I know what is best for my life and his job is to bless me. Living that way demonstrates a very warped understanding of who God is. It is no better than making terrible choices with how I treat my body and then asking God for good health.

Friends, the first step in the Christian life is asking God to forgive our sins. Then we study and learn to know him personally. We ask for guidance and follow where he leads. Through that process we grow to know him better and hear his voice more clearly. In the story above, the people finally got rid of their idols, sought the Lord, and implored Samuel to seek God on their behalf (1 Samuel 7). Then God gave them great victory over the Philistines. It wasn't that God couldn't have defeated the enemy in the first battle. When they sought the Lord's direction rather than just his blessing upon their decision, he answered mightily. God is more than able to meet our needs mightily too. May we never reduce our God to the status of a lucky charm when we are in trouble. Let us seek to know him and follow him every day of our lives.

Look on me with Favor

The Son of God was crucified between two criminals. Gospel writers Matthew and Mark both identify them as robbers. The robbers had earlier joined the spectators in heaping insults on Jesus. Luke's account is somewhat different. Luke tells us, "One of the criminals who hung there hurled insults at him: 'Aren't you the Christ? Save yourself and us!' But the other criminal rebuked him. 'Don't you fear God,' he said, 'since you are under the same sentence? We are punished justly, for we are getting what our deeds deserve. But this man has done nothing wrong.' Then he said, 'Jesus, remember me when you come into your kingdom.' Jesus answered him, 'I tell you the truth, today you will be with me in paradise'" (Luke 23:39-43).

"Jesus, remember me when you come into your kingdom." By the time this criminal figured out that the guy hanging next to him was the Christ, he had nothing whatsoever to offer him. With an agonizing hour or two left to live, and unable to even move his arms or legs, he asked for that which he knew he did not deserve: "Jesus, remember me." Jesus, in unspeakable agony himself, extended mercy. This man would never be a great evangelist, would never plant a church, would never write books or songs about God, would never share his faith with a single soul. The criminal had nothing whatsoever to offer, all he had was his need.

The same is true for you and for me. Most of us find it easy to list the skills we don't have. I can't sing or play an instrument. I have no athletic ability and no sense of style. I am not much of a hostess or a public speaker. I don't seem to have anything that God would want. I am a liability rather than an asset. I can relate to the robber.

Grace has been defined as "unmerited favor." Jesus saw that miserable wretch of a robber and looked on him with favor. I picture it as light coming out from him like a gentle spotlight and illuminating him. He does the same for each one who asks. No wonder the hymn writers call it "Amazing Grace." The assurance that Almighty God looks on undeserving Lynn Adams with favor is nothing less than amazing.

As we realize that we come to him with nothing to offer, we become more fully aware of the magnitude of his gift. We become a new creation in Christ (2 Corinthians 5:17). The Spirit gives us gifts of leadership ability, or generosity, or teaching, or speaking in tongues, (and many other gifts) that we might have something to give back for the glory of His Name. May each of us be overwhelmed, amazed, speechless, moved to tears as we realize the magnitude of God's grace extended to us.

All Alone

That terrible Thursday evening in the garden, Jesus prayed alone while his closest friends slept. He stood trial alone. There is no record of anyone speaking a single word in his defense, other than Pilate's statement that he found no fault in him. Although there were many people at the hill called Golgotha, and even two other men crucified alongside him, Jesus was alone. Weighted down with the guilt of my sins, he experienced the worst pain of all – "My God, My God, why have you forsaken me?" (Mark 16:34b). Jesus had to walk alone along the road that led to salvation.

Each one of us must walk that road alone, even as he did. Every single person who hears and accepts the call of the Spirit to repent and receive new life in Jesus must come alone. Even when hundreds or thousands of people stream to an altar at once, each one must come alone. The gift of salvation is for everyone, Jews and Gentiles alike, but there is no group plan. The only way is for me to acknowledge my own guilt directly to the Father; to confess my sins in broken humility. When I come to the cross, it is just him and me, one-on-one.

The walk of faith is one I must walk alone. Christian brothers and sisters walking along the road help to encourage me, but the choice to take another step with him is a choice nobody can make for me. My entire journey is one-on-one with the Spirit of God. The experience of sweet fellowship with him is one that is nearly impossible to explain to somebody else.

A Two-Tiered Drama

The spiritual warfare all around us is powerful and continual, even though we are seldom aware of it. The Easter story is two-fold; events in the physical realm and others in the spiritual realm unfolded simultaneously. Nobody knows for sure where Jesus went or what he did between the time of his burial on Friday and his first appearance to people on Sunday morning. Being no longer restricted by humanness, he did not need time to rest and recuperate from his ordeal. When Jesus appeared to Mary Magdalene he said, "Do no hold on to me, for I have not yet retuned to the Father. Go instead to my brothers and tell them, 'I am returning to my Father and your Father, to my God and your God'" (John 20:17). He did not show himself to the disciples until that evening (v. 19) so maybe he spent Sunday with his Father. God is not limited to a time continuum like we are, and he has not told us what happened on that Saturday.

There are some references that suggest he may have descended into hell, the domain of Satan, and reclaimed the souls of mankind which he had purchased with his own blood (see Ephesians 4:8,9). Then he defeated the final enemy - death (1 Corinthians 15:26). Even as that terrible yet wonderful drama unfolded on the stage of Golgotha's hill, a simultaneous battle was being fought backstage. In the unseen spirit realm, Jesus was fighting the enemy of our souls, buying back the deeds to our lives.

Then again, maybe we have it reversed. Perhaps the visible display of his death on the cross, covered in our putrid sins, was the backstage action and the most powerful part of the drama was what took place on the unseen center stage. During the days of his life on earth the Son of God displayed his authority over weather and creation. He demonstrated power over sickness, and blindness, and demonic possession, and he even raised the dead. We come to a better understanding of his power and authority as we note the ways evil spirits reacted to him. They had been opposing God for centuries, and knew their adversary. Notice their responses to him in these passages:

A man in the synagogue, possessed by an evil spirit cried out at the top of his voice, "Ha! What do you want with us, Jesus of Nazareth? Have you come to destroy us? I know who you are – the Holy One of God!" (Luke 4:35). "And Jesus healed many who had various diseases. He also drove out many demons, but he would not let the demons speak because they knew who he was" (Mark 1:34, see also Luke 8). "You believe that there is one God. Good! Even the demons believe that – and shudder" (James 2:19).

Brothers and sisters, the spirits recognized and feared the Christ far more readily than humans did. They knew his power far exceeded their own. Our Savior is so powerful that he defeated the enemy of our souls in order to buy us back as he own. He won the victory over death. There is no battle we are facing that will stretch or challenge him. He is stronger than the problems we can see, and more powerful than the evil powers that seek to destroy us. Let us praise and honor the One who is Risen Indeed.

Pivotal Servants

Since the beginning of time God has used some to lead others to him. Which of the following do you think were most effective?

- Adam and Eve knew God in a way that none of us has experienced. Their choices changed forever the relationships between human beings and their Maker.
- Noah's obedience allowed the human race to continue (although as in the days of Esther, God could have found another way if Noah had disobeyed).
- For the Jewish people, Moses stands out probably even higher than the patriarchs – Abraham, Isaac, and Jacob.
- King David led the people, and through the Psalms he still leads people to praise and trust God.
- The prophets were crucial in the life of the nation.
- Joseph and Mary, even Pilate and the religious leaders had roles to play.
- Letters written by the apostle Paul and others helped to shape the formation of the early Christian church and the spread of the gospel.

I think an argument could be made for any of these, each of whom was pivotal in his/her time and situation. The crucial issue is the willingness of each person to follow God's leading with whole-hearted surrender. Some of the people who had the greatest impact on following generations were "unschooled ordinary men" (Acts 4:13) whom Jesus called to walk with him through his years of ministry. Consider the role Peter, James, John, and other disciples were called to play in God's great plan. These men had to be willing to accept a total change of mindset about things they had been taught all their lives – rules for the Sabbath, animal sacrifices, clean/unclean animals, what the promised Messiah would be and do, and the unthinkable: inclusion of non-Jews as children of God. Some in Jesus' day could not wrap their minds around even one of these paradigm shifts, yet the disciples were called to change their whole way of thinking in a matter of a few short years. If they had not been willing to be totally "transformed by the renewing of their minds" they would not have been able to "test and approve what God's will is - his good, pleasing, and perfect will" (Romans 12:2). If these men had not whole-heartedly embraced God the Father in the ways that Jesus revealed him, they would never have set out to reach the entire known world with the Gospel message. What would that mean for you and for me?

I doubt that these men realized what they were signing up for when Jesus issued the invitation, "Follow me" (Matthew 4:19, Mark 1:17). Yet, God used them mightily to change the world, not only for Jews, but for Gentiles the world over. You and I will never have our names mentioned in the Holy Scriptures. Likely none of us will ever fill a role that is quite so crucial for the human race. Still, each of us has assigned tasks which are absolutely pivotal for our families, our church, our community, and for future generations. Have we surrendered fully to God's leading in our lives? Will we respond with obedience or resistance? "Our greatest fear as individuals and as a church should not be of failure but of succeeding at things in life that don't really matter."[9] If we are not ready to serve him in whatever ways he commands, he is not truly our Lord.

Don't Settle

When I was a young adult finding my way and making plans for my life, my mother was faithfully praying. Her consistent prayer went something like this: "Father, please do not let Lynn settle for less than the very best that you have planned for her." God alone knows how many poor decisions her prayers helped to prevent in my life. I am so grateful for her faithfulness. Her prayer for me has become my prayer, not only for my children, but also for you. I pray that you will not settle for less than the very best that God has planned for you (in your relationships, in your work, in ministry, and especially in terms of the depth of your relationship with your Savior).

One man who settled for less was King Solomon. God had appeared to him not once, but twice (1 Kings 3, and 9). God gave him abundant wealth and greater wisdom than anyone. The land enjoyed peace and prosperity throughout his reign. God had great plans for Solomon, but Solomon got distracted and self-absorbed. In the end he actually built altars for worshiping the gods of his foreign wives, and it cost his family the kingdom (1 Kings 11). There is no indication that he repented when confronted with his sin.

Friend, what does God dream for your life? His plan includes the fruit of the Spirit being evident in your life. Do "love, joy, peace, patience, kindness, goodness, faithfulness, gentleness, and self-control" describe who you are? (Galatians 5:22-23). He intends for your life to so overflow with love that others can clearly see Jesus in you. God longs, yes longs, to have time alone with you where you focus on no one and nothing except him. God's best plan for your life involves you hearing his voice and walking in step with him. Do you know him that way? God's plan for your life will lead you into a sense of fulfillment that cannot be found anywhere in the world except in the center of God's will.

Rather than settling for what is familiar or comfortable or easy, I challenge you – as I have been challenged – to pursue God desperately. Develop a mindset that is continually engaged in sincere worship. At least once during every waking hour I try to stop and picture God on his throne, thanking him for being my Father. I want to leave you with this prayer, written by A.W.Tozer. It has become my prayer for myself and my prayer for you as we choose not to settle for less than the best God has for us:

"O God, I have tasted Thy goodness, and it has both satisfied me and made me thirsty for more. I am painfully conscious of my need for further grace. I am ashamed of my lack of desire. O God, the Triune God, I want to want Thee; I long to be filled with longing; I thirst to be made more thirsty still. Show me Thy glory, I pray Thee, so that I may know Thee indeed. Begin in mercy a new work of love within me. Say to my soul, 'Rise up my love, my fair one, and come away.' Then give me grace to rise and follow Thee up from this misty lowland where I have wandered so long."[10]

Making Himself Known

For Mother's Day 2011 my wonderful husband surprised me with a trip to Arizona to see God's handiwork in the Grand Canyon and several other locations. It didn't take me long to conclude that this landmark is sadly misnamed. For one thing, "grand" does not begin to describe it. For another thing, it is far more than a "canyon." It is 277 river miles long, as much as 18 miles wide in places, and a mile deep. They claim some of the rocks at the base are 2 billion years old. I am skeptical about that, but only the One who was there knows for sure. (My imagination pictures him scraping his mighty fingers through the rock to give the river a

73

head start.) As we marveled at God's amazing creation in this vast network of spectacular canyons and elsewhere, I found myself awed once again by how big our God must be. Why would he make something so vast that the human eye can't even take it all in? If it comes to that, why would he make stars estimated to number in the hundreds of billions? Why make the oceans six miles deep in some spots? Why did he make giant Sequoia and Redwood trees more than 300 ft. tall?

We would have been impressed with just a single canyon, just a thousand stars, just a few different colors or a dozen kinds of plants and animals. Why did God make so much, so many, so extreme? I believe the answer is that creation glorifies its Creator. God has made himself known to all mankind through all that he has made (see Romans 1:20, Psalm 19:1, 2). All things were created, not just by God, but for God. "For by Him all things were created: things in heaven and on earth, visible and invisible, whether thrones or powers or rulers or authorities; all things were created by him and for him" (Colossians 1:16). I believe he enjoys creating and enjoys his creation.

God has made himself known through the beauty of his creation. When we take time to really see his handiwork, it helps us to know him a little more. The only appropriate response is to let the beauty of nature direct us toward our Lord. The more a person comes to know God, the more desperately he or she will long to know him more intimately and to live a life that pleases him.

One example of a person who had a profound experience of learning about God was Josiah. 2 Kings 22 and 23 recounts the story of one of the last kings of Judah before the people were taken into captivity in Babylon. Josiah became king at the age of eight, following the reign of two evil kings. When he was 26 years old, he ordered the cleaning and restoration of the temple of the Lord. During that process, the old book of the Law (part of what became the Old Testament) was found and brought to the king. When Josiah heard what God had commanded for his people, and realized how far his nation was from those laws, he tore his robes and immediately began to inquire of the Lord. Josiah carried out a great cleansing of Judah – removing high places and altars to idols that had stood for generations. He led the people in recommitting themselves to the Lord and obeying his laws.

King Josiah came to a new understanding of who God was, and it changed not only his life but his entire nation. Every time we come to a new or deeper knowledge of God, it should produce changes in our lives. We should be ever seeking to know him more. As we learn to know him more, we should love him more, and it should be reflected in the way we live our lives. He is no wimpy, needy Master begging people to give him a chance. He is all-powerful, all-knowing, everywhere-present at all times. He has revealed himself through his creation and he expects us to use the intelligence we have been given to recognize that and to seek to know him. Every individual is responsible to make the choice to know his/her Creator. He has made himself known. Do you really know him? As God shows himself and his glory to you and to me, may each of us grow to know and love him more.

The Wrong Finish Line

My daughter and some of her friends participated in a 5K run after several weeks of training. Watching the determination in their facial expressions as they crossed the finish line blessed me. The apostle Paul compared living a life of faith to running a race. "Do you not know that in a race all the runners run, but only one gets the prize? Run in such a way as to get the prize. Everyone who competes in the games goes into strict training. They do it to get a crown that will not last; but we do it to get a crown that will last forever. Therefore I do not run like a man running aimlessly; I do not fight like a man beating the air. No, I beat my body and make it my slave so that after I have preached to others, I myself will not be disqualified for the prize" (1 Corinthians 9:24-27).

The training and self discipline required of successful athletes has a parallel in the lives of believers training themselves to submit to the leading of the Holy Spirit rather than just doing whatever feels good. If life is comparable to a race, what is the goal, the finish line for which we are aiming? For the believer, to hear "Well done, thou good and faithful servant" (Matthew 25:21). Anything less is running toward the wrong finish line. So how did Jesus teach us to live? He said, "If anyone would come after me he must

75

deny himself and take up his cross and follow me" (Matthew 16:24, Mark 8:34, Luke 9:23). Friends, we don't get to skip right to the "follow me" part. It seems that somewhere along the way, many of us have turned aside onto a path that seeks a life free from pain, conflict, discomfort, or troubles. A path of ease and comfort is not the path Jesus invited us to follow. Imagine training hard and running a race, but turning off course and running across the wrong finish line. What good does it do to run a race like that?

There is only one finish line we should strive to cross. "But small is the gate and narrow the road that leads to life, and only a few find it" (Matthew 7:14). It is a lifestyle of self-denial, of total dependence upon God rather than on ourselves, of persecution and of being misunderstood and rejected by the world. Do we desire the sweet feeling of God's presence, or do we truly desire God himself? In the race of life, are we pursuing holiness and an ever - deeper love for God, or are we pursuing pleasures? It is the only race track that leads to that treasured eternal prize of hearing the Father say, "Well done." Therefore, I challenge you, as I myself have been challenged, to be absolutely sure that the life you are living, the race you are running, will lead to the prize you are seeking. "Therefore, since we are surrounded by such a great cloud of witnesses, let us throw off everything that hinders and the sin that so easily entangles, and let us run with perseverance the race marked out for us" (Hebrews 12:1). Run well the race, but make sure you are striving toward the goal that is eternal.

The King Gets the Glory

When a team wins a championship, the coach gets much of the credit even though he didn't personally score a single point. The players work as a team under their leader, and they are glad to share the glory with him. In the same way, our accomplishments as believers bring glory to our King, our Supreme Commander. Peter tells us that we will share in the glory that will be revealed. "And when the Chief Shepherd appears, you will receive the crown of glory that will never fade away" (1 Peter 5:4). As Paul was nearing the end of his life on Earth, he said, "I have fought the good fight, I have finished the race, I have kept the faith. Now there is in store for me the crown of righteousness, which the Lord, the righteous

Judge, will award to me on that day – and not only to me, but also to all who have longed for his appearing" (2 Timothy 4:7,8). That means you and me, Friends! Paul told us that runners who win a race receive a crown that will not last, but we will receive crowns that last forever (1 Corinthians 9:25). The Bible says people of God will receive a crown of glory, a crown of righteousness, a crown of life (Revelation 2:10), but these are not the goal. The ultimate goal is to hear him say "Well done, good and faithful servant" and to spend eternity enjoying life with God.

In John's visions of heaven, he saw four living creatures continually praising God and declaring his holiness. When the living creatures would say, "Holy, Holy, Holy is the Lord God Almighty, who was, and is and is to come" the twenty-four elders would fall down and worship him, laying their crowns at his feet (Rev.4:8-10). Like those elders, we too may one day have the privilege of casting our crowns in worship before the One who is worthy of all praise. On that day, what crowns will you have to lay at his feet? We will give him all honor and glory, recognizing clearly that anything good we might have accomplished was only though his help and strength. Are we living in such a way as to earn crowns to cast at his feet? Sometimes we seem to get so wrapped up in the issues and struggles of daily living that our goal is just to breathe in and out all day long. This may be necessary during a crisis, but we need to aim much higher than just survival. Each of us should be fighting to win victories for the glory of our King who is worthy of all honor and praise.

Summer

Summer is always a good time to stop and take a brief inventory. We think back to January and the expectations we had for the New Year, and the improvements we committed to making in our lives. By the end of June the year is half over already. For some, the bumps have been bigger than for others, but probably very few have had the first six months of the year go just the way they planned or hoped. Life has a way of throwing us unexpected curves. Summer is a time to re-evaluate and make some adjustments, resetting our course toward the goals we most want to meet. Are we closer to God than we were at the start of the year? Are we taking better care of our physical bodies than we did last year? Are we telling others about what Jesus has done in our lives? How are we doing at praying more earnestly for lost loved ones, and at reading through the Bible this year? Let us re-commit today to the decisions we have made to honor God in every area of our lives.

The Master Gardener

Some of you are experts at gardening. Not me. Although I like flowers and fresh produce, I know very little about growing them. Issues like the spacing of plants, type of soil, etc. are hit-or-miss rather than carefully planned. I am happy if they grow green and healthy, and if they happen to bloom, that is an extra bonus. But if they flop over and turn brown, I don't know how to help them. No matter how much more you know about gardening than I know, the fact is that plant growth is a miracle. We can try to provide optimal conditions, and study plant life, but only God can make something grow.

Writing to address divided loyalties within the church, the Apostle Paul wrote, "What, after all, is Apollos? And what is Paul? Only servants, through whom you came to believe – as the Lord has assigned to each his task. I planted the seed, Apollos watered it, but God made it grow. So neither he who plants nor he who waters is anything, but only God, who makes things grow. The man who plants and the man who waters have one purpose, and each will be rewarded according to his own labor. For we are God's fellow workers; you are God's field, God's building" (1Corinthians 3:5-9).

As ministers (and all believers are to be ministers) we try to plant seeds of the gospel in others by telling them about Jesus. We water them with testimonies and teaching so they understand what a difference Christ can make in a life. We do our best to create optimal conditions for growth. Some seeds flourish right off the bat. Some never develop at all. Some take a long time to germinate and begin to mature. Fortunately, the growth or rate of growth is not our problem. Only God can make believers grow. Like Paul and Apollos, each of us has been assigned a task as a minister of the gospel. Some plant seeds in unbelievers. Some water the seeds. Those who plant and those who water have one purpose – to create optimal conditions for the growth of God's kingdom.

What Paul said about ministering is also true about Christian parenting. We are instructed to train up our children in the way they should go (Proverbs 22:6). It is our responsibility to plant seeds of the gospel in our children and to water them faithfully with Biblical training and with our own daily example. We have a few precious years in which to train them, but only God can grow them into mature believers. Some will begin to blossom right away. Others may bloom and then lie dormant for several years. Still others may take years to develop in the first place. This can be incredibly frustrating, discouraging, even frightening for parents, but we must trust the Master Gardener. He will tend and prune each one as he knows is best. High School graduation marks the formal end of parents' opportunity to train up these young people according to Scripture. It marks the beginning of the waiting to see how these fresh young shoots will develop and grow in their walks with the Savior. What a blessing to know that the Master Gardener holds them in his hands and knows just how to care for them. We need to continue to water them with prayer as we wait on God.

Leave it There

One day in early June, my dad and my kids and I witnessed a remarkable sight. On a riverbank were two mama turtles laying eggs in shallow holes. We watched one turtle use her back feet to push dirt and stones back into place over the eggs. It was a slow process. When she finished, she walked slowly and directly back to the water without ever even looking at her work. She was done with them, so she left them there – forever. The rest was God's job through nature.

Her actions got me thinking about eggs we as Christians have trouble burying and leaving. First is the egg of worry. We bring a "big" problem to God and ask him to solve it, but instead of walking away, we keep walking around it, digging the egg back up and reminding God it is there. We need to release our worries into his care, praying and trusting that he will take care of each situation.

The second egg is past sins. Some who have come to Christ and been made whole, still see themselves as dirty and unworthy. They refuse to go forward, acting as children of the King and doing his work. When we do this, we tell Christ that his sacrifice was not enough to cleanse us. Romans 8:1 says, "There is therefore now no condemnation for those who are in Christ Jesus." Refusal to accept his forgiveness leaves us wandering around feeling guilty, and utterly useless in the work of the kingdom.

The third egg is forgiveness. This is a big one. When someone has wronged me, which is guaranteed to happen, the Bible tells me in no uncertain terms that I need to forgive – not just for that person's benefit, but for mine. "For if you forgive men when they sin against you, your heavenly Father will also forgive you. But if you do not forgive men their sins, your Father will not forgive your sins" (Matthew 6:14). If I keep acting offended, or continually replay the conversation in my mind, or hold a grudge, then I have not forgiven. A good measuring stick is my willingness to give that person the benefit of the doubt. We cannot keep picking the egg back up and carrying it around, any more than Christ does that with our sins. Such behavior destroys friendships, marriages, and even churches.

All of us can learn from the turtle . . . slow down, and when you give something to God, leave it there. Giving big problems to God and letting go can be a long, difficult process, but it is worth the effort. Never look back.

Starting Well

Graduation is a time of joy, of hopes, of optimism. During commencement, top students talk about how much they've learned and how ready they are to handle anything that comes their way. They have started well and they are totally committed to succeed in pursuing their dreams.

Scriptures tell us about someone else who started well. Asa, King of Judah, "Did what was right in the eyes of the Lord his God. . . He commanded Judah to seek the Lord, the God of their fathers, and to obey his laws and commands" (2 Chronicles 14:2-4). When enemies came against Judah, he cried out to the all-powerful Lord for help. Because of his faith, God gave him victory. King Asa led all the people of Judah to covenant to seek the Lord with all of their hearts and their souls. The people followed his example so completely that those who refused to seek the Lord were put to death. "They sought God eagerly, and he was found by them. So the Lord gave them rest on every side" (2 Chronicles 15:15).

Somewhere along the way, Asa's commitment to God derailed. In the 36th year of his reign, the king of Israel (the northern kingdom) came against him. Rather than seeking the Lord, he sought help from a neighboring king. God expressed his disappointment through a prophet, but King Asa refused to soften his heart and repent. Asa was angry and never returned to God, even when he was afflicted with a disease in his feet. He started well, but finished very poorly.

Each new believer starts out by accepting forgiveness of sins through Jesus, and committing to live for him. However, after starting well, some of us have reneged on our commitment. Some have sought help with our problems from friends, from counselors, or from books without seeking the Master. Others have sought escape through hobbies, entertainment, or addictions. Finally, some have continued going through the motions of serving God, through attending worship/church, visiting or bringing food to sick neighbors, or volunteering at the food pantry, while their hearts are filled with bitterness, critical thoughts, and complaints. That early passion to know God and live a life that pleases him dwindles to scarcely more than a memory.

My heart is deeply burdened for people who have started to walk with Jesus by receiving forgiveness from sins, but are not living in the abundant peace, joy, and hope that he longs to give. No matter who you are, what you have done, or what problem you are facing, God invites you to come near to him. Seek him humbly, and ask him to cleanse and to heal. His eyes are roaming through the earth looking for people whose hearts are fully committed to him (2 Chronicles 16:9). He longs to bless you and make you whole. Having started well, let us renew our unconditional commitment to Christ. Let us finish well.

Response to Rebuke

There is more to the story of King Asa (see 2 Chronicles 14-21). When a neighboring king came up against him, rather than seeking God, Asa formed a treaty with the king of Aram. God sent a seer, or prophet, to confront him with his actions and God's disappointment. In response, Asa turned his back on God – permanently (2 Chronicles 16). In the next chapter we meet his son Jehoshaphat, who succeeded him as king. He too started well, walking in the ways of King David (2 Chonicles 17:3). Jehoshaphat, in his turn, made an alliance with an ungodly king. "Like father, like son," but here comes the difference. When God sent Jehu the seer to meet him and confront him with his wrong decision, Jehoshaphat turned back to the Lord, and instructed the people to do so as well. He reminded the priests, Levites, and heads of Israelite families, "You must serve faithfully and wholeheartedly in the fear of the Lord" (2 Chronicles 19:4-9). When the vast army of Moabites and Ammonites and Meunites came to make war on him, he was right with God – which is right where he needed to be. He led the people in seeking the Lord. This is the response he received, "This is what the Lord says to you: 'Do not be afraid or discouraged because of this vast army. For the battle is not yours, but God's.'" The people believed, and marched out singing. God gave total victory without his people even having to fight, (20:23, 24) for his eyes had been roaming throughout the earth to strengthen those whose hearts were fully committed to him (16:9).

These two kings both started well, trying to lead their nation according to God's commands. One major difference is the pride or humility with which each responded to correction. We face the same issue. Obviously, none of us does the right thing in the right way with the right motives all the time. The problem is that some of us live as though we do. We have become so certain of our own point of view that we refuse to hear any other opinions. Some of us have become almost impossible to get along with, and don't even realize it. The action may not be wrong, but the way it is done and the motive behind it is sin. Some of us have been blessed with courageous, loving people who will gently confront us and call sin "sin." We all need those people.

The question I want us to honestly ask ourselves is this: How do I respond to someone who confronts me about what I am doing or how I am doing it or my motives for doing it? Do I become defensive, and like Asa, walk off in a huff? Or do I humbly listen, think and pray over this new point of view, and repent when necessary? Obviously, the first way is easier and more natural – and dead wrong. The right way is almost never the easy way. Each of us should ask the Lord to show us where we stand in this area of humility.

A Father's Footsteps

A young father walked out to check on his vegetable garden, trailed by four enthusiastic but ignorant young "helpers." To their inexperienced eyes, the garden looked like loose dirt with a few green plants sticking up here and there. The father cautioned his helpers to step between rows, but they were not sure where, exactly, the rows were. One after another they followed their father, jumping from one of Daddy's footprints to the next. In this way they navigated the garden safely without damaging any of the fragile plants. (This is one of my mom's favorite memories, as she witnessed her four children jumping through the garden, trying to follow in their Daddy's footsteps.)

Fathers have many things to teach their offspring. Training children the right way to walk before their God is one of the most important responsibilities that God has given to fathers. A man is instructed to be the spiritual head of his household, just as Jesus

Christ is the head of the church (1 Corinthians 11:3). Some of us had fathers that did a great job teaching us to work hard, or to be good athletes, or to earn and manage money, or to help others. Some of us did not have a good fatherly example at all. But all of us who have received forgiveness of sins through Jesus Christ have entered into relationship with The Heavenly Father. He is the consummate loving father, always ready to guide.

Like a dad leading his kids through the garden, we as Christians are to show those who are younger in the faith, the way to walk through life following Jesus' example. We have been commanded to, "Be imitators of God, therefore, as dearly loved children and live a life of love, just as Christ loved us and gave himself up for us as a fragrant offering and sacrifice to God" (Ephesians 5:1-2). Paul said, "Follow my example as I follow the example of Christ" (1 Corinthians 11:1). We should be saying the same to those who are younger in their faith, trying to learn to walk with the Savior.

A song written by Jon Mohr reminds us of our responsibility for the influence we have over other people. "May all who come behind us find us faithful. May the fire of our devotion light their way. May the footprints that we leave, lead them to believe, and the lives we live inspire them to obey. Oh may all who come behind us find us faithful."[11] The question before each of us is this: what Spiritual footprints are we leaving for others to follow as they grow in their faith?

Come In Awe

Hebrews 4:16 says, "Let us then approach the throne of grace with confidence, so that we may receive mercy and find grace to help us in our time of need." God invites us to draw near and approach his throne. He stands ready to give us the mercy, the grace, and the help we need. How then do we approach Almighty God? I think, too often, we come waltzing in like we would into the home of a friend or family member, and start talking before we are even inside. This is the Almighty Creator who formed the earth, who hung the sun and calls billions of stars each by name. He is the perfect, holy One. He is worthy of our respect and honor. Although he invites us to call him Father, and to approach his throne with confidence, we must come in the reverence that is due him. When God met with Moses at the burning bush, he told him to take off his sandals, for God's presence made the place holy (Exodus 3). Throughout the Old Testament, those who encountered him or even his messengers, fell face down in fear.

Queen Esther hesitated to go before the king, because the law stated that anyone who came, uninvited, into the presence of the king would be put to death. The only exception to this law was if the king held out his scepter, extending welcome to the intruder. To some extent, this is true for those who seek to approach the King of Kings. He is far more awe-inspiring than any human ruler. As God was teaching the Israelites to know and respect him, he commanded that the priests carry out their duties in the outer court of the tabernacle, but only one priest entered into the Holy of Holies, and that only once a year to offer sacrifices for the people (Hebrews 9:6,7). They did not take lightly the privilege of entering God's presence.

So what does Scripture teach us about how to come to God? The primary issue is the attitude of the heart. All those who truly draw near to God will become clearly aware of two things – God's indescribable holiness, and their own shameful sin. This heart of humility is the path for drawing near to God. Our posture, our demeanor, our words or silence ought to reflect a humble reverence for him. We are invited to come with confidence, but it is not self-confidence. It is assurance of the goodness, majesty, and grace of God.

The saying, "familiarity breeds contempt" carries some truth in it. Sometimes those of us who have walked with the Lord for a long time lose the awe, the sense of wonder, that God would want us to be his children. Let that not be true of you or of me. May each of us come humbly, reverently before the Lord. May we never forget the depths of despair from which we have been saved. Let us humbly approach his throne, "so that we may receive mercy and find grace to help us in our time of need."

Life in the Shadows

After Jesus' death and resurrection, he appeared to many people proving that he was alive. The first chapter of Acts describes his ascension into heaven as his disciples watched. Afterward the disciples and other followers of Jesus returned to Jerusalem. In a gathering of about 120 believers, Peter recommended that a man be chosen to replace Judas as the 12th apostle. The two men nominated were Matthias and Joseph, called Barsabbas. After prayer, Matthias was chosen and he was added to the eleven disciples. These two men had been following Jesus in the background throughout the years of his ministry. They had walked with him, heard his teaching, seen his miracles, but they had never been part of the well-known inner circle. They may well have been among the 72 men Jesus sent ahead of him into towns and villages where he was about to go (Luke 10).

After years of quiet devotion, following in the shadows, these two men were brought to the forefront. Both had been recommended. One would be selected to become the 12th apostle. I imagine that for Matthias this day was permanently etched in his memory. From now on his private Christian walk would be more visibly on display. There would be greater expectation for him to live as public example of godliness. He would be given more responsibility and held to a higher standard (James 3:1). Matthias is not mentioned by name in the rest of Scripture. He was, however, a member of the twelve who embraced the call to go tell the world the good news of salvation in Christ.

Friend, have you spent your Christian walk in the shadows? Have you lived a life of quiet devotion, going mostly unnoticed by others in the family of God? I ask you today to consider the account of Matthias and Joseph. Even though their names had not been mentioned previously in Scripture, the people of God knew them and recognized the depth of their commitment. Both were apparently asked and were willing to serve in a more public way. One was chosen. Can you identify with these men? Whatever your personality, God has a plan to use you in his kingdom. Are you available? If God calls you to continue serving in the background, like Joseph, are you content to serve whole-heartedly without recognition? If God calls you to step out of your comfort zone and take on a position of leadership, are you willing? Have you made your life available to God to use however he sees fit? God has given you personality traits. He knows what you are like. He will use the young and the more mature, the physically weak and the strong, the wealthy and the poor, the loud and the quiet. He just asks us to be willing to give our lives to him, even as Christ gave up his life for us. He will give us the courage, the strength, the wisdom to serve where he places us, if only we are willing. I invite you today to recommit your life, asking God to use you in the ways that will bring him the greatest glory. Will you surrender to him today?

What Are You Going To Do Now?

The hardest question facing high school students is the oft-repeated, "What are you going to do with the rest of your life?" Teenagers aren't the only ones dealing with this overwhelming question. The spouse who is suddenly single, because of separation or divorce or death, is asking himself/herself the same question. So is the parent whose youngest child is leaving home. The unemployed worker, and the new retiree are facing the same question. The one who has received the news of a terminal diagnosis or a permanent disability asks the question. Even the person stuck in a rut, lacking purpose is asking, what in the world am I going to do with my life? Friend how do we figure out what to do with our lives?

As always, the Word of God (The Bible) is the source of wisdom and direction. "If any of you lacks wisdom, he should ask God, who gives generously to all without finding fault, and it will be given to him" (James 1:5). 2 Chronicles 10-36 reads like a roll call of the kings of Judah, after the nation of Israel was divided. As each successive king is named, his life is briefly summarized in terms of wars he fought, building projects, successes and failures. Each new king, like a new high school graduate, was given the opportunity to make his mark. Like any class of graduates, some chose wisely and found success while others destroyed themselves with their choices. A seer (or prophet) told King Asa, "The Lord is with you when you are with him. If you seek him, he will be found by you, but if you forsake him, he will forsake you" (2 Chr.15:2b). King Joash "Did what was right in the eyes of the Lord all the years of Jehoida the priest" (2 Chr.24:2). In the end, however, he rejected God and was assassinated. His son Amaziah "did what was right in the eyes of the Lord, but not wholeheartedly" (2 Chr.

25:2). He too turned away from the Lord and was eventually assassinated. Of his son Uzziah, it is written, "As long as he sought the Lord, God gave him success." "But after Uzziah became powerful, his pride led to his downfall" (2 Chr. 26:5b, 26:16a). His son, Jotham, "grew powerful because he walked steadfastly before the Lord his God" (2 Chr. 27:6). The list goes on and on. Each one of these kings had God's law, and had access to priests and advisors who would help him discern the will of God. Only those who sought him were successful in the end. None of us will ever be a king of Judah, but the principle here still stands. We cannot expect God to walk with us and help us and bless us, if we are not seeking him and walking with him.

The Bible has several things to say about God's plans and discerning His will:

- Proverbs 3:5,6, "Trust in the Lord with all your heart and lean not on your own understanding; in all your ways acknowledge him, and he will make your path straight."
- Romans 12:2, "Do not conform any longer to the pattern of this world, but be transformed by the renewing of your mind. Then you will be able to test and approve what God's will is – his good, pleasing and perfect will."
- Prov. 16:3, "Commit to the Lord whatever you do, and your plans will succeed."
- Psalm 16:11, "You have made known to me the path of life; you will fill me with joy in your presence, with eternal pleasures at your right hand."
- Ps. 119:105, "Your Word is a lamp to my feet and a light for my path.
- Ps. 37:4, "Delight yourself in the Lord and he will give you the desires of your heart."
- Ps. 23:3b, "He guides me along paths of righteousness for his Name's sake."

God has plans to lead, to bless, and to work through every life that is fully surrendered to him. Those who choose to make their own way will never live the fulfilled, contented lives for which they were created. However, as long as a person is alive, it is not too late to begin really living. If you are asking today, "What shall

I do with the rest of my life?" I urge you to seek God and embrace his dreams for your life. You will never regret it.

Hope For The Captives

After the death of King Solomon, the nation of Israel was divided. The northern ten tribes continued to be called Israel, while two southern tribes were known as Judah. All of the kings who reigned in the north were ungodly, and refused to repent when the prophets warned them of disasters to come. In 722 BC, Israel was captured by the Assyrians and taken into exile, just as the prophets had said. The land of Judah faired a little better. They had some kings who served the Lord, some did not, and some tried to straddle the fence. In the end, the people and their king rejected God. They were captured by the Babylonians, as the prophets had foretold, and taken into exile in 586 BC. God, through the prophet Jeremiah, had told the people they would be in captivity for 70 years (Jeremiah 25:11, 29:10). At the end of that time God moved the heart of a heathen king, in order to accomplish his will. "In the first year of Cyrus king of Persia, in order to fulfill the word of the Lord spoken by Jeremiah, the Lord moved the heart of Cyrus king of Persia to make a proclamation throughout his realm and to put it in writing: This is what Cyrus king of Persia says: 'The Lord, the God of heaven, has given me all the kingdoms of the earth and he has appointed me to build a temple for him at Jerusalem in Judah. Anyone of his people among you – may the Lord his God be with him, and let him go up" (2 Chronicles 36:22-23). The books of Ezra and Nehemiah tell of a remnant of Israelites returning to their homeland, rebuilding the temple and the city. King Cyrus, and later King Darius, not only allowed the captives to return home, but even commanded other people to help fund the rebuilding (Ezra 1:4, 6:8-9).

Something similar had happened four centuries earlier. When Moses led the slaves out of Egypt, God instructed the people to ask the Egyptians for silver and gold, and articles of clothing. "The Lord had made the Egyptians favorably disposed toward the people, and they gave them what they asked for; so they plundered the Egyptians" (Exodus 12:36). In this reference and also in Ezra, God not only set his people free from their captors, but also caused the captors to give his people generous gifts. He poured unexpected blessings on those who sought him.

Friend, can you relate to the people of Judah? Perhaps your life, thus far, is not working out as you had hoped or planned. Has your devotion to God been inconsistent, or lukewarm? Have you tried going your own way, only to have your dreams dissolve into a pile of sand? Have you found yourself in captivity to an addiction or to depression or to unforgiveness, or an endless search for fulfillment? Perhaps, rather than personal failure, you are grieved by the sin of our nation, or the local community, or ungodliness within your own family. The story of the Israelites clearly shows that struggles and trials come, and that there are consequences to be paid for sinful choices. But there is always hope for a nation, for a community, for a church, for a family, for an individual who will admit sin and ask God's forgiveness. Take heart. God is "able to do immeasurably more than all we ask or imagine, according to his power that is at work within us" (Ephesians 3:20). He can set the captive free and bring the wandering one home again. He is able to restore, renew, and reconcile, when we repent. He still has a plan to make something beautiful of your life. Have hope in him today.

Because He said So

"Why?" whines the child. "Because I am the parent and I said so" replies the parent firmly. If you grew up in a family, some form of this mini conversation is probably familiar to you. At the root level it is a question of authority. There are times when both children and adults should submit to those in authority over us, even when we disagree with them or don't understand their logic. (I am not suggesting that those suffering in an abusive relationship should continually submit. There is a major difference between healthy, Biblical submission and abuse.)

The Bible uses many words to describe the character of God, and in so doing, demonstrates his ultimate authority over all of us. He is the Creator. He is all-powerful and nothing is too hard for him. He is present in all places at all times. He knows and understands everything. He is righteous and totally without fault or blemish. Everything he does is right for he can do no less. He is so holy that man cannot look upon his face and live. He is the judge of all mankind. Once a person knows God, unquestioning obedience to his will is the only path that makes any intelligent sense.

There are multiple examples in Scripture of God telling people to do things that they did not understand or did not want to follow. For example, when told to go out fishing, Peter said to Jesus, "Master, we've worked hard all night and haven't caught anything. But because you say so, I will let down the nets" (Luke 5:5). Joshua followed the strange instructions to conquer the city of Jericho by marching around it (Joshua 6). Gideon went to fight a battle with a just tiny fraction of an army (Judges 7). As always, Jesus is our consummate example of submission to the Heavenly Father, illustrated so clearly in the Garden of Gethsemane where he said, "Father, if you are willing, take this cup from me; yet not my will, but yours be done" (Luke 22:42).

All of these obeyed just because God said so, even when it was frightening or painful or didn't seem to make any sense. All were richly rewarded. Peter and friends caught enough fish to weigh down two fishing vessels. The Israelites watched the walls of Jericho fall and totally defeated this powerful enemy. Gideon and his men saw the destruction of a much larger army. Jesus defeated the enemy and provided a way of salvation for all mankind. Obedience to God always brings his blessing. The reverse is also true. Disobedience to God blocks the flow of blessings he has for his children.

Friend, what is God asking you to do? Reach out to a neighbor or co-worker? Turn down a promotion? Break off a relationship or reconcile a broken one? Give more money or resources to those in need? To teach a class or visit someone who is sick, or tell somebody what God has done for you? God is always calling us to come closer. Are you resisting his call, or are you willing to say as Peter did, "Master . . . because you say so, I will obey"?

Hidden Issues

My daughter has wonderfully curly hair – beautiful to look at, but a nightmare to comb. When she was young she dreaded that part of preparing for the day, and I couldn't blame her. One morning we waited until we were almost ready to go out the door, then I found a whole mess of tangles. Neither of us had the patience for combing through it, so we put it into a ponytail, which looked nice and disguised the mess underneath.

Right in the middle of this operation, God pointed out to me that many people in churches are just like Sierra's ponytail. They come to church looking right and acting right and sounding right, but underneath that exterior is a tangled mess. Some have never truly given Christ control of their lives and received forgiveness of sins, but have just gotten in to the church habit. Others committed their lives to Christ a long time ago, but they have allowed the relationship to grow stale. They don't bear any fruit or do any work to grow the kingdom. Finally, there are people trying hard to do all the right things and failing miserably because they have not been filled with the Holy Spirit and tapped into his power.

The longer I put off combing my daughter's hair, the harder it was to get through it at all. Some church goers have gone so long without actually responding to the Spirit that they have grown complacent and no longer even yearn for a deeper walk. Some of us have let our lives get so tangled under our ponytails that we almost need to cut it off and start over. Only God can do the work that is needed. But he won't chase you down with a comb like I sometimes had to do with my daughter. He waits for your invitation. In Psalm 51:10 David wrote, "Create in me a clean heart, O God, and renew a right spirit within me." Let's begin asking Christ to untangle our lives, renew us, and make us whole. Let's not settle for anything less than the life God created us to live. Having the tangles combed out can be painful, but it is healthy and necessary for abundant life.

Created For God

God told Isaiah that his people were created for his glory (Isaiah 43:7). In fact, "All things were created by him and for him" (Colossians 1:16b). He made stars which remind me of his majesty, but what do they do for him? Does he enjoy gazing at them from above as I do from beneath? The waves on the seashore remind me that he is constant, powerful, faithful. Does he enjoy their sound like I do? Jesus spent a lot of time by the lake. Maybe the waves refreshed him because they were still doing what they had been created to do. Spring and summer bring so many beautiful, sweet-smelling flowers. Do they bring a smile to him as they do to me?

The psalmist said, "The heavens declare the glory of God; the skies proclaim the work of his hands" (Psalm 19:1). Maybe all of nature is constantly engaged in a symphony of praise to God. Once in a great while I take the opportunity to eavesdrop on the concert. Oh for ears to listen more often! The purpose, then, of this wondrous creation is not just to remind me to look to him. It is an expression of praise to him, regardless whether anyone else notices.

What then of me? I too must have been made by him and for him. I am not simply one of a million stamped from the same mold. What a lofty calling, to have been made for him! I am not here by coincidence but by careful design. I do not know what work God may call me to do, but for now he has called me to be right here. That is all I need to know today. Let us ask God to help each of us hear his instructions as to what do and when, that we may live to honor him. May we have ears to hear creation's symphony of praise.

The Gift of Forgiving

While I was growing up my mom routinely made four-layer birthday cakes for us. I watched her work many times, and I'm sure my help was invaluable to her. I decided to follow her example and make a layered cake for my own daughter's fifth birthday. As I fought the frosting, and tried to keep Sierra from knocking it all off the counter in her efforts to help, my appreciation for my mother's efforts increased significantly. I never before appreciated the work Mom went to in making these special cakes. There is nothing like trying to make a gift to help us appreciate gifts that others have made.

There is another gift we don't really appreciate until we try to give it - forgiveness. Jesus offered us forgiveness at an unimaginable cost to himself. He instructs us to forgive as he did. He said, "But if you do not forgive men their sins, your Father will not forgive your sins" (Matthew 6:15). We may be, should be, thankful for his gift, but we don't fully appreciate the cost of forgiveness until we need to give it to someone who has grievously wronged us. Many years ago I was deeply wounded by someone I considered a friend. Learning to forgive was a long, difficult process. I don't ever want to repeat the experience, but I am immensely grateful for the lesson I learned about offering forgiveness. The other person was wrong, and deserved my wrath, but I needed to forgive. That is what Jesus had done for me. "But God demonstrates his own love for us in this: While we were still sinners, Christ died for us" (Romans 5:8). Jesus offered to forgive me when I did not deserve it. He instructs me to do the same for others. It was a hard lesson to learn, but I no longer take for granted the costly forgiveness Christ offers to me.

If you have never been terribly hurt, you probably will be. Holding a grudge is easy and natural. Offering forgiveness is extremely difficult, but it is the only choice if we are to be obedient, and it will increase our gratitude toward our Savior as nothing else in life ever can. If there is someone in your life who has wronged you, I urge you to start asking God to help you begin to forgive, for your own good. You cannot take one more step spiritually if you have not dealt with the sin of unforgiveness.

It Takes More Than Hard Work

One summer day while my daughter was playing in a plastic sandbox, I was watching a small ant crawl around in the inverted dome lid. This poor little guy tried repeatedly to crawl up the concave wall. He would make it most of the way to the rim and then slide right back down with all six legs flailing. He tried all different sides with the same result. He even tried crawling along at an angle, which worked better, but still was not successful. I watched him for more than fifteen minutes. He worked as hard as he could the entire time, but he was still trapped.

As I watched the ant, I concluded that perseverance is good, but it is not always enough. Sometimes help is needed from an outside source. I can see a clear parallel in my own attempts at walking with Jesus. As the daughter of a pastor, I asked Jesus to forgive my sins at a young age. I really wanted to please him and do the things that were right, but I could never seem to do it. For years I tried and failed. Every time I heard a sermon about salvation I would go to the altar and confess my sins again, thinking I must not have meant it enough or tried hard enough all those other times. My spiritual life was much like that of the ant I saw trying to escape from the sandbox lid. My desire was strong to escape the pull of sin, but I kept sliding back down. I really needed help from an outside source, but I didn't understand it was available.

After my senior year of high school, while at camp, I realized that what I needed was not just more perseverance. I needed the help of the Holy Spirit. Christians are to be "Filled with the Spirit" (Ephesians 5:18b). Paul instructed the Christians in Galatia, "Live by the Spirit, and you will not gratify the desires of the sinful nature" (Galatians 5:16). That night at the altar I prayed earnestly to be filled with the Spirit, and God heard my cry. Of course, I was not perfect from that day forward, but I had far greater strength than I had ever had before. The Holy Spirit began teaching me to know God personally, rather than just trying to follow his rules. He began giving me guidance when I didn't know what to do, and words to say to others who were hurting. He filled me with joy and peace and a new perspective on life. He helped me to understand what I read in the Bible and what I heard in sermons, and apply it to my own life. My spiritual walk ceased to be a long trail of failure and frustration, and became a life of victory which God could use to reach others.

What about you? If you have believed in Jesus, and confessed your sins, and received his forgiveness, you are a child of God. Praise the Lord! It may be, however, that your Christian walk is marked by failed attempts to live for Jesus, rather than by victory and joy. If your heart is yearning for more of him and you need strength from an outside source, it is readily available. I urge you to begin today praying fervently to be filled with the Holy Spirit. Keep asking and seeking until God answers your prayer. Your life will be far sweeter and your usefulness in his hands far greater.

Idolatry

Have you bowed down to any idols lately? The books of Isaiah and Jeremiah express God's heartache at the unfaithfulness of his chosen people. Rather than being wholeheartedly devoted to him, they began to worship the gods of neighboring peoples, while continuing the religious rituals recorded and taught by Moses.

In our culture it is very hard to imagine someone physically bowing before a wood or stone or metal carving. In Old Testament days, however, this was common practice. The Israelites continued their routine sacrifices, but also put their faith in idols worshipped in neighboring lands. God repeatedly compared this duplicity to adultery and prostitution (for example, read the book of Hosea). "The house of Israel and the house of Judah have been utterly unfaithful to me," declares the Lord (Jeremiah 5:11). He sent at least sixteen different prophets warning the people of all the trouble that would come upon them if they did not repent and serve only the One True God. It all seems far removed from 21st Century America. But is it really?

We too, worship things other than God. Gluttony is not just unhealthy, it is a form of idolatry. Some believers refuse to give up a particular kind of music, even though it glorifies an ungodly lifestyle. Some put their trust in money and material possessions. Some have given health foods and exercise the top spot in their lives. For others it may be success in a career, or a need to be liked by everyone. For many it is the Internet or the latest technology gadget.

These things do not sound like idols. Many of them are good things. An idol is anything in my life that I treat as more important than God. If I focus more of my time, energy, money, thoughts, or skills on something of this world than I do on loving and seeking God, I am guilty of idolatry. The very first commandment God gave to Moses was: "I am the Lord your God . . . You shall have no other gods before me" (Exodus 20:2-3).

What about you? What holds top priority in your life? My prayer for myself and for all of God's people is that we would learn, not only to recognize sin, but to hate it as he does. I encourage you to make this your prayer as well.

Built to Last

We used to have a large cottonwood tree in our front yard. Every spring it would blanket the entire neighborhood in white.

Due to concerns about it falling on the house or power lines, we had it cut down. After decades of providing shade, it became fuel for a furnace. All that remained were wood chips and a few photographs. In some ways, our lives are similar to that tree. James 4:14b says, "What is your life? You are a mist that appears for a little while and then vanishes." Psalm 103:15,16 tells us, "As for man, his days are like grass, he flourishes like a flower of the field; the wind blows over it and it is gone, and its place remembers it no more." (There is a similar reference Psalm 40:6-8).

Though our lives on earth are comparatively brief, they are to be filled with purpose. When your brief life is over, like a mist that vanishes, what will be left? Beyond photographs and the memories treasured by friends and family members, what will you leave behind that will make a difference for generations to come? If you leave a big house, it may burn down or be left to deteriorate. If you leave a large sum of money, it will likely be used in ways you never desired. Eventually one of your descendants will bring disgrace to the family name. All of these things fade away. Some people write their memoirs so as not to be forgotten – but most of us forget any way. Is all of life futility? Are we merely chasing after the wind as the writer of Ecclesiastes says in the first chapter? The wise teacher concluded that chasing after pleasure, or riches, or knowledge, or buildings was all futility in the end.

The Apostle Paul told the Christians in Rome to build on the foundation that is Jesus Christ. The quality of each person's work, building on that foundation, will be tested (see 1 Corinthians 3:11-15). You have been given the priceless opportunity to build a life of relationship with Almighty God. What are you building? When the test comes, will what you are building burn up, or stand through the fire? When you are gone, will you leave behind a greater influence than withered grass or fading photos?

We are to spend our energy and talents storing up treasures in heaven. I encourage you to invest in people. Follow the example of Jesus. Be a part of as many spiritual family trees as possible – the one who led someone to Christ who led others to Christ. Teach by example what it means to walk in close relationship with the Savior. All else is meaningless. Let us invite the Savior to examine the work of our lives, and show us where we are building with hay and straw rather than with gold and silver (1 Corinthians 3). May we each be willing to receive correction from the Father, and to be more faithful in doing the eternal work he has asked us to do.

In Every Situation

When we focus on God rather than on ourselves, we come to know him and converse with him throughout the day. More than thanking him for what he has done and has given to us, we praise him for who he is. God is omniscient – knowing and understanding all things. God is omnipotent – nothing is too hard for Him. God is eternal and unchanging. God is also omnipresent – in all places at all times. His omnipresence is clear in the following passages:

"Am I only a God nearby," declares the Lord, "and not a God far away? Can anyone hide in secret places so that I cannot see him?" declares the Lord. "Do not I fill heaven and earth?" declares the Lord (Jeremiah 23:23). "O Lord, you have searched me and you know me. You know when I sit and when I rise; you perceive my thoughts from afar. You discern my going out and my lying down; you are familiar with all my ways. Before a word is on my tongue you know it completely, O Lord. You hem me in – behind and before; you have laid your hand upon me. Such knowledge is too wonderful for me, too lofty for me to attain. Where can I go from your Spirit? Where can I flee from your presence? If I go up to the heavens, you are there; if I make my bed in the depths, you are there. If I rise on the wings of the dawn, if I settle on the far side of the sea, even there your hand will guide me, your right hand will hold me fast" (Psalm 139:1-10). God is not only in all places at all times, but he is in all situations. He knows our thoughts before they become words, or even if they are never spoken. He knows us in the innermost parts of who we are.

A grandmother in our church had a stroke. She was unable to speak for a while, but she continued to pray faithfully for many people. Through the whole ordeal, God was right there with her. He is with a sick child, when parents do not know how to help. When a person is frustrated, beaten down by depression and lack of purpose, God is there. He is with the discouraged caretaker stuck in the day-to-day grind, trying to find a way to help lift a loved one out of the pit of despair. When the single parent cries alone in the night, God is there. He is not only in all places, he is present in all situations.

Friend, my heart is burdened for those who are struggling under a burden of heartache or despair. Although the Bible teaches that we can have joy and peace and victory in Jesus, many Christians are not experiencing those blessings. Some have been afflicted with depression, having little or no energy to fight back. Even in the darkest of days, God is there. Through a lot of prayer and encouragement, through counseling and sometimes with medication, God can bring new life. Be encouraged, beloved. God is always with you. He will keep "in perfect peace" the one whose mind is steadfast, trusting in him (see Isaiah 26:3). Do not despair. God has a plan and a purpose for your life. I once heard a youth evangelist say, "God is not a bridge over troubled water. He is more like a submarine carrying you through it." There is hope and help in him. May you experience the wonder of his presence and the hope that only he can give.

What He Has Said

The Prophet Isaiah foretold the painful life and horrible death of the Messiah. The words are familiar, but what I want you to notice is the tense that is used. "He was despised and rejected by men, a man of sorrows, and familiar with sufferings. Like one from whom men hide their faces he was despised, and we esteemed him not. Surely he took up our infirmities and carried our sorrows, yet we considered him stricken by God, smitten by him, and afflicted. But he was pierced for our transgressions, he was crushed for our iniquities, the punishment that brought us peace was upon him, and by his wounds we are healed" (Isaiah 53:3-5).

Isaiah served as a prophet from approximately 740-681 BC. Why did the Holy Spirit give him these words to write in past tense, centuries before the events occurred? I believe it is written that way, at least in part, to show the certainty of it. God had decided how he was going to bring salvation to sinners. The plan was set and would not be changed "God is not a man that he should lie, nor a son of man, that he should change his mind," Numbers 23:19). God is "the Alpha and Omega, the First and the Last, the Beginning and the End" (Revelation 22:13).

When political candidates promise to fix the economy, when officials from oil companies claim responsibility for a massive oil spill, when athletes declare victory before the competition . . . we sit back, fold our arms and wait to see if they will do what they have said they would do. We have, wisely in most cases, developed an attitude of "I'll believe it when I see it." Sometimes, however, we choose to believe a person's words before they are fulfilled. In 1998, Bart Adams committed himself to me for a lifetime in our marriage ceremony. I have complete trust that he will keep those vows. We can have even greater confidence in the words of God than in the words of any man. Just as he completed his plan to send a Messiah, so also he will fulfill his plans for the second coming of Christ. Trials and plagues will come upon the earth. "There will be terrible times in the last days. People will be lovers of themselves, lovers of money, boastful, proud, abusive, disobedient to their parents, ungrateful, unholy . . ." (2 Timothy 3:2). "Nation will rise against nation, and kingdom against kingdom. There will be famines and earthquakes in various places" (Matthew 24:7). Jesus will come again and take his people to the place he has prepared for them (Matthew 24:30-31, John 14:2-3). Every person must face judgment, "For we must all appear before the judgment seat of Christ, that each one may receive what is due him for the things done while in the body, whether good or bad" (2 Corinthians 5:10). God has declared these things and they will happen.

When Jesus came the first time, people were not ready to accept and follow him. His second coming may very well happen in our lifetime. Will we be ready? God is guaranteed to do what he said he would do. It is our responsibility to know what he has said and to be ready and watching for our Master (Luke 12:36-37). Are you ready and waiting for the Savior's return?

Waiting for a Growth Spurt

During the teen years many students have what parents call a growth spurt – growing several inches taller over a very short period of time. It is remarkable how quickly it happens for some. For others, like me, it doesn't happen at all. Beyond taking care of your body, there is not much a person can do to control this physical growth. No amount of stretching can make it happen sooner or last longer.

The Bible relates our spiritual journey to physical growth and development. Those who are new to the faith, who have just recently come to repentance and forgiveness of sins are compared to babies, no matter what their chronological age (1 Corinthians 3:1). They need nourishment from others – instruction and help in learning to know God and to hear his voice. They need to have basic truths of the Bible explained and reinforced. As with newborn babies, however, this period is supposed to be brief and marked with significant growth. Those who have been walking with Christ for a period of time, though still benefitting from preaching and teaching, should be feeding themselves. All of God's people should be seeking to know him through reading and studying his Word. All of God's people should be spending time regularly with him in prayer. We should be showing love to others. "By this all men will know that you are my disciples, if you love one another" (John 13:35). God's people should be attentive to the call of the Holy Spirit and should be growing ever closer to him. They should be taking steps of faith and sharing with others what God has done in their lives. All nine fruit of the Spirit – love, joy, peace, patience, kindness, goodness, faithfulness, gentleness, and self-control – should be evident in the lives of God's children through the work of the Holy Spirit (Galatians 5:22).

When it comes to physical height, my growth spurt will probably never come and there is nothing I can do about it. The same is not true, however, in the area of spiritual growth. Some have been in the church for years, even decades, waiting for their spiritual growth spurt. Brothers and sisters, this should not be! The writer of Hebrews found fault with those who were not moving forward (Hebrews 5:11-13). Each one is to take responsibility for his/her own maturation. Just as healthy young children insist on doing things for themselves, climbing and walking, holding a spoon, drinking from a cup, etc. so healthy believers of every age should be striving to take steps of faith. Each person must take his own personal journey with Christ. There will be struggles and difficult lessons along the way. There will also be unspeakable joy and inexplicable peace in his sweet presence. It is my prayer that you will take another step with him today.

What Should I Do?

Stuck – in a miserable job, in a house that is falling apart, in a painful relationship or the grip of loneliness, in a city far from the place you would really like to live. Should you fight with all you've got to improve your situation, or should you try to learn to be content and wait for God to change it? There is really no easy answer to this question. American mentality says, "God helps those who help themselves" but this phrase is not found in Scripture. It is just an over-simplified human philosophy.

When God led the Hebrew people across the Jordan River and into the Promised Land, it was inhabited by large, powerful nations. God clearly and repeatedly told his people to drive out the people groups living there. They were to fight continually and relentlessly to make the land their own. God promised to help them, as long as they followed his instructions. When they stopped fighting the enemy, God refused to help them any longer.

After the people had settled in the Promised Land they turned their hearts further and further from their God. They ignored endless warnings by the prophets so God sent his people into exile. The northern kingdom of Israel was captured by Assyria in 722 B.C. The southern kingdom of Judah was conquered by King Nebuchadnezzar and sent into exile in Babylon in 586 B.C. God instructed Jeremiah the prophet to send a letter to the exiles (Jeremiah 29). He told them to settle in the land, planting gardens and raising families. He told them, "Seek the peace and prosperity of the city to which I have carried you into exile. Pray to the Lord for it, because if it prospers, you too will prosper." He told the people to make the best of their situation rather than trying to change it. God also promised, "When seventy years are completed for Babylon, I will come to you and fulfill my gracious promise to bring you back to this place." This is the context of the familiar words, "For I know the plans I have for you," declares the Lord, "plans to prosper you and not to harm you, plans to give you hope and a future" (Jeremiah 29:7-11).

So, in the first instance, the people were instructed to keep fighting until they had conquered the land and made it their own. In the second situation, the people were told to settle in, to be content and make the best of their circumstances while they waited on God. Our Heavenly Father is far too creative and individualistic to have a cookie-cutter response for every situation we face. When we ask, "What should I do?" he knows everything and understands all of the ramifications of every decision we might make. He is able to use any situation to accomplish his will. He uses both pleasant pastures and difficult valleys to make himself known to people and draw us near to him. He is the only one who knows the best response in any given dilemma. Those who are wise will seek him and wait on him to show them the best way to handle an unpleasant situation, rather than fighting to change the very circumstances God is trying to use to speak to them.

Free Indeed

Freedom is a central part of who we are as a nation. We, as Americans, are very passionate about this topic. Let's look at what freedom means for the believer, by looking at examples of a prisoner and a free man. Exhibit A is a very intelligent Chinese man. At the age of 17 he dedicated his life to Christ. He was given numerous revelations from God, which enabled him to explain many of the truths of the New Testament. He experienced great struggles in life, including poverty, very poor health, and opposition from both Christians and others. "On May 30, 1972, after twenty years of imprisonment for his belief in Christ and his participation in the local churches, [he] rested with Christ, Whom he loved and served at the cost of his life. Before his departure, he left a note under his pillow to testify of the truth: 'Christ is the Son of God who died for the redemption of sinners and resurrected after three days. This is the greatest truth in the universe. I die because of my belief in Christ.'"[12]

Exhibit B is an intelligent young man who found success in his work. As he began to accumulate wealth and possessions, he became consumed with the problem of how to store and protect and enjoy his stuff. He had it made.

Which one of these two men was free, and which was the prisoner? Watchman Nee was in prison in China for twenty years, and yet his writings on living a life of faith comprise a sixty-two volume set, and have greatly influenced Christians the world over. Nee and Witness Lee (a son in the faith) were instrumental in planting hundreds of local churches which have since multiplied to over 2,300 worldwide. The rich young man of Exhibit B is one that Jesus described in his parable about the rich fool (Luke 12:13-21). Although he had everything he could wish for in this life, God called him a fool and demanded his life that very night. I would argue that, in God's system of measurement, the rich fool was the prisoner of his wealth, while the man who had been imprisoned was free in Christ.

The question for personal application is this: with which of these two men do you relate most? Is your time spent listening to the Holy Spirit and using his messages to encourage other believers, or are you focused on the things you have and the things you hope to get? Is the majority of your disposable income spent on things for yourself or things to help others? God has blessed America abundantly, and it is a privilege to live in this country. There is, however, a constant danger that we might become prisoners to our wealth and possessions.

Jesus said, "If you hold to my teaching, you are really my disciples. Then you will know the truth, and the truth will set you free" (John 8:32). Freedom in Christ does not mean freedom from struggles or heartache. Rather it means a life completely at peace, trusting fully in the Savior no matter what comes your way. "So if the Son sets you free, you will be free indeed" (John 8:36). "It is for freedom that Christ has set us free. Stand firm then, and do not let yourselves be burdened again by a yoke of slavery" (Galatians 5:1).

As we thank God for this nation and for our freedoms, let us seek the deeper freedom that is only found in personal relationship with Jesus Christ. Let us determine once again to serve him rather than our possessions.

A Blameless Life

In reading through the Bible, I struggle with the book of Job. His pain and heartache are excruciating to read. The counsel of his friends is infuriating. I find myself peeking ahead to see when God is finally going to answer (not until ch. 38). There are several lessons for us in this old story. Good people, even very good people, can never be good enough. Job lived a nearly blameless life. He tried to walk uprightly. The people of his family and his community recognized him as a godly man. Even God himself commended Job as being "blameless and upright, a man who fears God and shuns evil" (1:8). Yet, all his righteous acts were not enough to meet his deepest need. Job needed an advocate, an intercessor (16:19-21) who could bridge the gulf between the man and his God.

Living a good life is not enough to earn heaven, any more than a boat with only one hole in the bottom is a good buy. The Bible clearly teaches that all have sinned (Romans 3:23). There is no one who is truly righteous. Job was not a man who had never sinned, but a man who tried to live for God. He was a very good man, but it was not enough. James 2:10 tells us, "For whoever keeps the whole law and yet stumbles at just one point is guilty of breaking all of it." Job could not be holy enough to draw near to God. He needed the forgiveness that God freely gives.

Friends, none of us is living a blameless life before God or before others. Hopefully we are trying our best, and we are quick to seek forgiveness when we fall. Still, it can never be enough. We must be washed and cleansed by the Savior or we cannot be in right standing with Almighty God. Our righteousness and obedience do not earn us salvation, but rather, they are an expression of our love for God. Jesus said that if we love him, we will obey him (John 14:15). Let us live holy lives that reflect our love for God and our gratitude to our Savior. He is our advocate. In response to his love, may we strive to become people that God would describe as "blameless and upright" like Job.

Seek God, Not Just His Help

The first chapter of the book of Job describes a remarkable conversation between God and Satan. Satan stated his desire to attack righteous Job, in order to get him to turn away from his faith. God allowed Satan to take all ten of Job's children, and his great wealth all on the same day. Although he was shaken, bent and battered like a reed in a hail storm, Job maintained his steadfast devotion to his God. Later, God allowed the enemy to inflict Job with painful boils all over his body. Job, broken, wished he had never been born and he longed for the relief that death would bring (although he clearly was not suicidal). He questioned why God had stricken him, but he still clung to his faith. Three well-meaning friends came to comfort Job in his terrible grief. Chapters 3 through 37 relate the discussion between these four men as they struggled with the question of why these terrible things had happened to Job.

Some of us have discovered, as these men did, that there are no easy answers or explanations for the heartaches that life brings. We can see Job's grief reflected in his anger, his despair, his attempts to plead and bargain with God, and finally his acceptance. There are twenty chapters that record Job's anguish, his cries to God, his attempts to defend himself against the accusations of his friends. As you read these chapters, you see Job longing for the way things were. His chief heartache, evidenced in his words, is not the loss of his great wealth. Nor is it the rejection from the community that once revered him. It is not even the loss of his children. The constant thread in Job's discourse is distress over the relationship with his God that has become so distant. He who had walked with God, and enjoyed fellowship with him, longed to be restored to right relationship with God. Look at his words:

"Your hands shaped me and made me. Will you now turn and destroy me?" (Job 10:8). "If only you would hide me in the grave and conceal me till your anger has passed! If only you would set me a time and then remember me!" (Job 14:13). "You will call and I will answer you; you will long for the creature your hands have made" (Job 14:15). "I know that my redeemer lives, and that in the end he will stand upon the earth. . . . I myself will see him with my own eyes – I, and not another. How my heart yearns within me!" (Job 19:25,27). "How I long for the months gone by, for the days when God watched over me, when his lamp shone upon my head and by his light I walked through darkness! Oh, for the days when

I was in my prime, when God's intimate friendship blessed my house . . ." (Job 29:2-4).

None of us ever wants to walk the road that Job had to walk. All of us, however, face trials that knock us down and leaving us bruised and battered. In those times, the natural human response is to ask "Why?" Oftentimes, though, the question seems to go unanswered. Years down the road we may be able to look back and see good that has come out of the heartache, but we may never really know why these things happened. In the midst of such pain, we are tempted to complain and to wallow in self-pity day after day. We beg God to fix the problem, or to at least take the pain away. Eventually, each of us must deal with the heartache in order to go on living, rather than just existing as a shell of a person. Job worked through his horrific trial. Here are a few of the lessons we can learn from his experience: First, there is no shortcut through the pain. Each of us must walk through it. Attempts to deny it or ignore it or cover it up, only delay the process. Second, when our friends are walking through terrible heartache, we don't need to come up with reasons or answers or advice. It is far more helpful to just walk beside them and listen to them, than to lecture or speak empty platitudes. Most importantly, in the midst of grief, rather than continually pleading with God to fix the problem, we should seek to draw near to him and cling to him in faith. His presence brings help, strength, comfort, and peace in the midst of any trial.

The last few chapters of the book of Job record God's response to the questions. God described part of the process of creation, the weather patterns and limitations he had set on nature, the mighty creatures that he alone controls. God reminded Job that even when terrible trials come and we don't see or feel God working to bring relief, he is there. He is in control. He knows and he sees and he cares. The one who formed you in the womb and knows the ever-changing number of hairs on your head, will never leave you or abandon you. Whether you feel it or not, he sees you as a precious treasure. Take heart. Just as he did with Job, God will carry his children through, if we will trust in him.

Catch the Foxes

In my experience, church camp has been a place where people leave behind the routines and struggles of daily life and spend a week focusing on God. Those who are willing to hear His Spirit speak to their hearts always receive a blessing, a sense of spiritual renewal and re-focus, the call of God to draw nearer. It is a feast for the soul, made even richer by fellowship with other believers. One summer I was wounded by some harsh words spoken to people I love by people I love. My peace and joy quickly turned to hurt and discouragement. My desire to see the issues dealt with and friendships reconciled kept me awake at night. I struggled in prayer, as my mind continually reverted to this hurt. God was still there, calling me near to himself, but my focus had shifted. I lost out on two days of fellowship with God and with his people because I allowed my mind to be consumed with these issues (which were actually very small in the scheme of things).

The book entitled Song of Solomon or Song of Songs is a strange part of the Old Testament. It is a bold, poetic description of the love between a man and a woman. It is also a picture of the intimate, personal love God desires to have with each person he has created. As the book expresses this beautiful, healthy love it gives an admonition, "Catch for us the foxes, the little foxes that ruin the vineyards, our vineyards that are in bloom" (2:15). The foxes referred to here are the petty things, the little annoyances of life that crowd out my joy and take my focus off of my first love.

For me, the little foxes were careless words spoken that brought out my defensiveness. Sometimes, the foxes may be worries over finances or decisions or relationships. The little foxes may be unfulfilled longings, or physical pain, or any number of things that take our focus off God and his desire to be near to his children. They rob us of our joy. It is like a man sitting on the beach, in view of a beautiful sunset over the water. The beauty that would enrich his spirit is right in front of him, but he is busy looking down at a hangnail and completely misses the spectacular display.

Friends, God is doing something beautiful. He longs to draw you close and to make himself known to you. When you focus fully on him, the cares of this world will lose some of their power, and you will be filled with an indescribable joy and peace. The enemy of our souls will feed us lies and try to keep us distracted by the little foxes. It takes a deliberate, and repeated, act of the will to catch the foxes – the lies of the enemy that damage your relationships with God and others – and to set your eyes upon the Lord. I encourage you not to let those little foxes rob you of the joy of the Lord. That joy can only be found in a close, personal relationship with him. Recognize the lies of the enemy and rid your life of those foxes, so that you can live victoriously in Jesus.

How Do You View God?

One summer day as the kids and I were making plans to walk to the beach, my young daughter could not find her swimming goggles. ("Everything in its place" is not a philosophy that guides her days.) As we searched and she became distressed about trying to swim without them, I heard her begin to pray, asking God to help us find the goggles, and explaining how much she wanted to have them for swimming. My heart was richly blessed by hearing my daughter spontaneously take her need to God. We found the goggles and went on our way. This episode illustrates in part how my child views God. She has learned to believe that he can help with any problem, and that he cares about the things that matter to her. What she believes about God influences her actions. The same is true for all of us.

In his book, *GOD: As He Longs For You to See Him*, Pastor Chip Ingram states "What you think about God shapes your whole relationship with him. In addition, what you believe God thinks about you determines how close you will grow toward him." He also quotes A.W. Tozer, "Worship is pure or base as the worshiper entertains high or low thoughts of God. For this reason the gravest question before the Church is always God Himself, and the most portentous fact about any man is not what he at any given time may say or do, but what he in his deep heart conceives God to be like."[13]

Friend, deep in your heart, what do you conceive God to be like? Is he a permissive, indulgent parent? Is he a strict judge waiting to mete out punishment as soon as you fail? Is he a passive observer of mankind, or directing every event? I invite you to examine your honest conceptions about who God is, and then begin earnestly seeking to know more of him. Scriptures make it very clear that God wants people to know him (for example, Deuteronomy 7:9). Ask God to make himself known to you more clearly, and then to begin to study the Word to find out what he has revealed about himself.

We have a wall hanging with the following verse on it; "Delight yourself in the Lord and He will give you the desires of your heart" (Psalm 37:4). It has a nice sound to it, doesn't it? Especially that last part. My heart has, at times, desired many different things. Think for a moment though, about the first part of the verse, "Delight yourself in the Lord." Do you find delight in him? Is time alone with him the central focus of your day? As we seek to really know him, we learn to delight in relationship with him and to see with more of his perspective. As a result, the "desire of our hearts" becomes a desire for deeper intimacy with the Savior. That is the desire of his heart, and he will give it to us as it becomes the desire of our hearts. Let us learn to "delight ourselves in the Lord" not to gain stuff, but to begin to know him more deeply. No riches on earth can compare to the delight of being close to him.

Be Still and Know God

Do you sense God calling you to come to know him more deeply? I would like to share two more quotes from, *GOD as He Longs for You to See Him*, by Chip Ingram. Ponder this thought: "Until you know God as he is, you'll never become all that he's created you to be."[14] Perhaps instead of focusing our efforts and attention on improving ourselves, we need to focus on coming to know God. Then he will shape us into all that he created us to be. Here is a second thought, related to Psalm 46:10, "Be still and know that I am God." Rev. Ingram notes, "Until we are ready to be still, we will not be ready to know God." Friend, are you ready to be still? It is much harder than it sounds and takes a lot of discipline, but it is the only way to begin to really know God.

One way I am growing to know God better is through studying his attributes. Think for a moment about God's invisibility. Honestly, I always saw it as just one of his quirks that we had to put up with. I have come to see that he is invisible for our good. Many have seen it as a stumbling block, refusing to believe in something they cannot see although the same folks have no difficulty believing in gravity. Consider these two points related to God's invisible nature. First, review the description provided in the first chapter of Ezekiel. It reveals an awesome God, too awesome, in fact, for human eyes to look upon. He "looked like glowing metal, as if full of fire." God himself said that no man could see him and live (Exodus 33:20). Second, consider God's omnipresent nature. He is everywhere, all the time (Psalm 139:1-12.) There is no place where we can go to get away from him.

If God is too brilliant for us to look at with human eyes and he is everywhere all the time, humans literally could not function with a visible God. Even if he allowed us to live, his awesome presence would preempt our free will. Everyone would believe in him and obey him, even fall on our faces before him, but it would be from trepidation, not out of faith and love. Almighty God could have made us a race of robots, but that would not have fulfilled his desire for intimacy with people. The longing of his heart is for us to know him and choose to love him. The invisibility of God is, in actuality, a gift to us. Let us thank him for his goodness to us – the things we see and appreciate, and the things we cannot yet comprehend.

Olympic Pursuit

In August 2008, swimmer Michael Phelps won more Olympic medals than any other athlete in the history of the games. One thing that draws me to watch contest after contest in the Olympics is the clear reminder of what it means to dedicate one's life in pursuit of a goal. In this country, athletes give up "regular life" in terms of schooling, schedules, relationships, etc. In other countries it is far more extreme and young children are actually taken from their families and groomed to be athletes. Even though we don't know these individuals personally, but we can understand just a little of the sacrifice required. A few receive a large reward in the form of a medal, but most do not.

In Philippians 3:12-14, the Apostle Paul, describing his driving desire to know Christ – in his power, in his suffering, even in his death and resurrection says, "Not that I have already obtained all this, or have already been made perfect, but I press on to take hold of that for which Christ Jesus took hold of me. Brothers, I do not consider myself yet to have taken hold of it. But one thing I do: Forgetting what is behind and straining toward what is ahead, I press on toward the goal to win the prize for which God has called me heavenward in Christ Jesus." Brothers and sisters, what would it look like if believers pursued intimacy with God the way Michael Phelps pursued gold medals? What would it look like in our church? In our nation? In our world?

The few believers that do pursue God that way stand out – Brother Andrew, Mother Teresa, Billy Graham – like Olympic stars. My friends, this should not be! Just as many athletes never receive much public acclaim, so most Christians will never be known by those outside our immediate sphere of influence. Still, each of us is called to give our all. Jesus told us what it would take. "If anyone would come after me, he must deny himself and take up his cross and follow me. For whoever wants to save his life will lose it, but whoever loses his life for me and for the gospel will save it" (Mark 8:34b). The truth is, all of us could be doing more than we are to pursue God. All of us could discipline ourselves to be still and listen better, to seek him more earnestly, to reflect him more clearly. Nobody who decides today to become an Olympian is ready to compete tomorrow. It takes time. It takes work. And it takes continual re-focusing on the big goal. Let us start today. Not for fame or reputation or gold medals, but for a life wholly devoted to intimacy with Almighty God.

Expectations

Early in the 2008 Olympic Games both the men's and women's gymnastic teams participated in team competition. Both USA teams earned Olympic medals, but the reaction was markedly different. You see, the women's team was the reigning world champion team and expected to perform very well. The men's team, including three alternates because of injuries, was not expected to contend for a medal. When the men won Bronze they were ecstatic at having accomplished so much. When the women won Silver they were disappointed at having accomplished so little. Going into the games with an expectation of winning a gold medal, and then winning "only" a silver made it harder for the women to rejoice in their accomplishment. Expectation plays a significant role in how we perceive events.

Expectations also affect the way we see the Christian life. If we expect to be comfortable and positive, we will get frustrated and discouraged. However, if we heed the Biblical teaching that we are engaged in spiritual warfare, we expect trouble and prepare to meet it. That mindset helps us to avoid getting so easily discouraged.

As believers, we are to be on our guard. We are to be aware of what is going on in the world around us. We are not, however, to be afraid. We are to expect trouble and watch for the signs Jesus foretold. All of these things bring us closer to promised return of Christ. "At that time the sign of the Son of Man will appear in the sky, and all the nations of the earth will mourn. They will see the Son of Man coming on the clouds of the sky, with power and great glory. And he will send his angels with a loud trumpet call, and they will gather his elect from the four winds, from one end of the heavens to the other" (Matthew 24:30-31).

Friends, let us live in expectation . . . expecting to see the Lord do great things and expecting to see the enemy fight against us harder than ever. With this expectation, we may heed the words of Peter. "Therefore, prepare your minds for action; be self-controlled; set your hope fully on the grace to be given you when Jesus Christ is revealed" (1 Peter 1:13). Live in Biblical expectation.

Live By the Word

"How come the golden rule only applies to kids and not to parents?" This was the angry question from my child after yet another confrontation about what tone of voice is acceptable for speaking to a person made in the image of God. At first I just tossed the question aside and kept my focus on the need to change my child's behavior. The faithful Holy Spirit brought me up short, repeating the conversation over again in my mind. He has often reminded me to be very careful to say only what I really mean, and say it with love.

113

The focus on words in my home has carried over into Scripture reading, helping me pay closer attention to the words God chooses to use. When God says "forever" he really means forever. Not like "I had to wait forever at the doctors office," but like never ending. God told Abraham he would have as many descendants as there are stars in the sky (Genesis 15:5). He is not given to using empty words. I wonder how the count stands, Jews compared to stars. God told the Jews they would be held in captivity for 70 years (Jeremiah 25:11). Guess how many years they spent in Babylon? It wasn't 69 or 71. God said what he meant and he meant what he said. Because God means exactly what he says, wise people study what he has said and live their lives accordingly. Let's look at just a few of the things God has said in His Word.

- God said to love your God with all that you are, and to love your neighbor as you love yourself (Matthew 22:37-39).
- God said repeatedly to keep the Sabbath day holy (Exodus 20:8, Jeremiah 17:21-27).
- God said to take care of widows and orphans (James 1:27).
- God said speak only the truth, for Satan is the father of lies (John 8:44).
- God said children are to honor their parents (Exodus 20:12).
- God said he would send a Messiah, and he did – fulfilling at least 18 prophecies.
- God said he would destroy everyone not in the ark. Now every person alive is a descendant of Noah.
- God said we are to be ready and working (Matthew 25).
- God said he will return for his own (John 14:1-3).
- God the Son made it clear that there is a heaven and a hell (Luke 16).
- God said that children are a gift (Psalm 127:5).
- God said his followers must take up their crosses and follow him (Matthew 16:24, Mark 8:34, Luke 14:27).
- God said we are to "Be holy and blameless" (Ephesians 1:4).
- God said, "In your anger, do not sin" (Ephesians 4:26).

Brothers and sisters, are we living as if every word God has spoken is true? Will he find us ready, working and watching when he comes, or will he find us sitting around complaining? Each of us must take responsibility to learn to know God and study His Word. Then, we must live in accordance with every word he has spoken. Finally, as we imitate him (Ephesians 2:10) we ought to carefully choose both our words and our tone. The golden rule actually applies to parents even more than to their young children. I exhort you to be a man/woman of your word and a man/woman of God's Word.

Worth The Price

Early in July as we celebrate the birthday of our beloved country, we thank God for the privilege of living in the "Land of the Free and the Home of the Brave." Though we love our country and believe it is the greatest land on earth, still we recognize many discouraging trends. Many of the founders and early leaders of this nation declared their faith in Almighty God at every turn . . . in their speeches and written documents, in national monuments, in our pledge and on our currency. Apparently they wanted it to be clear in their own time and to all future generations that this was "One nation under God." I wonder, if they could see the USA today, what they would say. In so many ways we have great freedom and prosperity, yet, the foundational belief in God is being consistently and deliberately chipped away. The faith they built upon is now an object of scorn and ridicule from many directions. The future looks bleak in that regard. Would those who sacrificed their wealth, their reputation, their comfort, and their very lives for this new nation think it was worth the price 200 years later?

All of us have things in our past that we now realize were not worth the price we paid. Have you ever said, "If I had known then what I know now, I would have made a different choice"? Many of those choices center on how we have handled relational issues . . . relationships we never should have started or never should have ended, or maybe people we should have treasured rather than despising. By this point we have all learned the hard way that life doesn't give "Do-overs." No amount of regret will allow me to take back things I have said or done. Sometimes I have an opportunity to reconcile a damaged relationship, but it can never be the same as it was before.

How often does God look at the human race he created and think about how much easier things were before us? We are far from God's ideal plan. Still, he knew before Genesis 1:1 what we would be like, and he created the earth any way. Throughout Scripture he has demonstrated his ability to look both forward and backward through time. He is both the beginning and the end (Revelation 21:6; 22:13). With all his vast knowledge, he has chosen not only to put up with us, but to continue to extend abundant love to people. What an amazing God we serve!

Even though he knew we would repeatedly fail him, he still chose us. Even though he knew how His Son would be treated, he still sent him to be our Savior. If you follow him you need not have cause for new regrets. He has already determined that you are worth the price he paid for your salvation.

Fed By God

God is faithful. No exceptions. One of the things he is faithful to do is to speak personally to our hearts when we choose to be quiet and seek his face. I cannot ever remember a year when God did not speak to me at camp meeting, but I don't always like the message I hear. One year he told me it was time to grow up. Here is the quote that got it all started, "You will know you are his servant when other people treat you as a servant, and you don't mind" (Dr. Bob Laurent).

A waiter in a restaurant serves people for several hours. When his shift has ended, does he sit at his favorite table and wait for someone to bring him food? No. He gets himself something to eat. The one who serves is responsible, not only to serve others but to take care of feeding himself.

Apparently I have reached the point where even camp is not a place primarily for me to be fed, but a place to serve so that others may be fed. When my kids complained about having to stand up so long to sing in church, I would tell them it was very little to sacrifice compared to what he gave for us. God began to tell me the same thing about missing services to work in the nursery. He asked me to throw out my self pity and "be transformed by the renewing of [my] mind so that [I] can test and approve what His will is – His good, pleasing and perfect will" (Romans 12:2). Those who are spiritually mature in the faith receive only a small portion of their spiritual food through others. I must learn to be fed directly by the Holy Spirit. I must continue to learn to walk more closely in step with the Spirit. It would be more comfortable to just stay as I have been and enjoy being spiritually fed by others, but God has called me to go deeper and take the next step in being transformed. I will follow where he leads.

What about you? Are you willing to take the next step in the transformation process – becoming more like Jesus? Even though we all like to go to a restaurant – or a worship service – and be fed, God is calling us to practice feeding ourselves. We need to be learning His Word, not just reading, but studying, meditating, and memorizing. We need to practice quiet listening in prayer. I encourage you to try to feed yourself. You will be blessed, and God will be glorified. The last time someone treated you as a servant, did it bother you to be taken for granted and unappreciated? We all have a long way to go in this transformation process. Thankfully, God is in it for a lifetime.

The Family Name

One Tuesday morning the call finally came. After years of longing and hoping and praying, Tony and Julie had finally been selected as adoptive parents for a new baby. The caller informed them that a baby had been born on Sunday and they should make plans to come to the hospital to meet him and take him home. So they packed suitcases, called work, and made arrangements to be gone a few days. Then they drove two hours to the hospital and met their new son. Talk about an adjustment! No nine months of waiting, preparing, and counting weeks. Instead there were seemingly endless months of hoping, months of testing, months of paperwork and interviews, months of waiting and preparing a nursery, years of praying. God heard their prayers and they were chosen as adoptive parents.

To give your name to a child (whether biological or adopted), to welcome him or her into your family, is no small thing. There are many blessings in parenting. Still, the commitment to provide the necessary physical care is huge, not to mention the emotional commitment. There are great risks and no guarantees. Even if your child makes it safely to adulthood without life-threatening injuries or diseases, there are other risks. What if this child whom I love chooses to live in a way that goes against what I believe and what I stand for? Giving him my name opens up opportunities for my reputation to be greatly damaged. Giving away my heart allows it to be broken. Still, parents find it worth the cost. Created in God's image, we were made to give love. We trust God to help us to train up our children in the way they should go (Proverbs 22:6). Without his help, how could we even hope for a positive outcome from their lives?

The book of 1 Chronicles describes family leaders and the clans that were named after them, illustrating the importance of the legacy we leave for our children and grandchildren. If a branch of your family ends up being known by your name ("Oh, that's one of the Adams boys") what kind of connotation will that bring to the minds of people? What kind of reputation do you leave for others to live up to or to try to live down?

Scripture tells us that those of us who have received forgiveness of sins have entered into a familial relationship with Almighty God. We are not distant cousins twice removed. Rather, he has adopted us as his sons and daughters (Ephesians 1:5). We're immediate family with the perfect, all-powerful Creator! We carry the name of Christian ("little Christ"). What an indescribable honor for us. What a terrible risk for him, yet he considers it worth that cost just to have a personal relationship with humans. He has, in part, entrusted his precious, unblemished reputation to us. Unbelievers in our family, our community, and our work places make decisions about what God is like and whether they want to know him, based on what they see of him in our lives. What a huge responsibility we have!

If I am kind and gentle at church, but critical and complaining throughout the week, will people want to know the God who supposedly leads my life? If we teach our children to read and pray, to be honest and fair, but we do not model that for them, we are only teaching hypocrisy. Whether the issue is drunkenness or foul language or misuse of money or treating people as being lower than us, the result is the same. We smudge the reputation of the God who has forgiven us and to whom we have sworn allegiance. We will be held responsible for our influence on those around us.

Here is an example of true allegiance, found in a collection entitled: *Grace Under Fire: Letters of Faith in Times of War.* "In 1943, Private First Class William Kiessel, who was about to take part in the invasion into France, wrote to friends that he did not want prayer for his safety, because 'Safety isn't the ultimate goal. True exemplary conduct is.' And he added, 'What is important is that whatever does happen to me I will do absolutely nothing that will shame my character or my God.'"[15] Would you be able to say the same? Would I? How well do we represent the Name of Christ? Does your life lead people to want to know him or to reject him?

The God Who Hears

After becoming Israel's third king, Solomon built and dedicated the magnificent temple in Jerusalem. Even with all the descriptions of the building and the use of so much gold, I cannot imagine what it must have been like. Talk about offering to God extravagant love and devotion! King Solomon knelt in front of all the people of Israel, and offered a prayer of dedication for the newly completed temple (2 Chronicles 6). In this passage, Solomon acknowledged that God's greatness was indescribable, and that even such a beautiful temple was inadequate for Almighty God. Still, he boldly asked the God of the universe to keep his eyes open toward the temple and to claim it as his own. Looking forward to the days to come, Solomon asked God in advance to hear the prayers of his people whenever they would look toward the temple – his earthly dwelling – and repent.

During the trek through the wilderness, and the years of conquering the Promised Land, God had made the tabernacle his dwelling place among the Israelites – the symbol of his presence with them. The new temple was to take the place of the old tent. Still, the most important part was the presence of God. Without that, it was just a fancy building. God answered Solomon's prayer. "When Solomon finished praying, fire came down from heaven and consumed the burnt offering and the sacrifices, and the glory of the Lord filled the temple. The priests could not enter the temple of the Lord because the glory of the Lord filled it. When all the Israelites saw the fire coming down and the glory of the Lord above the temple, they knelt on the pavement with their faces to the ground, and they worshiped and gave thanks to the Lord, saying, 'He is good; his love endures forever'" (2 Chronicles 7:1-3). God is still good and his love continues to endure.

Hundreds of years later, after Jesus was taken back to heaven, God gave the Holy Spirit to dwell within us. He has made us his temple. What then, is the lesson for us in this passage? Although the particulars have changed, the struggles we face are similar to those faced by the people of Israel in Solomon's day. We still need God's help to do what is right and just. The enemies that defeat us are not the Philistines or the Amalekites, but rather greed, bitterness, and pride. Sometimes needed rains are shut off because of our sin, and we do not have what we need – physically, financially, emotionally, Spiritually. Sometimes we face diseases and afflictions and all kinds of other problems. Whatever the need, the answer is the same. Seek the face and the presence of God. He is all the help we will ever need. He is good and his love endures forever. Today we do not need to get out a compass in attempts to pray toward the temple of God in Jerusalem. We don't even need to figure out which direction our own church building is at any given moment and pray in that direction. Rather, we need to humble ourselves and repent. Kneeling down with our faces to the ground, acknowledging God's great holiness is a good place to start. We need to submit ourselves anew to the leading of the Holy Spirit, who dwells within us and turn from our sin. Friend, I encourage you to turn your mind and your heart toward God and remember this beautiful response he gave to Solomon's prayer: "I have heard your prayer and have chosen this place for myself as a temple for sacrifices. When I shut up the heavens so that there is no rain, or command locusts to devour the land or send a plague among my people, if my people who are called by my name, will humble themselves and pray and seek my face and turn from their wicked ways, then will I hear from heaven and will forgive their sin and will heal their land" (2 Chronicles 7:12b-14). God hears our prayers as well and stands ready to help us when we seek him. Let us seek to draw near to him today.

Are We Listening?

During the glorious days of King David and King Solomon, the Jews followed the Lord. In the decades that followed, some leaders served God, but many did not. Some were half-hearted in their pursuit of godliness. "The Lord, the God of their fathers, sent word to them through his messengers again and again, because he had pity on his people and on his dwelling place" (2 Chronicles 36:15). He eventually sent them into exile in Babylon. We learn a few verses later that God allowed the land to rest 70 years, making up for the years when the Sabbath rest had not been observed (2 Chronicles 36:21-22).

It has long been said that wise people learn from history rather than repeating its errors. Are we wise? Is there a message that God seems to keep speaking to you again and again, as he did to the Israelites of old? Has he been calling you to be more faithful in personal Bible study? Perhaps he has been telling you to end an unhealthy relationship – or to reconcile a broken one. Has God been speaking to your heart about becoming more active in ministry and using the Spiritual gifts he has given you? Maybe he is challenging you to be a person of integrity and take a stand for righteousness in your family or your workplace. Have you answered his call to deliberately, consistently disciple your children or grandchildren? God is a good communicator. He speaks to his children and shows us the right way to go – the way that is very best for each of us. As we listen and obey, we know more peace, more joy, and see his character reflected more clearly in our lives. If we ignore his call, there is a limit to his patience. He sent the people of Israel into exile in a foreign land for 70 years.

What will it take to get you to listen? Will God have to do something drastic because of your disobedience? As painful as it is to be disciplined by God, it would be even worse to be written off and left to wallow in misery. When King Saul disobeyed, God rejected him as king and refused to listen to him or help him any more (I Samuel 15:23). I would call that worse than discipline.

In the passage above, God mentioned the Sabbath not being kept. He had repeatedly told his people to keep the Sabbath day holy (see Exodus 20:8, 31:14, Leviticus 25:2, Deuteronomy 5:12, Isaiah 56:2,6,13). It is a commandment every bit as important as "do not murder," or "do not covet." It is a day to rest our bodies from work, and also a day to rest our minds from the daily pressures and To Do lists. God invites us to be still and know that he is God (Psalm 46:10). We must push out the thoughts and responsibilities that fill our waking moments, in order to focus fully on God. When we come to see Sunday as a precious gift, a priceless opportunity to get alone with the Savior, our lives will be greatly enriched and God will receive the glory. Let us be careful to hear and obey what the Holy Spirit is saying to us.

Reflecting God

In preparation for a 40th wedding anniversary celebration, I was given the job of typing up a family tree. These names and notes and memories help to document the legacy of the Adams family, and enable us to pass it on to the next generation. God has truly blessed me through my in-laws. I am honored to be a part of their family.

The book of Ezra carries a clear reminder of the crucial role played by the senior generation. The Israelites had been exiled in Babylon for 70 years (almost a whole lifetime), just as God had said. At the end of that time, God moved the heart of Cyrus, King of Persia, to release the Jews and allow them to return to their homeland. (God moved the heart of a pagan king to make a ruling which cost him silver, gold, and workforce, without any notable political benefit. Reading this my heart cries, "O Lord, move my heart to do as you will, even when it makes no sense to those around me.")

Forty-two thousand, three hundred and sixty Jews packed up and went to Israel. Likely a very small percentage had been alive in Israel prior to the exile and those people were now past the age of 70. Over those decades in exile, some people had been faithful to teach the succeeding generations the history and heritage and faith of their nation. When the opportunity came to return to Israel, even many who had lived their whole lives in Babylon were ready to go – a clear sign that elders had passed on the legacy of what it meant to be a Jew. When the exiles arrived in Jerusalem they immediately set to work rebuilding the altar and sacrificing to their God. Then they began the work of rebuilding the temple. These priorities show that the focus was not on just reclaiming the land, but on drawing near to the God of Israel. That focus demonstrates the influence of the older generation teaching their children and grandchildren to seek the Lord.

When the work on the temple foundation was complete, the celebration began. "With praise and thanksgiving they sang to the Lord: 'He is good; his love to Israel endures forever.' And all the people gave a great shout of praise to the Lord, because the foundation of the house of the Lord was laid. But many of the older priests and Levites and family heads, who had seen the former temple, wept aloud when they saw the foundation of this temple being laid, while many others shouted for joy. No one could distinguish the sound of the shouts of joy from the sound of weeping, because the people made so much noise. And the sound was heard far away" (Ezra 3:11-13).

Brothers and sisters in Christ, even more than representing our own families, each one of us is a representative of the God family. We have a responsibility to teach the next generations – testifying to God's faithfulness and helping others to know him. No matter how high gas prices go, no matter how many companies close, no matter who wins the next election, no matter how bleak the country looks – even when big storms come – God is still faithful. Those of us who have seen him work through hard times in the past, must encourage others to hold fast to him, just as others have been faithful to train and encourage us.

All Sin is Ugly

During my teen years, participating in the youth program at Brown City Camp was always one of the highlights of the year. One of the first years that I was old enough to be in the program, organizers planned a team competition in a mud pit. They had worked up the ground and added lots of water to make the pit for relay races and other competitions. Lacking the self-confidence to join in, I enjoyed watching the rowdy event. Some participants tried to move gingerly through the knee-deep mud while others just jumped right in. Both techniques eventually yielded the same result. Everyone came out the exact same shade of gray no matter how he looked when he went in. The soil there is mostly clay.

Quite slippery, it stuck to everyone and everything. Very soon it was nearly impossible to tell one participant from another. To those of us standing outside the pit, they all looked very much alike.

As believers we have a tendency to rank sins in order of severity, and treat sinners accordingly. This is not Scriptural. Although God does not approve of taking the life of someone he created (either through murder or abortion), these are not unforgivable sins. Sexual immorality of any kind, stealing, and lying are all displeasing to God, but so is gluttony, one of the most obvious and least mentioned offenses. Putting something or someone before God is sin, so is failing to honor your parents. Any of these sins separates a person from God. To the one who is pure, all sinners are equally guilty and covered in filth, like participants in the mud games. The Apostle James tells us, "For whoever keeps the whole law and yet stumbles at just one point is guilty of breaking all of it. For he who said, 'Do not commit adultery,' also said, 'Do not murder'" (James 2:10-11). One sinner is not more lost than the other. Judging someone who has committed a "worse sin" than I have is like one mud-covered participant telling another that he is dirty. It is foolishness. "For all have sinned and fall short of the glory of God" (Romans 3:23). And, for all who have sinned, "The wages of sin is death" (Rom.6:23). It is the same wage no matter what the sin. Consequences differ, but the eternal cost is the same.

The good news is that Jesus' Blood is one-size-fits-all. No matter which sins I am guilty of, his blood is sufficient to cover them and to make me clean. There is no room for pride here. We all need his cleansing. Let us never forget how desperately lost-in-sin we were, and let us never lose compassion for those who are still lost.

Participants in the mud pit were instructed to be thoroughly sprayed with a hose before going to clean up. The water was cold and the line was long, so some skipped this step and just tried to go clean themselves. The result was a clogged drain system all over camp (and the end of mud pit games forever). In the same way, none of us can clean our own hearts. We must allow God to clean us on the inside. Only then can we really begin the empowered work of cleaning up our lifestyle to better reflect him.

Is Your Toothbrush Packed?

Friends of ours are serving as missionaries in Ireland. Several years ago God brought Denny and Linda together after each had been widowed. Mutual friends wondered what God had planned for them. Denny had served as a missionary to Spain even after the death of his first wife. Linda was very much a "home body" both before and after the death of her first husband. As Denny and Linda grew together and sought the Lord's direction, there came a day when Denny asked her how she felt about going to the mission field. I love her response: "My toothbrush is packed." Although they had not physically packed anything, spiritually she was so ready to follow God that if he said "Go" she was ready to go without delay. After all, daily necessities like a toothbrush are packed just before leaving. What a great word picture of surrender to God's will!

Friends are you ready and willing to go wherever God calls whenever God calls? It is not a question of personality type (introvert / extrovert, home body / adventurer). It is a question of Lordship. It is not a question of how old and how settled you are. It is a question of Lordship. When an individual decides to make Jesus Lord of his life, he gives him permission to direct every part of his life. That means God says "go there" or "do this" and we say "Yes, Lord. Right away" and then we obey. If we are not willing to follow wherever he leads, then he is not Lord.

There are many examples in Scripture of God calling very reluctant people to leave home. They had doubts, they asked for proof, they were afraid, but ultimately they obeyed, if not perfectly or with the results they expected. Abraham was called to leave his country and his people without knowing his destination (Genesis 12:1). Moses was called to confront Pharaoh and lead the Hebrews out of Egypt (Exodus 3:10). Gideon was called to lead Israel in fighting against Midian (Judges 6:14). Jonah was sent to call the pagan city of Ninevah to repentance (Jonah 1:2). Paul was sent to preach the Gospel message to the Gentiles (Acts 9:15). Moses learned that God does not like excuses. Jonah learned that God does not like disobedience. Each of these men decided to go where God called him to go.

Is Jesus your Lord? Have you truly surrendered your will to his? Can you say honestly that you are willing to go when God calls you? Maybe he wants to use you in another country, or maybe in a different city or state. Maybe he is calling you to go to Bible college and prepare for ministry (no matter what your age) or to change jobs. Scripture tells us that God has good plans for his people (Jeremiah 29:11) and that he planned "beforehand" good works for each of us to do (Ephesians 2:10). Notice that Scripture never says that God has plans to keep us comfortable. He doesn't. He has plans to glorify his Name.

Growing up in the parsonage, we experienced obedience to God's call. Dad served as pastor for four churches in 37 years. When God said "move" we moved. For us, moving to another church was always a possibility. The same is true today. As delighted as we are to live near family (a rare treat in ministry), and to have such a wonderful church family, we live with the knowledge that it may be temporary. There may come a day when God calls us to serve elsewhere. As hard as that would be, we would be doing our family and two churches a terrible disservice if we disobeyed. The same is true for you. Are you willing and ready to serve wherever your Lord leads? If not, he is not Lord. Have you ever sincerely asked him where he wants to use you, or do you avoid the question like a student avoiding eye contact so the teacher will call on someone else? Ask him today. Abundant life is only found in the center of God's will. Is your toothbrush packed?

Center of the Home

The responsibilities of adulthood are not as easy or fun as they seemed when I was a teen – tired of people telling me what to do. Trying to establish and maintain a home centered on Christ is one area that is much harder than I ever realized. Creating a godly home does not come naturally or easily, no matter what kind of family you had. It takes work and deliberate choices. It also yields immeasurable rewards, both in this life and in eternity. Fathers, the Bible gives you the primary responsibility for establishing a godly home. You will be held accountable for this. Mothers, you must do your best in this, regardless of whether you have a husband who provides spiritual leadership.

Whether your household consists of one person or of twenty people, the first step is always the same. Surrender your own life fully to God, and commit to following him in everything. Determine to live a life of loving obedience to God's Word. Discipline yourself to read God's word daily and spend time alone with him in prayer. Learn to hear his voice speaking to you. A life surrendered to God will be a life of integrity, a life of purity in speech, in thought, and in action. Make it your goal to make your home a place where the Holy Spirit is always welcome. It is a good practice to kneel together as a family in the center of the house and dedicate the house to God for his use. It is also appropriate to do a family prayer walk through the house asking God to be Lord over everything that happens in each room. Invite him to take up residence in the home he has given you.

If you have children at home, Scripture tells you to "Train a child in the way he should go, and when he is old he will not turn from it" (Proverbs 22:6). Although this is a proverb – a general principle rather than a promise, it is very wise advice. God, through Moses instructed the Hebrew people, "These commandments that I give you today are to be upon your heart. Impress them on your children. Talk about them when you sit at home and when you walk along the road, when you lie down and when you get up" (Deuteronomy 6:6,7). How do we as parents go about training up our children as disciples? What kinds of things do we need to teach them? Sometimes the task seems so overwhelming that we are tempted to just give up, or to abdicate our responsibility to Sunday School teachers and others. Neither of these options will hold up when our Heavenly Father calls us to give an account of what we did with what we were given. If we are going to be obedient to Scripture, we must disciple our children.

Here is a list to get us started. In each area we must teach and model these traits in age-appropriate ways throughout the years we are raising our children so they will learn to make God the center of their lives, and eventually their own homes.

1) Most important of all is helping our children to understand that the Christian life is all about a personal relationship with Jesus Christ. We teach and model personal quiet time.

2) Biblical Mastery – with very young children this often begins with teaching basic Bible stories. It must, however, go further and teach foundational principles. Some examples include: God loves us, God is good, the Bible is the Word of God and is to be treasured as such, and Jesus died to forgive our sins. As children get older, we need to teach other basics of Christian living such as Biblical use of money and standing up for what is right. 3) Fellowship – healthy relationships with others in the church family, and prayer for others. 4) Ministry/Service – from the preschool years on we should include our children in opportunities to serve others. In a generation of self-centered people, this is the most effective way to help children learn to actively care for others. 5) Family Interaction – Healthy relationships with parents and siblings, including obedience, respectful speech, and sharing the responsibilities of the home. A good rule of thumb is this: Don't treat your family members in a way you would not treat Jesus.

Even if you do not have young children at home, every member of the church family has a part in training up disciples. It is no secret that Satan is attacking the institution of the family. At any given time, in any given church, there are families falling apart. Obviously, this was never God's plan. Each of us should be praying fervently for families . . . for protection and also for help in making God the center of the home.

What I Feared Most

I once heard a speaker ask how many people in the congregation were dealing with fear of some kind. I was shocked to see more than half of the people raise a hand. Even within the church, many people are desperately longing to be set free from fear. When Job faced devastating loss, he said, "What I feared has now come upon me; what I dreaded has happened to me. I have no peace, no quietness; I have no rest, but only turmoil" (Job 3:25, 26). Job was a fine, upstanding citizen, with a stellar reputation and a firm faith. Still, he was apparently plagued by fears.

My friend, what is it that you fear most? Failing health? Financial ruin? Death? Losing a child? Rejection? Smudged reputation? Failure? Criticism?

In the end, Job was comforted by God's personal reminder of his power over all creation and the depth of his knowledge. I believe this reassurance that God is God, he is good, and he is in control, meant more to Job than the restoration of his worldly wealth. Without God as the foundation, everything is meaningless "Like chasing after the wind" (Ecclesiastes 2:11).

Friend, whatever it is that you fear may or may not actually happen. Remember, fear of the future does not come from God. Do not dwell upon such thoughts. (If the enemy can keep you paralyzed with fear, he will render you completely ineffective in God's kingdom.) Leave the future in God's hands. If what you feared has come upon you, as it did upon Job, cling tightly to the Lord. Read the last five chapters of Job. Rediscover that God is God, he is good, and he is in control. Determine, as a matter of your will, to put your faith in God and hang on to him as you wait for him to bring you through the storm. God has said, "So do not fear, for I am with you; do not be dismayed, for I am your God. I will strengthen you and help you; I will uphold you with my righteous right hand" (Isaiah 41:10).

The Perfect Campfire

One night at church camp, I stopped to greet some friends gathered around a campfire. I was struck by the beauty of their fire. Its perfect teepee shape and bright flames made me wonder if an eagle scout had been responsible. Arriving back at our own campfire, I noticed that the burning sticks and logs were all lying in a haphazard pile. Still, it gave off beautiful light and warmth which are the most important aspects of a fire.

The Scripture refers to both God and the Spirit with fire. "Do not put out the Spirit's fire" (1 Thessalonians 5:19). In Hebrews 12:29 God is called a "consuming fire." When the disciples first received the gift of the Holy Spirit after Jesus had returned to heaven, the Spirit came to each of them like tongues of fire (Acts 2:3). The Holy Spirit is to burn within the heart of every believer. It seems to me, though, that some of us are more concerned with looking like an attractive fire than we are with living a life that glows with love for those in the dark and cold of sin. Some of us look very "put together" in our physical appearance, or in our actions and words. Some of us look more like a haphazard pile of sticks. God is far more concerned with the light and warmth of our spirits than with our appearance. Let each of us examine our own hearts with the following questions. When I pray, do I cry out to God earnestly, desperately, or do I just politely place my order at the drive thru? Friends, if I am not faithfully reading, if I am not faithfully praying for lost souls and new disciples, if I am not daily sacrificing my will to his . . . I may look good but I am not a useful fire.

The morning after I had seen that beautiful fire I walked past the same fire pit again. It was just a pile of ashes. I couldn't see even a glowing ember. It needed to be rekindled, re-ignited. My heart has become burdened regarding the apathy of God's people. I pray for every believer to become passionate about the things of God. I long to see us cry out desperately for our own spiritual depth and for the lost souls all around us. May the fire of the Holy Spirit burn strongly, warmly, and brightly in your life. May people be drawn to Jesus because of his light shining out through your life.

An Answer Out of the Storm

Job's friends are among the most annoying personalities in the Bible. After 37 long, painful chapters we read, "Then the Lord answered Job out of the storm" (Job 38:1). In the previous chapter Elihu talked about how God had made himself known through clouds, thunder, and lightening. Job faced the worst storm imaginable, most of it all in one day. Later he got boils, and then came a rain storm. Chapter 38 verse 1 tells us that God answered him "out of the storm." To me this can only mean that God was in the storm with Job.

This is good news for you and me. Chances are you have not lost all ten of your children, your oxen and donkeys, your sheep and camels, and all of your servants all at once, only to be plagued with boils, cursed by your spouse, and accused by your friends. Still, I am sure you understand how it feels to have the storms of life pounding down on you. Maybe your heart is breaking, as mine is, for a loved one. The clouds just seem to roll in thicker and darker every day, with no visible reason for hope. Is that true for you? Whether your storm is health related, financial, relational, or emotional, it can rock your world. Maybe it is deep grief over a relationship that ended too soon, or a dream that has never come to be. Whatever it is, friend, God is with you in the storm. Reverend Steve Jones described Emmanuel (which means "God with us") as being "closer than your clothes." He is all around us. "In Him we live and move and have our being" (Acts 17:28a). God may never explain the reasons for the storm, but he is right there and he will carry you through day by day and moment by moment.

Good News and Bad News

The Bad News:

After King David died, his son Solomon reigned. Solomon's son Rehoboam followed him (2 Chronicles 10). As soon as he became king, the people of Israel came to Rehoboam asking him to lighten the heavy load that Solomon had placed on them. The wise men who had served as advisors to Solomon recommended that Rehoboam grant their request. Rejecting their advice, and listening instead to his peers, Rehoboam answered the people harshly. He promised to burden them more than his father had. As a result of this one decision, ten of the twelve tribes rejected him as their king. Only the tribes of Judah and Benjamin remained loyal to the descendants of David. One choice and Rehoboam went from ruling 12 tribes to ruling 2!

Although we have never been considered royalty, many of us can relate to the consequences of a single choice. Those big choices are often made in a moment, with repercussions for a lifetime. . . Dropping out of school, speeding or drinking which leads to an accident, aborting a baby, having an affair, breaking the law, or angry words that end a relationship. All of these choices have consequences, some of which last a lifetime.

The Good News:

Still, that does not mean there is cause for despair. 2 Chronicles 11:13-16 tells us that the priests and Levites, the spiritual leaders - relocated to the southern kingdom, and "people who sincerely wanted to worship the Lord, the God of Israel, followed the Levites to Jerusalem." The southern kingdom for many years was spiritually much stronger than the northern kingdom and enjoyed God's blessing. If you have made poor choices, do not despair. God still loves you and wants to draw you near to himself. He still wants to lead you into abundant life.

The Most Important News:

Of all the choices one makes in life, by far the most important is the decision of what to do with Jesus. Are you willing to give God authority over your life or not? God will gladly forgive any of the choices listed above. He is not, however, willing to settle for second place in your life.

Look at King Rehoboam's epitaph, "But he was an evil king, for he did not seek the Lord with all his heart" (2 Chr. 12:14, NLT). We tend to define an evil person as someone who does mostly evil most of the time. God's definition is far more stringent. Rehoboam sought the Lord when he was in trouble, but not at other times, and the Bible described him as evil.

Friends, you and I need to closely examine our hearts. None of us is ever allowed to go back and change decisions we have made in the past no matter how much we wish we could. Rather, we must go forward and make right choices today. The most important decision you and I can ever make is to repent, receive forgiveness of sins, and commit to live our lives seeking and obeying Almighty God, our Loving Father. I pray that you will choose him today.

Two Epitaphs

Let's look this week at two epitaphs found in 2 Chronicles. "Jehoram was 32 years old when he became king, and he reigned in Jerusalem 8 years. No one was sorry when he died. He was buried in the City of David, but not in the royal cemetery" (21:20, NLT). Just a few chapters later we are told, "Jehoida (the priest) lived to a very old age, finally dying at 130. He was buried among the kings in the City of David, because he had done so much good in Israel for God and his temple" (24:15,16 NLT).

What a stark contrast! These two men lived at the same time. One was born into royalty. The other was born into the priesthood at a time when Judah was not committed to serving God or following the priests. King Jehoram earned the saddest epitaph ever written: "No one was sorry when he died." Jehoida earned a royal burial.

Looking at these two lives, we can clearly see that, no matter what situation you were born into, you can choose what kind of person you will be. While this is true for all of us, we are going to focus on fathers. Biblically, being a father is a tremendous responsibility. The father is the head of the family (Ephesians 5:23). He is responsible to provide for his family (1 Timothy 5:8). As the head of the household, fathers are also responsible for keeping the family centered on Christ. No matter what kind of home a boy grows up in, with God's help he can build a home centered on God.

In his extensive research, George Barna found a very sad trend among church-going families. Parents consistently set high goals for their children in many areas such as academics, athletics, and career. None of these is bad, but they are all temporary. Research found, however, that when it comes to things that are eternal, most parents set the bar very, very low.[16] Just hoping a child will attend church occasionally as an adult, and refrain from killing others, is not much of a goal. Obviously, as each child reaches adulthood, he/she becomes responsible for his/her own choices. We cannot choose for them to follow God. Still, we are responsible for the influence we have on them.

Fathers, as head of the household, this responsibility is especially strong for you. If you are to be a family of disciples who make disciples, you must take the lead. As in other areas of life, God is eager to help make up for the skills you lack as you fully surrender your life and your family to him. I encourage you, no matter what kind of father you had, to raise the bar and to prayerfully lead your children into the very best that God has planned for their lives. As it was with King Jehoram and Jehoida the priest, so it is with you. You will be held responsible for the choices you make, the priorities you set, and the influence you have.

Today more tombstones do not include an epitaph because engraving costs are charged by the letter. Still, it would be a healthy exercise to try to write your own epitaph. Decide how you want to be remembered, and then live in such a way as to leave those memories in the people around you.

Unquestioning Obedience

In our small town, five churches from five different denominations work together in various types of ministry, including Vacation Bible School each summer. When my children were young, I served as teacher for the preschool class. When my youngest started kindergarten, I decided to move up to an older (easier) age level. I talked to the representatives from the other churches and prayed and waited for God to send along someone who, unlike me, was actually gifted in that area. A few weeks before our start date, nobody had volunteered to teach the preschool class. Begrudgingly I started to make the preparations. As I was working I kept reminding God that this was not something I wanted to do. I kept thinking of the title of a book I used to see on my parents' book shelf, *Lord, Here Am I – Send Aaron*. Although I never read the book, I wholeheartedly agreed with Moses' mindset. Finally, God filled my mind with the question, "Since when did serving me become about what you want to do?" Ouch! I agreed to stop complaining and just give him my best. A couple of days later I read what Jesus had to say about the attitude of a servant of God.

"Suppose one of you had a servant plowing or looking after the sheep. Would he say to the servant when he comes in from the field, 'Come along now and sit down to eat'? Would he not rather say, 'Prepare my supper, get yourself ready and wait on me while I eat and drink; after that you may eat and drink'? Would he thank the servant because he did what he was told to do? So you also, when you have done everything you were told to do, should say, 'We are unworthy servants; we have only done our duty'" (Luke 17:7-10).

Does that sound like my attitude? Or yours? It is hard for most of us in America to really understand the attitude of servanthood day in and day out. Our God is worthy of unquestioning obedience. Here are two short stories about the costs and benefits related to our choices to obey.

First, is Tom's story. In 2002 Tom was invited to join a medical missions team to Guatemala. He and his teenage daughter both felt called to go on the trip and they obeyed. After that trip, the host missionary visited our church. In that service the Holy Spirit moved my husband to organize and lead a team from our church. Since then, at least one missions team has been sent out every year. Every team member who was open to God's work has been changed by experiencing these trips. How greatly God has blessed because of Tom's obedience!

Second, is Michelle's story. Michelle and her family came to the Lord when her oldest son was nine years old. Since that time they have tried to follow God's will for their lives, but she wishes she had known God earlier and had more years to train up her children in the way they should go (Proverbs 22:6). She wonders why God waited so long. That question got me wondering how many times God asked one of his people to share his/her faith with Michelle but he/she refused. How much did someone's disobedience cost Michelle and her family? When you and I choose to disobey the prompting of the Spirit, how much does it cost others?

We need to examine the attitudes of our hearts. Do we give him unquestioning obedience, or do we whine and complain when asked to do something we don't want to do? We may never know the precise cost or benefit resulting from our obedience or disobedience, but we may be sure that God knows and it matters. As reward for my obedience that summer, he sent nearly 40 preschoolers! Still, he was faithful and sent seven helpers. If even one child follows Christ, it is all worth it!

How Is Your Walk?

After my first year as a school psychologist, I spent the summer volunteering in Camden, New Jersey. One of my team members made a powerful impression on me. All through the summer, sometimes in serious conversation and sometimes in gentle rebuke she asked the question, "How is your walk?"

135

Now I ask you, "Who, of all the people you know, asks you about the status of your walk with the Lord?" It seems to me that most people in the church are more comfortable talking about anything else. I often have people confide in me about very private health issues, legal trouble, serious relationship struggles, or even how far they are in debt – very personal disclosures. It is rare, however, for anyone outside my family to volunteer information about his/her personal relationship with God or to ask about mine. Why is that? Why do we talk least about the stuff that matters most?

Let's look at the Word. "As iron sharpens iron, so one man sharpens another" (Proverbs 27:17). "Therefore confess your sins to each other and pray for each other so that you may be healed" (James 5:16a). "But encourage one another daily, as long as it is called today, so that none of you may be hardened by sin's deceitfulness" (Hebrews 3:13). "Two are better than one, because they have a good return for their work: If one falls down, his friend can help him up. But pity the man who falls and has no one to help him up (Ecclesiastes 4:9-10).

There are men and women in your church family who are floundering in their faith and feeling totally defeated. They put up a good front on Sunday morning, but it is just a mask. These people need someone to care enough to ask, "How's your walk?" Do you care enough to be that person? Do you care enough to spend time building a relationship and walking alongside someone? Most people seem to agree that one of the keys to healthy, lasting relationships is honest communication about the big issues. Are we mature enough to do that with members of the family of God?

Finally, if you are a person who is hurting desperately inside and struggling spiritually, my earnest hope and prayer is that you will let someone walk alongside you and help carry the load. Please, please, don't stagger on alone thinking the rest of us have it all together spiritually. It just isn't so.

Every Opportunity

I have often wondered about all the people in the chain who were instrumental in bringing the gospel to me. How did the good news about salvation in Jesus Christ travel through the years and miles from New Testatment Jerusalem to me? So far I only know about a few links in that chain. One was my Aunt Verda, who found Christ at the age of 16. She prayed earnestly for her younger sister, and saw the answer to that prayer when my Mom came to the Lord on her 12th birthday. Aunt Verda prayed for my Mom's salvation, and told her about Jesus. What an impact those prayers have had on Mom and our whole family!

In May, 2006 Verda Matteson went to meet her Savior. Our loss was certainly her gain. In the small cards commemorating her life, I read something I don't ever remember reading before. It said she lived "67 years, 6 months, 11 days." At first, this struck me as strange. Why didn't they just write "67 years"? Then I started thinking about how every day matters. After I learned about her prayers for my Mom, I wondered if those "extra" 6 months and 11 days were the time she spent praying for her little sister. Suddenly those days seem to me like some of the most important days in her life. Every day is a chance to make a difference – a chance you never get back.

In James 4:13-17, we are warned, "Now listen, you who say, 'Today or tomorrow we will go to this or that city, spend a year there, carry on business and make money.' Why, you do not even know what will happen tomorrow. What is your life? You are a mist that appears for a little while and then vanishes. Instead, you ought to say, 'If it is the Lord's will, we will live and do this or that.' As it is, you boast and brag. All such boasting is evil. Anyone, then, who knows the good he ought to do and doesn't do it, sins." I think all of us know the good we ought to do. Are we doing it? Today is the only day you are guaranteed – and maybe not even all of today. Someone's eternity could be changed by the way you spend this day. As of this writing, I am 43 years, 4 months, 19 days old. Who needs to see and hear God's love from me today? I encourage you to, "Be wise in the way you act toward outsiders; make the most of every opportunity. Let your conversation be always full of grace, seasoned with salt, so that you may know how to answer everyone" (Colossians 4:5-6). Let us not waste the opportunities God gives us today. We may not get a chance at tomorrow.

A Job for Everyone

The books of Ezra and Nehemiah tell the story of the Jews returning to their homeland. The people of Judah were sent into exile in Babylon – having persisted in disobedience to God despite the warnings of many prophets – they stayed there 70 years. After that time, as God had said, the king of Persia allowed those who wished to return to Jerusalem to do so. Ezra led them in repairing the temple and confronted them about areas where they were living contrary to God's law (for example, intermarriage with neighboring peoples). A short time later, Nehemiah returned to Jerusalem with a second wave of Jews. He was greatly distressed that the city wall was still a pile of rubble. He challenged and encouraged the people there to work with him on rebuilding it. So they set to work, each one taking a section and working on it diligently. These men were not all builders by trade. Many were probably farmers, along with blacksmiths, potters, etc. Still, there was a job to be done. Every hand was needed, so each one did his part. Many of their names are listed in Nehemiah 3. Soon they had the entire wall rebuilt to half its height, in spite of criticism and opposition from neighbors, "for the people worked with all their heart" (Nehemiah 4:6). As each one worked diligently, God blessed the work of their hands. "So the wall was completed . . . in fifty-two days. When all our enemies heard about this, all the surrounding nations were afraid and lost their self-confidence, because they realized that this work had been done with the help of our God" (Nehemiah 6:15,16).

What is the message for us? No matter what your job is, God has a job for you. Our pastor emphasizes a difference between your career and your life's work. No matter what career you are working in, either in the home or outside of it, your life's work is to further the kingdom of God. Each one of us is to do his/her part in sharing the gospel, ministering in the church, and serving others. When this has been done well, people will realize "that this work [has] been done with the help of our God." Some of us are not working to further the kingdom. If you are attempting to serve the Lord, I encourage you to do a simple job performance review. Are you doing your life's work to the best of your ability? You will only find fulfillment, and abundant life, in the center of God's will. The strength to keep doing your best comes, not from yourself or from others, but from him. Let us seek his will and obey.

Lessons from Washington DC

On my third visit to our nation's capital, I saw several things and places I had never seen before. I want to share with you a challenge and a word of encouragement.

Challenge

I was blessed and challenged as I read speeches of some of our founding fathers, who made no secret of their complete faith and dependence on Almighty God. As we heard tour guides mention the burning of the White House and the Capitol Building during the War of 1812, and looked at the magnificent structures of marble and granite and concrete which now stand on every corner, I was reminded that the attacks which have caused the greatest damage to our nation, were not those which destroyed our treasured buildings. Far greater damage has been done through subtle attacks on our consciences, our moral standards, our priorities. We have forgotten what the Apostle Paul told the church of Ephesus. "For our struggle is not against flesh and blood, but against the rulers, against the authorities, against the powers of this dark world and against the spiritual forces of evil in the heavenly realms" (Ephesians 6:12). My friends, we as a nation have done better in preparing for physical battles than for spiritual battles. The office of Homeland Security – no matter how well they do their assigned task – is totally incapable of protecting this land from its greatest enemy. That job belongs to you and me. Are you praying faithfully and consistently for America? Am I? This is the only way the battle can be fought. This is the only source of protection. Each of us needs to do his part. Read Isaiah and Jeremiah and hear God's heart calling out for his people to faithfully seek him, so he will not have to destroy them.

Encouragement

One of the most moving sites in Washington DC is Arlington Cemetery. We stood for thirty minutes watching the sentry at the Tomb of the Unknown Soldier, and the ceremony of the Changing of the Guard. It is a very solemn experience. I was reading about the Tomb of the Unknown Soldier, and how unidentified soldiers were selected, after the various wars, to be buried here. There were more than 2100 unknown soldiers from the Civil War alone. The grave markers go on, row after row after row. America has chosen to honor the memory of these unknown soldiers continually. Still, no one knows who they were, how they fought, how they lived their lives, or who they left behind. They served without recognition, and did not live to see the results of their sacrifices.

John 6 describes Jesus' miraculous feeding of more than 5,000 people. Jesus gave the food to the disciples to give to the people. Each disciple received a very small amount of the original meal, yet he had to start giving it away in order to see the miracle of multiplication. There are, in the church, many unknown soldiers. Although God has called each of his children to be a part of his army, many think they have little or nothing to offer. They quietly give their little bit without recognition or honor. No accolades or medals adorn their uniforms. If you are one of these unknown soldiers, wondering if your small contribution matters, I want to encourage you today. There are no unknown soldiers in God's army. Nor will there ever be a changing of the guard. God is unchanging throughout all of eternity. Jesus sees what you do, how you do it, and the motivation of your heart. You will receive your reward in heaven. Please do not be discouraged, but keep on striving for his glory in whatever battlefield God has placed you. "Let us not become weary in doing good, for at the proper time we will reap a harvest if we do not give up" (Galatians 6:9). "So whether you eat or drink or whatever you do, do it all for the glory of God" (I Corinthians 10:31).

A Sabbath Gift

Our District Superintendent, Rev. Jim Keller, once compared church camp to a family Thanksgiving dinner. Some people start preparing and planning months in advance. Others arrive early to work and prepare. Some just show up for the meal. As he was sharing this observation, God nudged me with the following thought: How sad it would be to work so hard to plan and bake and clean and cook, only to fall asleep in your plate before ever eating a bite!

Many ministry responsibilities take great effort and preparation. This is true for camp, true for Sunday morning services, true for Vacation Bible School, and true for many other areas of service such as prison ministry. Sometimes we work so hard in preparing, that when the actual ministry takes place, we are too tired to focus and to listen to the Spirit as he tries to speak to our own hearts.

I believe that God's gift of a Sabbath Rest is one of the least used and appreciated gifts we have received. God told the Israelites, "Remember the Sabbath day by keeping it holy. Six days you shall labor and do all your work, but the seventh day is a Sabbath to the Lord your God. On it you shall not do any work, neither you, nor your son or daughter, nor your manservant or maidservant, nor your animals, nor the alien within your gates. For in six days the Lord made the heavens and the earth, the sea, and all that is in them, but he rested on the seventh day. Therefore the Lord blessed the Sabbath day and made it holy" (Exodus 20:8-11).

As I grew up I always viewed Sunday as a day of rules and don'ts. We didn't play ball or do homework or go shopping or plan other activities. We had mandatory nap time in the afternoon. I remember neighbor kids standing in the yard yelling up to the second story window asking if we could come out and play yet. I remember how hard my Mom worked on Saturday night to make sure the house was clean, the laundry was caught up, and as much prep work as possible had been done for Sunday dinner. Some weeks we would arrive home late on Saturday from a trip, and my exhausted mother would be up until midnight working. But by 12:01 a.m. she was in bed whether all the work got done or not. Why? It was now Sunday and no further work would be done except what was necessary for feeding her family. No laundry, no cleaning, and cooking of only one formal meal. Although I usually enjoyed church services, I never particularly enjoyed Sunday.

It wasn't until many years later, when I was out on my own, that I finally came to understand that the Sabbath rest was a gift from God. In his wisdom he recognized two things about human nature: First, humans need regular down time; Second, we would never admit it unless it was forced upon us. Left to ourselves, we would just run and run and run 24/7.

The Sabbath (which we now celebrate on Sunday rather than Saturday in honor of our Lord's resurrection) is a beautiful gift. It is a license to relax, as well as to quiet our spirits so we can hear him. In Bible times, and still today in that part of the world, the Sabbath begins at sundown on Friday and runs through sundown on Saturday. Isn't God smart? He knew long ago that if we would stop working at sundown, having made all the necessary preparation earlier, we could relax in the evening. We could awake well rested and in good spirits rather than being irritable and ill-tempered with family members while we try to get ready for church. We would be alert and focused and attentive to the Spirit during the service rather than falling asleep or thinking about many things that need to be done as soon as we get home. We could enjoy the feast in his presence rather than falling asleep in our plates. If we treat Sunday like any other day, except for a couple of hours spent at church, we trample God's gift in the dirt and it is clearly our loss. Imagine how much more God would be accomplishing in our lives and in our churches if we arrived at church fifteen or twenty minutes before the service, not to finish preparations or to visit with others, but to pray and seek his face! If our hearts were fixed on him and sensitive to his Spirit before the service ever started, we would begin to experience regularly what God has wanted for us all along.

Thanksgiving is not until November, but we have opportunity to come together as a family and feast in his presence each week. Let's prioritize better, so that we don't fall asleep in our plates. Remember, the Sabbath Rest was not a suggestion or an afterthought. God considered it so important that he made it the fourth commandment. We would do well to heed what he considers important.

Just One Day

"There just aren't enough hours in the day!" Have you ever felt that way? Sometimes it seems there are more things that *need* to be done than a person could ever reasonably do in a day. In the USA this thought pattern seems to be the norm rather than the exception. I think most of us buy into it much of the time, and spend every waking hour (and some half-asleep hours) trying to do all that important stuff.

I would like us to look at our All-Knowing Father's gift of one day at a time. God has created our bodies to run in 24-hour cycles, which include a significant period of rest. Of course, since he is a God of order, this coincides with his plan for the entire universe. He made us that way, because he knew it was optimal for our well-being. I want to give God thanks today for giving me only one day at a time. Whether you are just busy with day-to-day chores, or whether your world has been turned inside out by grief or heartache or another kind of crisis, aren't you glad God has only given you one day?

When I was single and turning 25, and then 30, I kept asking God if I would ever marry. Sometimes I was impatient. Several times I begged him to let me peek through a window of time just to see if it was ever going to happen so I could stop worrying about it. Of course, he never did. Instead, he would ask me gently, "Lynn, can you be content to be single and serve me for one day? All I am asking for is today."

I don't know what struggle you are facing or helping someone else to face. Chances are your heart is burdened about something. Do you, like me, tend to look forward and think how terrible it will be if this problem goes on for another year or five years or ten? If I had known when I was twenty that I would still be alone when I turned thirty, what despair I would have felt! But God in his wisdom gave me only one day at a time, and taught me as many things as I was willing to learn in those days. Likely your problem won't last forever either. To spend time dreading the future is foolish, since things are always changing. Your life will be considerably different a year from now than it is today. In the Sermon on the Mount, Jesus tells us, "Therefore do not worry about tomorrow, for tomorrow will worry about itself. Each day has enough trouble of its own" (Matthew 6:34).

I leave you with the question God has so often asked me. "Can you serve me in the midst of this heartache for just one day?" Carry on, one day at a time and thank him daily for the gift of rest in between the hours of struggle. Rest in him and refuse to worry about tomorrow.

Blockage in the Heart

Over the years, we have seen many friends and family members face cardiac issues. There are numerous similarities between physical heart problems and spiritual heart problems. The physical heart transports blood throughout the body. The spiritual heart transports Jesus' blood throughout the believer. Without blood there is no life. Without the blood of Christ there is no spiritual life. I need steady blood flow in order to be productive. I need Jesus' blood flowing through me in order to produce spiritual fruit. Sometimes the physical heart becomes clogged with plaque, which greatly hinders the flow of blood. Plaque in the spiritual heart comes in the form of bitterness, worry, unforgiveness, insistence on having my own way, self-focus, a critical spirit, or disobedience. These things greatly hinder the flow of Jesus' blood through me.

When plaque builds up in either the physical heart or the spiritual heart, denying the problem or postponing treatment only makes it worse. In both cases, I need help to treat the problem, either from a heart doctor or from the heart maker, our great physician. Treatments for blockage in the physical heart include outside help (medication), improved diet, and increased exercise. Treatment for blockage in the spiritual heart requires outside help (Holy Spirit), diet on the written Word of God and on the words he speaks as we listen in prayer, and exercising Christ-like characteristics. I must let his blood enable me to do things like it enabled him to do – love God and love people.

Physical heart problems are found and treated when a person admits he is in pain and seeks help. Spiritual heart problems can only be treated when a person repents of sin and seeks help. Specific tests reveal physical problems. Only the Holy Spirit can reveal the blockage in our spiritual hearts.

Along with so many similarities, there is one major difference: If blockage in my physical heart goes untreated I lose only my life. If blockage in my spiritual heart goes untreated, I could lose eternity. In John 15 Jesus said, "I am the true vine, and my Father is the gardener. He cuts off every branch in me that bears no fruit, while every branch that does bear fruit he prunes so that it will be even more fruitful. . . I am the vine; you are the branches. If a man remains in me and I in him, he will bear much fruit; apart from me you can do nothing" (John 15:1,2,5). The Bible clearly states that Christians will bear fruit. As I allow blockage in my spiritual heart, the Gardener/the Great Physician comes to prune or to clear the blockage so I can be as fruitful as possible. If I resist his work and refuse to repent, the blockage becomes more and more extensive until the flow of his blood is completely blocked and I am totally unfruitful. The Bible calls this hardening my heart. If I refuse to be pruned and stop bearing fruit, I may be cut off from his kingdom. This is serious business. It is my challenge and plea that each of us ask the Holy Spirit to do a Spiritual heart catheterization – and wait quietly upon him in prayer as he reveals the results of his search. A lot more than our lives could be at stake.

Not Just Crumbs

There is a great verse in Psalm 63 that I would encourage you to commit to memory. "O God, You are my God, earnestly I seek You; my soul thirsts for You, my body longs for You, in a dry and weary land where there is no water" (Psalm 63:1). Have you ever longed for God with that kind of desperation? I tend to use 99% of my waking hours fulfilling a long list of "shoulds." I should read to my kids, I should prepare a Sunday School lesson, I should fix a meal for someone, I should call a hurting friend, I should clean the house. My list gets longer rather than shorter throughout the week. These are all good things, but if all my energy is directed toward doing, there is no time left for being renewed in his presence.

One day while as I was walking, God shared this picture with me. Visualize a tall cliff or rock-climbing wall. At the top sits God with an unbelievable banquet spread out, ready to renew my heart, my mind, my soul, my body. At the bottom of the cliff I am running around in circles doing "good stuff." God is calling me to climb up and feast in his presence, but that would take discipline. God invites, and even commands us to "be still and know that I am God" (Psalm 46:10). It seems that as soon as I start thinking about climbing up to him, dozens of "shoulds" invade my mind. Instead of climbing up to feast with him, I try to make do with little crumbs that fall . . . a song here, a short devotional there, maybe a testimony I hear on the radio. Before I realize it, I have gone days without nourishing my spirit.

Spending time in his presence renews us, like a powerful battery re-charger. He is ready and waiting, longing for our undivided attention. He wants to pour himself into us and renew us. Isn't that what we want too? But the batteries will just run slower and slower if they aren't taken out and connected to the charger. He is ready, our endless power source. We need to come apart and feast with him. Let us seek him "as the deer pants for water" when there is none to be found (Psalm 42:1).

Here are some suggestions for getting started.

- Carve out a block of time, even ten minutes, when you can be totally alone.
- Try kneeling or sitting in a chair that will not make you sleepy.
- Before you start to read or even pray, be silent. This is a very difficult discipline to develop, being silent without letting your mind wander, but it is crucial to learn to listen to the still quiet voice of the Savior
- Read and pray out loud. This helps to keep your mind focused and fights off thoughts that threaten to invade.
- Play soft music that reminds you of the awesomeness of God
- Try journaling the burdens on your heart or the questions on your mind or the things you believe God is saying to you.

Like any other discipline that is good for you, (exercise, diet, quitting smoking, etc.) the most important thing is to start today. When you fall down, don't give in to attacks of the enemy that say you'll never succeed. Just get up and try again. You will never believe what a feast you have been missing!

Check Your Feet

The prophet Isaiah said, "How beautiful on the mountains are the feet of those who bring good news, who proclaim peace, who bring good tidings, who proclaim salvation, who say to Zion, 'Your God reigns!'" (Isaiah 52:7). A week-long vacation in the Smokey Mountains, hiking to view waterfalls, helped me to realize that traveling on the mountains to bring good news would be very hard work. The feet that make such a trek are not beautiful in a way that would appear in a fashion magazine. They are tired and smelly and sore. The prophet called such feet "beautiful" not because of their appearance, but because of the reason behind the difficult journey. The feet would be put to such a difficult task in order to proclaim peace, to bring good tidings, to proclaim salvation, to declare that God reigns. For those living in the darkness of despair, without any purpose or future hope, such a message is so precious a gift that those who bring it seem beautiful.

At the Wright-Pat Air Force Museum I watched a short video about U.S. soldiers who arrived at concentration camps in Germany after the war ended. Some of the prisoners had been incarcerated and mistreated for eight long years. Can you imagine how those soldiers looked to the prisoners? Their sore, smelly, dirty feet were a beautiful sight because they brought peace and good tidings and release for the captives.

Of course, the ultimate example is Jesus Christ. The last walk of his mortal life was to climb the hill called Golgotha. The walk that brought good news, that proclaimed peace, hope and salvation, and that proved God reigns . . . the feet that staggered on that walk were nailed to a tree. Talk about a difficult walk, and yet, "How beautiful on the mountains are the feet of [Him who brought] good news."

All of us have the opportunity to carry the message of peace and hope to those who dwell in misery and despair. Some missionaries (both long-term and short-term) have trudged up mountains, through polluted rivers or dense jungles, and across fields of mud in order to bring the best good news imaginable – forgiveness of sins and salvation through Jesus Christ. Some have walked through prison doors in order to proclaim the good news of salvation and peace. Others have walked through the miles of red tape in order to serve as foster and/or adoptive parents for kids who are unwanted and neglected. Some have stayed closer to home, but have made the difficult walk to build relationships with neighbors and co-workers in order to share the good news of salvation through Jesus Christ.

What kind of feet do you have? When your feet walk into a room, do people see a person who brings peace, comfort, and encouragement – or do they see a person who brings criticism, complaints, and conflict? The world around us is lost in darkness. Do you just add to the problem? Do you ignore the need and go about your business? Or do you have the kind of feet that are beautiful because you do the difficult work of bringing good news, proclaiming peace, hope, salvation, and declaring that God reigns? Rather than soft, protected feet, every Christian should have well-worn feet that are beautiful like those of Christ. We don't need a podiatrist – we need a deep passion fueled by the love of God for those created in his image. Carl F. H. Henry remarked, "It's only good news if it gets there in time."[17] Will your feet carry the good news?

Family First?

A man from Malaysia had broken the law prohibiting individuals from witnessing about Jesus to Muslims. This man came to faith after a Christian prayed for him and he was healed. Soon the man and his wife and son started attending church. They were discovered and threatened. The wife chose to live as a Muslim, but the man would not renounce his faith. The courts divorced him and awarded their son and all the possessions to his wife. He spent two weeks sleeping in a train station, but still testified to God's goodness in his life.

The Bible teaches that the institution of family was God's idea based on what our Creator knew to be best for his creation. Still, he knew there would be conflict, even with regard to the way individuals received him. Jesus told his followers, "Do not suppose that I have come to bring peace to the earth. I did not come to bring peace, but a sword. For I have come to turn 'a man against his father, a daughter against her mother, a daughter-in-law against her mother-in-law – a man's enemies will be the members of his own household.' Anyone who loves his father or mother more than me is not worthy of me; anyone who loves his son or daughter more than me is not worthy of me; and anyone who does not take his cross and follow me is not worthy of me. Whoever finds his life will lose it, and whoever loses his life for my sake will find it"

(Matthew 10:34-39). In another place he said "If anyone comes to me and does not hate his father, and mother, his wife and children, his brothers and sisters – yes, even his own life – he cannot be my disciple" (Luke 14:26).

Although these words sound harsh, they are the truth. Jesus did not come to take second-place in your heart and your loyalty. When you choose to give Jesus first place in your life, whoever or whatever had previously held that position, must be displaced. As a result, unsaved family members sometimes feel rejected or judged when a loved one surrenders his life to Jesus Christ. Relatives and friends will not understand, and very often, relationships will become strained or even broken as in the example above. This man recognized that following Jesus was worth so high a price. Jesus is worth whatever it costs in your life as well.

Many have nobly suggested that a person's family should be his highest priority. It is true that we have both the responsibility and the privilege of caring for our families as the Scripture teaches. Our first loyalty, however, must always be to the King, even when loved ones do not understand or accept our choices. Although they don't always see it, family members are better off to take second place in your life, because the One in first place teaches and enables you to love them far better than you could on your own. The most powerful testimony in the world is that of a transformed life. Surrender your life whole-heartedly to him, and pray without ceasing for those you love who are lost in darkness.

So, if you are struggling today with family relationships as a result of your faith, I want to encourage you. God knew it would happen. He desires to shine through your life as a witness to those he loves who are lost. No matter what you may have to give up, Jesus is worth it. No exceptions. Jesus said, "And everyone who has left houses or brothers or sisters or father or mother or children or fields for my sake will receive a hundred times as much and will inherit eternal life. But many who are first will be last, and many who are last will be first" (Matthew 19:29,30). Be of good courage. Fight the good fight with holiness, gentleness, and perseverance.

A Heart To Know God

In the Old Testament, God was the original parent practicing tough love. Yet, even as God was sending his chosen people into exile in Babylon because of their unfaithfulness, he loved them. He said, "My eyes will watch over them for their good, and I will bring them back to this land. I will build them up and not tear them down; I will plant them and not uproot them. I will give them a heart to know me, that I am the Lord. They will be my people, and I will be their God, for they will return to me with all their heart" (Jeremiah 24:6,7). God allowed the worst case scenario in order to turn their attention to him. He desired to give his people hearts to know him, and to give them "singleness of heart and action" so that they would always respect him (Jeremiah 32:39). That is still God's desire for his people today.

The worst case scenario is not always a punishment or even an attempt to get our attention. In this world bad things happen. God has a myriad of reasons for the things he allows and he has not explained them to me. I do know, however, that he only allows that which will, in some way, bring glory to his Name. When we face problems, we are often quick to ask him to fix a difficult situation. We must remember, however, that God wants to do so much more than help us out of trouble. He longs to bring every individual into an intimate, personal relationship with himself – for a lifetime and for all eternity.

Some of us are, even now, watching people we love limp through a worst case scenario in their lives. I talked with a young lady whose choices had landed her in jail. After her anger subsided, she discovered within herself a need and a longing to know God. God was giving her a heart to know him. This is something he longs to give to every single human being – but not all are willing to receive it.

If you are watching loved ones struggle through life's problems without the Savior, I encourage you to start asking God to give them a heart to know him. Only those who have such a heart can understand and receive the Gospel message – which leads to a transformed life.

God said of the Jewish exiles, "I will make an everlasting covenant with them: I will never stop doing good to them, and I will inspire them to fear me, so that they will never turn away from me. I will rejoice in doing them good and will assuredly plant them in this land with all my heart and soul" (Jeremiah 32:40-41). Although this was written about Jewish people several centuries ago, it reveals the heart of our unchanging God toward his people. He longs to do good for his people. The best he can give them is a personal relationship with himself and that is what he wants to give. Let us be asking God to give people everywhere, all who are willing, a heart to know him.

For Every Generation

The founders of this great nation, those who drafted and signed the Declaration of Independence had great intentions, hopes, and dreams for this group of states united as a new country. We have some understanding of the values and underlying motives of our founding fathers based on their writings, but each generation must decide the degree to which they will follow the course of those who preceded them. Many generations have rejected some of the core values and practices of their fathers, choosing to move in a different direction. What is true on a national scale is also true on a smaller scale. One day our children will make their own decisions about how to live and how to raise their own kids. We cannot determine what course any of them will take. The best thing we can do to influence the values and choices of upcoming generations is to share with our children that which we have learned. The other powerful way to influence generations to come is to pray regularly for them, even for those we will never meet.

There is only One who will still be here to directly guide our children's children and those who follow them. He is eternal and unchanging. "Know therefore that the Lord your God is God; he is the faithful God, keeping his covenant of love to a thousand generations of those who love him and keep his commands" (Deuteronomy 7:9, see also Exodus 20:6). When God placed the rainbow in the sky, the covenant was not only for Noah, but for all generations to come after him (Genesis 9:12). "He remembers his covenant forever, the word he commanded, for a thousand generations" (Psalm 105:8). "But the plans of the Lord stand firm forever, the purposes of his heart through all generations" (Psalm

33:11). All of these passages make it clear that God is committed for the long haul and he will call every generation unto himself.

Scripture clearly teaches that God's people are to teach his love, his deeds, and his faithfulness to the generations that follow (Deuteronomy 4:9, Psalm 78:4, 89:1, 145:4). Personal testimony is the primary way in which knowledge of God is spread through the human race. Each of us is to do his/her part. "Let this be written for a future generation, that a people not yet created may praise the Lord" (Psalm 102:18). Unfortunately, the people of God have failed at times to pass the baton to their descendants (see Judges 2:10). Fortunately, God is willing and able to call our children despite our short-comings, but it is often harder for them to hear without a human messenger. His salvation is available for all generations (Isaiah 51:8b). Our job is to teach those who come behind us to know and love our God. That is the most important lesson we will ever teach, and must be taught continually through words, actions, and attitudes.

Every American wants to see this nation thrive, rather than fall apart. Far more important even than the future of our nation is the future of our families. Every believer wants to see his/her children, grandchildren, and great grandchildren know the Lord and spend eternity in heaven. Let us be faithful to share the message of the Gospel with the generations to come, so they will be ready no matter what the future brings.

The Plumb Line

I watched two men working to put purlins on the roof of a new building. (Purlins are 2 X 4s nailed horizontally across the trusses in order to provide stability, and to hold the steel that will cover the roof.) It was somewhat tedious work as they carefully measured the placement of each board before nailing it in place. Step by step they measured and cut and nailed each piece, working up toward the peak. This job has parallels in the Christian life. From the day I repented and received forgiveness of my sins, until the day I meet Jesus face to face I am to be growing, maturing, climbing (See 1 Peter 2:2, Hebrews 5:11-14). The same is true for every believer.

As we grow in Christ, we learn to submit every part of ourselves and our lives to his will. The Word of God is the plumb line by which we measure our decisions. In Amos 7:7 God told the prophet "Look, I am setting a plumb line among my people Israel; I will spare them no longer." Webster defines a plumb line as "A line perpendicular to the plane of the horizon; or a line directed to the center of gravity in the earth." The plumb line used in Amos was "a symbol of the searching moral investigation which would be followed by a precise and exact judgment."[18]   God sees and judges both our actions and our motives.

All throughout life the Holy Spirit reveals areas that need to be measured against the will of God. Each believer is to search the Scriptures to learn what God teaches about the way we should use the time, money, and talents he has given us. We must examine our habits and bring them into line with what the Bible says about how to treat our bodies. God also calls us to examine our motives, and operate from a heart that loves God and loves the people created in his image. From time to time we face major decisions about education, jobs, and relationships. Who should enroll in college or enlist in the military? When is it time to leave a job or change careers or end a relationship? Only God knows what is best for every person in every situation. Like the men measuring where to nail each purlin, we should measure every decision against the word of God and the leading of the Holy Spirit before we make a choice. As we move closer to the peak, more and more of our lives are in line with his desires, but sometimes the decisions get even harder. The more we know God through His Word, the more deeply we are challenged to reject the pursuit of wealth and comfort, choosing instead to pour ourselves out for the poor and the lost all over the world. This kind of living is clearly in line with God's word, but many people in the church never seem to climb that high or reach that level of maturity. Why is that? How effective (and how stable) is a roof that is only covered half-way to the peak? How effective is a Christian who does not seek to live in line with the will of God? The only way to shine the light of Christ to a world in darkness is to live in a way that reflects his light. "In the same way, let your light shine before men, that they may see your good deeds and praise your Father in heaven" (Matthew 5:16).

Never stop growing. Never cease climbing. Pursue with desperation the goal of knowing and loving God as much as is humanly possible. Let each one of us ask the Holy Spirit regularly to show us areas where our lives do not measure up to his will, and be willing to change as he leads us. The goal of a Christian's life should be to bring glory to God in our words, actions, and motives.

What Matters Most

In the greatest scheme of things, what is it that really matters? One of the best places to find answers to that question is at funerals. When a whole life is summed up in a matter of minutes, it illustrates not only what was important to the deceased, but what about that person's life most deeply impacted the people around him/her. Have you noticed that a eulogy rarely goes on and on about a person's nice house, or her jewels or his toys or a great job? If I had continued in school psychology until retirement age, I would have tested at least 2500 children in my career. That is a huge chunk of my life, but it wouldn't be mentioned at my funeral, because, compared to other things, it wasn't all that important. Whatever it is you spend your time doing may be necessary for the moment, but may or may not be meaningful in the larger scheme of life.

Jesus taught that the most important commandments were to love God with every part of our being, and then to love other people as we love ourselves (Mark 12:31). We need to prioritize relationships, first with God and then with other people. A personal relationship with God defines values, priorities, and long-term goals, as we choose to live in line with his Word. Those who learn to hear the voice of the Holy Spirit, receive clear direction for where to go and what to do. Knowing, loving, and serving our Creator is the greatest purpose possible for a human being, so that relationship is what gives life meaning. After a relationship with God has been established, the most important thing we can pour our lives into is relationships with the people around us. Spending time with people, helping them, listening to their hearts, sharing our lives with them, will have a far greater impact than anything else we can do. So often, those left behind share memories of how a beloved friend or family member invested in their lives. When your life is over, and people attempt to capture the essence of you in a brief service, what will they say? Is anybody stronger, richer, closer to God, because of your role in their lives? The most enduring legacy any of us can leave is to shine like stars in the universe by leading many to righteousness (Daniel 12:3). I would encourage each one of us to spend the remainder of our days and hours on this earth pursuing those things which truly matter most.

God's Plans for Us

On my very first day as a school psychologist, a co-worker showed me around the buildings and introduced me to several staff members. Nearly every one of them, after greeting me, would ask my guide, "Has she seen The List?" I began to get very nervous about this list of kids awaiting assessments. By the time I was hired in mid-September, there were enough kids on the list to keep me busy throughout most of the school year. Even though I worked hard, more and more struggling students were always being referred for evaluation, so the list never came to an end.

In pondering God's plans for my life, I wonder, does he have a list of things that he would really like to do in and through me in the number of days I live on this earth? If he does, there are a finite number of specific things, unlike the ever-growing list of assessments. If he has a list for me, then he also has a list for you. Some of the things on the list are universal. God wants every person to repent of his/her sins, receiving the gift of grace, and entering into a personal relationship with the Savior. "For He is not willing that any should perish, but that all should come to repentance" (2 Peter 3:9). God wants and expects us to use the gifts he has given for the health of the church body and the glory of His Name. God's plan involves his people serving as witnesses to those in darkness, so that they too may know him.

Other parts of God's plans for my life are very different from his plans for your life. He is a personal, one-on-one God. Imagine with me the list of things God has planned to accomplish through your life. Picture check marks by a few entries: repent and receive forgiveness; baptism; telling others what God has done for you; becoming part of a church body, etc. Now envision the rest of the list. Maybe it contains names of people God deliberately brought

155

across your path so that you could be his witness. Maybe it includes opportunities to serve or to help those in need, or even a specific foreign country where he wanted to use you to bring people to Christ. Imagine, after starting well, you become comfortable and complacent just attending church and praying most every day. For the rest of your life you just stay in the same routine, comfortably oblivious to the rest of the plans God has for you. What would it be like to arrive in heaven and discover that 80% of that which God longed to do in your life never happened because you were not about his work. The thought of letting him down or disappointing him breaks my heart.

Salvation is totally about what Jesus did on the cross, not at all about any good works I might do (see Ephesians 2:8,9). The issue is not whether or not I have done enough good things to get into heaven. If it were, the entire human race would be condemned to hell. No, the issue is about loving God so much that our entire lives are consumed with the desire to bring honor and glory to him.

Jesus told his disciples, "My food is to do the will of him who sent me and to finish his work" (John 4:34). The prayer of my heart is that, during my days on earth, I will accomplish every single thing God has for me to do. May the desire to see all of God's plans fulfilled in my life be stronger than my desire for physical food or any other pleasure. May the same be true in your life – to the glory of His Name.

Get Radical

I read about a small town in rural Texas with an average annual income below $30,000. Believers in one church adopted a total of 72 children, just because Jesus wanted them to show love to these needy kids.[19] It's an inspiring story, but seems kind of radical, doesn't it?

Why is it that stories about people giving up their own comfort and convenience in the name of Jesus Christ seem so outrageous to us? His plan for you and for me probably includes some challenges that might be classified as radical. Scripture provides instruction for the way God wants his people to live. One of the repeated commands in Scripture is that we are to take care of widows and orphans because God cares about their plight. "Religion that God our Father accepts as pure and faultless is this: to look after orphans and widows in their distress and to keep oneself from being polluted by the world" (James 1:27). (See also Psalm 68:5, Exodus 22:22, Deuteronomy 10:18, Psalm 146:9, Isaiah 1:17.)

Does it seem that God's people have been conveniently ignoring this directive? We have quite a few widows and widowers in our family of faith. We as the family of God are commanded to look after them, which means we must take the time to find out what they need, and then work to meet those needs. How well are we doing that?

I had never been as burdened about the command to look after orphans because I don't know any personally, but God is challenging my lack of concern. There are 20,498 children in foster care in Michigan. Of these, 7,061 are right now waiting for adoptive families in Michigan.[20] The fact that I don't know them does not excuse me from obeying the command. Wouldn't you agree that the people of Christ are the ones most qualified and equipped to show them love and hope? I have come to believe that what we consider radical Christianity (like moving to a foreign country, or adopting kids we can't afford, or selling a nice home to live in the slums where people need Jesus) is what God would consider normal life for his people. It is certainly the way believers lived in the early days after Jesus returned to heaven.

What can I do, what can you do, to live out a religion that is pure and faultless before God? What can/should we be doing to look after the widows and orphans around us? The answer may differ for each family. Maybe God's radical plan for you includes changing jobs or homes or leisure activities so that he can use you more effectively. I have been challenged to start praying, "Lord I am willing to be made willing to do whatever you call me to do." Are you willing to be made willing even if it brings great upheaval in your life? It is becoming clear to me that the life to which God calls his people is far more radical than most of us have begun to imagine. He has good plans for his people, but the goal of those plans is to advance his kingdom and bring as many people as possible into a relationship with the Father. How does he want to use us to accomplish those plans? Are we willing and available to be radically obedient to our Master?

157

Living It is Hard

High School graduation is a major milestone in the lives of most American teens. It marks a monumental shift from a small, closed set of people and experiences to a wide open field of possibilities. The accomplishment of graduating from high school is relatively easy for most students – attend classes, pay attention, do the assigned work. But living as a responsible adult is hard – earning money to pay for things that had been provided free; clothes, housing, food, travel, entertainment. Making big decisions regarding jobs, college, military, and relationships is not easy. It feels nearly overwhelming when several big questions must be answered all at once.

Enlisting in the military is easy – pass a couple of tests, sign on the dotted line, and you're in. But living as a soldier is very hard – enduring the grueling training and uncomfortable living conditions, and agreeing to take orders, is very difficult even without the danger and the separation from loved ones. It's a hard life.

Becoming a Christian is easy – admit that you are a sinner, repent, and ask Jesus to forgive your sins. But living as a child of God is hard – the Bible teaches us not to gather material possessions but give to the poor. We are to be slow to anger and quick to reconcile, to do what pleases God rather than doing what feels good, to exhibit self-control and integrity at all times, and to imitate Christ.

Being a mature, responsible adult requires more than a high school diploma. Being a skilled, reliable soldier takes more than enlisting and wearing a uniform. Being a true child of God requires far more than regular church attendance. All three require discipline and self-denial. All three require recognition of the ultimate goal, and willingness to work hard to achieve it. In each case, the stakes are very high, but none is more crucial than the way we live out our faith. Brothers and sisters, this holy living is not for wimps. Truly living as God expects his children to live takes a lifetime of self-denial. Every true disciple has a heart that is broken for lost souls and is actively engaged in trying to help people know the Savior. Those who are wholly surrendered to God stand out in this culture, because they are focused on giving to the needs of others rather than on accumulating things for themselves. If people in the world around us do not know we are Christians by the way we love others (John 13:35), something is seriously wrong. Even more important than what we do, is the motivation behind our actions. Deep love for God should be the defining characteristic of our lives. A desire to honor the one we love should be the motivation for right living. Empty rituals or attempts to win the praise of men do not bring God glory.

Are we living a life of deep love and devotion toward God, or just living for ourselves? Let each one of us today, like new high school graduates, make plans to take steps toward growth. Spiritual maturity will not just happen. It takes effort and discipline.

Be Careful How You Listen

Jesus said, "No one lights a lamp and hides it in a jar or puts it under a bed. Instead, he puts it on a stand, so that those who come in can see the light. For there is nothing hidden that will not be disclosed, and nothing concealed that will not be known or brought out into the open. Therefore, consider carefully how you listen. Whoever has will be given more; whoever does not have, even what he thinks he has will be taken from him" (Luke 8:16-18). What does it mean to "consider carefully how you listen?"

Spending a week with 150 kids at camp gave me ample opportunity to study a variety of ways that people might listen. Sometimes, while instructions were being given, kids just kept on talking – making little or no attempt to listen. Some would just lower their voices to a whisper and continue their conversation. Others would be quiet while receiving directions, but afterward have no idea what to do next because they had not focused their attention on what was being said. Others listened to the message and seemed to understand it. Some of these listeners immediately went to do as they had been instructed, while others just went on with their own plans. (And we adults, who think we know the instructions, tend to be worse than the kids.)

In the passage above, Jesus warned people to be careful about how we listen. Let's look at the example of the prophet Jonah. When God told him to go to Nineveh and preach a message of repentance, Jonah listened well enough to hear the instructions and then went in the opposite direction. God could have just chosen somebody else, but instead he took steps to get Jonah's attention. After the fish spit him up on the shore, the Word of the Lord came to him again and repeated the original instructions (Jonah 3:1,2). This time Jonah listened a little better. He went and did as God had commanded him to do, but with a resentful attitude. Chapter four describes Jonah's anger and God's compassion toward him, even as he addressed his hard heart.

Friends, there is much we can learn from Jonah's example. When it comes to the voice of our Lord, listening involves far more than just hearing the message. It involves doing what he says to do, but it also involves the motives of our hearts. God expects us to do what he has commanded – speak the truth, give to the poor, keep the Sabbath, treat others the way you want to be treated, etc. But he is looking for a kind of listening that hears not only his words, but the attitude of his heart. He calls us not only to do what is right, but to be motivated by a heart that loves him supremely.

When we read the Word of God, we should be careful how we listen – expecting the Holy Spirit to speak to our hearts, and ready to obey what he says. When we listen to a sermon that God has given to his servant to declare, do we listen casually, hoping the words will make us feel good, or do we listen with rapt attention – expecting the Holy Spirit to speak and show us something we ought to do in response?

Brothers and sisters, this message is for us. Each of us should be careful how we listen. God has something to say to us. Are we listening to both God's words and his heart, eager to know him more and to bring honor to him by our actions?

Autumn

The fall season brings a myriad of beautiful colors in Michigan. As you view the amazing variety in creation, may it remind you that God works the right things in each life at just the right time. If you are patiently waiting on him for something, and it seems he gives it to others but not to you, keep waiting. Just as he causes different leaves to change at different times, so he works in each life as he knows is best for us. He cares for the birds of the air and the grasses of the fields, and you can be sure he cares for you (Matthew 6:25-34). The beauty is in the variety, both in leaves and in lives.

The Big Picture

I did not enjoy driver's training, but I did learn one useful life lesson from the instructor. He advised us to look at the big picture, rather than just trying to keep the front of the car between the center line and the deep ditch. Focusing too intently on the things closest to you distorts your perception, in driving and in life.

It seems there is always some issue or worry blocking our pathway. From the time we start school (earlier for some) until the day we die, most of us find things to worry about. Children often fear new situations. Older students worry about homework and tests and conflicts with peers. Teens stress about sports, driving, dating and making career choices. Young adults are often preoccupied with starting careers and families. Nearly all adults feel pressures regarding bills and deadlines and home or car repairs. As we age, we face new concerns about health and retirement income. Throughout our lives there are various relationship issues that bring stress. No matter what your age or stage in life, Satan is fighting to keep you worried about something. If he can keep you focused on a temporary problem, he saps your energy and attention from kingdom work.

Worry and peace cannot co-exist in your mind. Peace comes from God. Worry does not. In writing about the verse, "Peace I leave with you, my peace I give unto you" (John 14:27), Oswald

Chambers described the peace of Jesus as "a peace which comes from looking into his face and realizing his undisturbedness." [21]

No matter what worries try to distract you, I invite you to look into the face of Jesus your Savior. In order to look into someone's face you have to choose to stop looking at the things around you. Look and see his "undisturbedness" and receive his peace. God is a Big Picture God. Our problems may seem insurmountable today, but in his perspective they last but a moment. Find rest in the knowledge that he is in control not just for today but for all eternity.

The people of Judah, as punishment for their idolatry and disobedience were sent into captivity in Babylon. God, through Jeremiah, told them to settle down and build houses and raise families. Then, "When seventy years are completed for Babylon, I will come to you and fulfill my gracious promise to bring you back to this place" (Jeremiah 29:5-10). He was seeing the big picture and reminding his people to find rest and hope in the knowledge the he was, and always would be, in control. May each of us find that same peace in him today no matter what struggles we face.

Coming Home

Homecoming has come to mean a season in the fall when high schools and colleges welcome alumni back to campus. The focus seems to be mostly on activities to build school spirit, such as football games, parades, and dances. The whole week leading up to the big game and the dance is even called spirit week.

What does Homecoming mean for the believer? I see three types of homecoming that we all need. The first is coming home to Jesus for the first time. Christ invited, "Come to me, all you who are weary and burdened, and I will give you rest" (Matthew 11:28). He also stated, "I have come that they may have life, and have it to the full" (John 10:10b). Full and abundant life is available only through a personal relationship with Jesus Christ. Have you come home to your Heavenly Father by asking him to forgive your sins?

The second type of homecoming for the believer is that of renewing a commitment to Christ after a season of lukewarm faith or living in disobedience. As Christ said to the church at Ephesus, so I believe he would say to some of us, "Yet I hold this against you: you have forsaken your first love. Remember the height from which you have fallen! Repent and do the things you did at first" (Revelation 2:4-5a). God called to the people of Israel through the prophets, and he still calls to his wandering children, "Return to me" (Zechariah 1:3, Joel 2:12). Do you need to come back home to your first love today?

The final homecoming for the children of God is the glory of being welcomed home to heaven when this life is over. In Jesus' parable, when the assigned labor was finished, the master said to the hard workers, "Well done, good and faithful servant! . . . Come and share your master's happiness" (Matthew 25:21). Eternal life with our Father is assured by the Son who came from heaven and returned thirty-three years later. Jesus said, "In my Father's house are many rooms; it if were not so, I would have told you. I am going there to prepare a place for you. And if I go and prepare a place for you, I will come back and take you to be with me that you also may be where I am" (John 14:2,3). Are you looking forward to that glorious day?

What kind of Homecoming does your heart need? Just as school spirit is a big part of any school's homecoming celebration, so the work of the Holy Spirit is absolutely necessary for any kind of Spiritual homecoming. It is the Spirit who draws us and calls us to come home to God. It is the Spirit who brings conviction of sin when we allow the things of this world to take precedence over our love for God. It is also the work of Holy Spirit to counsel us in the way we should go, and to comfort us. When the end of life is near, it is the comforting presence of the Holy Spirit that fills the heart with peace in preparation for that final homecoming. Will your heart respond and come as close to God as he longs for you to be?

Praising in Problems

Thelma, the big-hearted office assistant at our church is a blessing to all of us. Every time I ask Thelma "How are you today?" I get the same answer: "Couldn't be better!" Whether the sun is shining or the snow is falling, whether she enjoyed an evening with family, or she had a stressful night of work at the hospital, even when she is tired and muscles are aching, the answer is the same. A person's outlook on life is not merely the result of circumstances. Rather, it is a deliberate choice we make regardless of our circumstances. Even in her seventies, Thelma is a beautiful example of choosing the right attitude day by day.

Scripture includes many examples of individuals who chose to praise God in spite of their feelings. Originally written as songs, many of the Psalms read like entries in a personal journal. The authors expressed their pain, loneliness, discouragement, and longings. As different writers worked through these issues, they chose to turn their hearts to God and give him praise. The truth is that God is worthy of our praise no matter how we are feeling. My emotions do not alter the character of God any more than they determine the temperature of the sun, or the depth of the ocean, or the number of stars in the cosmos. God is good all the time. Even when things are not going the way I want them to go, God cannot be anything other than good. That is the essence of who he is.

Friend, what struggles are you facing right now? Long-term health problems, or tight finances, or longing for a friend, or strained relationships can drag us down leaving us weary and discouraged. In our humanness, the natural response is self-pity and/or anger. As we travel on our journey to become more Christ-like, however, the appropriate response is to praise our God. The issue is not my feelings, but his worthiness.

Let us look at some of the qualities of God for which we choose to give him praise. God is eternal. He always has been and always will be. God is merciful. He does not treat us as our deeds deserve (Psalm 103:10). God is faithful. He will do everything he has said he would do. God is omnipresent, meaning he is everywhere at all times. He is always with each of us. He is omnipotent, or all-powerful. Nothing is too hard for him (Jeremiah 32:17). God is omniscient, which means all-knowing. There is nothing that he does not know or understand. Your problem has not left him scrambling for a solution. God is holy and perfect. He is light in the darkness. He is righteous and just. He is infinite and unchanging. And God is thinking about you (Psalm 139:17,18).

The Prophet Habakkuk declared, "Though the fig tree does not bud and there are no grapes on the vines, though the olive crop fails and the fields produce no food, though there are no sheep in the pen and no cattle in the stalls, yet I will rejoice in the Lord, I will be joyful in my Savior" (Habakkuk 3:17,18). No matter what circumstances you are facing today, I encourage you to give God praise. Turning our thoughts toward Jesus our Savior truly does put the struggles of this world into perspective. He is worthy of all praise.

The Harvest

Once upon a time there was a pastor of a small city church. A teenage girl, whose family attended the church, invited her friend to come. This friend started attending services, and received the free gift of salvation. The pastor moved on without ever seeing this teenage girl, whom he had helped to find the Lord, begin bringing her family to church. The girl's mother was saved, and later her father and both of her brothers. Years down the road, both of her brothers became pastors. Eventually both of that young girl's sisters also came to Christ. It took many years, but this whole family found the Lord as a result of the pastor's ministry and of the girl who invited her friend to church. God, in his faithfulness, brought fruit from their labors, fruit that continues to this day.

In Matthew 13 Jesus told a parable about the different ways people respond to hearing the message of Salvation. He used the illustration of a farmer planting seeds in different types of soil. Some people hear the word, but do not understand it, and immediately reject it. Others receive it joyfully, but do not put down deep roots of faith, and turn away when troubles come. Still others accept the word, but remain more concerned about the things of this world than about things of eternal importance. Finally, there are those whose hearts are fertile soil. When they hear the word and understand it, they become spiritually fruitful, yielding a crop that is thirty, sixty, or even one hundred times what was sown.

Those of us who are fully committed to Christ should be producing spiritual fruit. All of us want to see people receive the Word and give their lives to the Savior. It is very rare, however, for a believer to have opportunity to bring one hundred, or sixty, or thirty, or even ten people to faith at once. Unless you are Billy Graham, you are more likely to see individuals come one at a time,

165

like the teenage girl in the story above. That young woman was my Aunt Pauline. At the invitation of her friend Phyllis, she came to church and heard Rev. Bruce Pierson share the word. After giving her life to Jesus, she got my Grandma to start going, and later my Dad. At the age of twelve or thirteen, my Dad asked Jesus to forgive his sins and be his Lord. He and his brother both followed the Spirit's call to full-time pastoral ministry. How many lives were touched because of the faithfulness of God's servants? I don't know whether these individuals had any idea of the impact they made on my aunt and her family, much less the effect on those of us whom Dad has touched.

What does this mean for you and for me? It reminds us to be faithful in sharing the good news of salvation with those around us. We never know which hearts are ready to receive the message and become spiritually fruitful. We must remember, however, that the crop may take many years to mature. We might not ever know all the people who come to Jesus partly as a result of our testimony. That is okay. Keeping track of the harvest is God's job. Our responsibility is to be faithful. Are you sowing the seed? Even if you are not seeing as much fruit as you had hoped, keep on sharing your testimony. The harvest will come in God's time.

Clean Up the Mess

Autumn is my favorite season. God paints the leaves, the bushes, even the grasses of the field in bright colors to declare his glory. Those pretty leaves do not stay on the trees very long. Eventually they end up on the ground. We have only a few trees in our yard, most of them small, but each year we spend several hours raking. Leaves from six large maple trees across the street find their way into our yard. Even though they aren't really our leaves, it is our job to clean up the mess.

This also happens in human relationships. As we go through life, people hurt us and leave the debris of scars and distrust and bitterness. Sometimes people are aware of the damage they do; sometimes they are not. Sometimes they apologize and try to make it right, but no person can heal the hurts in someone else. Even though the debris in my life is not all my fault, it is still my responsibility to get it cleaned up. Nobody can do it for me. If I choose to ignore it, decay begins and my own life is the one that suffers.

Jesus taught about forgiveness. "For if you forgive men when they sin against you, your heavenly Father will also forgive you. But if you do not forgive men their sins, your Father will not forgive your sins" (Matthew 6:14-15). "Then Peter came to Jesus and asked, 'Lord, how many times shall I forgive my brother when he sins against me? Up to seven times?' Jesus answered, 'I tell you, not seven times, but seventy-seven times'" (Matthew 18:21-22). "And when you stand praying, if you hold anything against anyone, forgive him, so that your Father in heaven may forgive you your sins" (Mark 11:25). Forgiveness is not easy. God knows that better than anyone. It cost him far more than it will ever cost you or me. Offering us forgiveness cost him the terrible pain of seeing his son mistreated, slandered, falsely accused, beaten, and crucified. Forgiving someone a grievous wrong is a process that takes time. I may have to decide five times, ten times, fifty times that I will not hold something against another person. Still, with Jesus' help, we can forgive those who have left scars on our lives. He longs to bring healing, but we must choose to be healed. Some wounds are terrible and take a long time to heal. Others are smaller and just take a conscious choice to forgive. Either way, my life and all of my relationships will be richer if I allow Jesus to help me get rid of the debris of bitterness and unforgiveness.

Give Thanks to God

Have you listened to a young child pray recently? One of the richest blessings for Christian parents is the privilege of hearing a child talk to God. Young children, as they learn to pray, string together a long list of sentences that start with "Thank You for. . ." They give thanks for their family, their blanket, their toys, their food, their grandparents. As kids get a little older, you hear a few requests being added to the prayer. Adults, in contrast, tend to include a whole list of requests, and hopefully a note or two of thanks. Why is that? We could certainly learn from our children.

One day ten men with leprosy came to Jesus and pleaded with him to have pity on them. He instructed them to go and show themselves to the priests (which the law required people to do after

167

they had been healed). Along the way, they were all cleansed of their leprosy. One of them, a Samaritan, came running back and fell at Jesus' feet, overwhelmed with gratitude. "Jesus asked, 'Were not all ten cleansed? Where are the other nine? Was no one found to return and give praise to God except this foreigner?' Then he said to him, 'Rise and go; your faith has made you well'" (Luke 17:11-19).

Every time I read this story I wonder about the other nine men. Apparently, they followed Jesus' instructions to go to the priests, and then just went on their way. I wonder if Jesus was tempted to reverse the healing process in light of their ingratitude. I have no doubt in my mind that those men were thankful for the healing they received, but there is a difference between being thankful and giving thanks. It is like wrapping a gift for someone you love, but never giving it to him/her. Even a whole closet full of such gifts is less meaningful than one or two gifts actually given.

I have noticed a disturbing pattern in my life. I will pray earnestly for some need (physical healing, financial stability, freedom from worry, reconciled relationships, hunger for the Word, reconciled relationships, etc.). Over time, I lose the intensity, and pray for the need less and less, until I have all but forgotten about it. God, in his unfathomable patience, continues to work and to answer those prayers beautifully in his time. Sadly, I have so quickly moved on to other things that I hardly even notice his answers to my requests. I am more like those nine lepers than I want to admit.

Each one of us should not only be consciously looking for things to be thankful for, but should actually give thanks to God for those blessings. May we pray more like little children, and may our hearts overflow with thanksgiving. As we discipline ourselves to give thanks daily to God, we will also become better at giving the gift of gratitude to people in our lives.

A Goal Worth Chasing

In November 2009, NASCAR fans watched driver Jimmie Johnson set a new record – the first ever to win four consecutive championships. There was quite a celebration. Imagine the euphoria, the heady feeling of too-good-to-be-true victory.

Through the ages, there have been those who found great success in various types of arenas, from sporting events to reaching the summit of Mt. Everest. For each one there were moments of that indescribable feeling of being on top of the world but those moments are all too fleeting. That euphoria fades and the crowds disperse. When the great victor lays his head on the pillow at night he relives the moment, trying in vain to hold on to those wonderful fleeting emotions. It cannot be done. The memories last for many years, as do the trophies. But the sweetest part of the whole experience – the taste of victory – slips away. The victor is left forever hungry for another taste of that heady feeling.

The Christian life too has pinnacle moments, often referred to as mountain-top experiences. The sensation of being in the presence of the Holy Spirit, of feeling him almost tangibly surrounding you is a powerfully moving experience. Somewhat like the euphoria of victory, it leaves you wanting more and more. The psalmist invites each of us to "Taste and see that the Lord is good" (Psalm 34:8). Peter, on the mount where Jesus was transformed wanted to build dwellings so they could remain in the wonder of the moment (see Matthew 17 and Mark 9). Not even the thrill of a fourth consecutive racing championship can compare to one taste of true relational interaction with Almighty God. There is nothing like it in the world, because it is not of this world.

Both the thrill of victory in a sporting contest, and the wonder of being in the presence of God bring a sweet feeling, but it does not last. Feelings are, by nature, fleeting. No matter how hard we try to hold on to them, they slip away. We are left searching for ways to recreate that indescribable emotion. For a sports champion, the brief moments in the lime light are always preceded by countless hours of work and frustration, joy and discouragement. For the believer, sweet moments of untold glory are only rare treasures. None of us is allowed to stay on the mountain top in this life, for it is so wonderfully consuming that everything else dims – including the work he has for us to do. Much of the Christian life involves struggles and self-discipline. Along the way, the Holy Spirit confirms his help and encouragement gently in our hearts, filling us with peace throughout the work of running the race.

We must be careful not to spend our lives chasing after a feeling. This is a sure road to defeat. Rather, we must pursue the goal of knowing God with every ounce of our being. Along the way, there will be an occasional taste of glory. Enjoy it, and then continue pursuing godliness. That is the only goal that will truly last and lead to endless blessings. (See Philippians 3:14, Hebrews 10:35, 36; Matthew 6:19). If you are discouraged today because you do not feel Spiritually victorious, I admonish you to fix your eyes fully on the Savior and re-join the race. He will meet with you again in his time. "Come near to God and he will come near to you" (James 4:8a). Only when we reach heaven will that indescribable joy of his presence become a constant reality. Those who have had a taste of it, long for that day.

God Hears You

Scripture clearly demonstrates that God is listening to his children. Genesis 19 tells the story of God's plan to destroy Sodom and Gomorrah. He listened to Abram's pleas for the city and promised to spare his nephew. A few chapters earlier an angel had assured Hagar that the Lord heard her. When she saw how God met her need, she said, "I have now seen the One who sees me" (Genesis 16:13). When the people of Israel rebelled in the desert, God listened to Moses' prayer and relented from wiping out that nation (see Exodus 32:11-14, Numbers 14:10-20). God sent an angel to tell Daniel that his prayer had been heard, and later did the same for Zechariah. God heard and responded to the prayers of these individuals and many more.

These passages reassure us that God – the One who is mighty and strong and rules over all the universe – knows our names and hears our prayers. Be encouraged. God understands the burden of your heart and he is at work whether you can see evidence of that work or not. Choose to keep believing in God. He is already answering your prayer.

The Scriptural truth that God hears us brings comfort when the trials are long and hard, but it also brings a warning. Christian, God hears you. He not only hears what you say, he hears your thoughts. No matter how kind our words and deeds may be, if our hearts are complaining, bitter, or critical, God hears that too. If we pray, asking God to meet our need, but dwell on thoughts that he is not going to answer, God hears. The sarcastic comments we mumble under our breath, God hears. In fact, David said "Before a word is on my tongue you know it completely, O Lord" (Psalm 139:4). God hears our thoughts and he judges them, even if they never become spoken word or action. Jesus told his disciples, "There is nothing concealed that will not be disclosed, or hidden that will not be made known" (Matthew 10:26).

Friend, God hears you. What is he hearing from you? Insincerity? Self-pity? A complaining spirit? A heart filled with emptiness or bitterness while your body goes through the motions? Or is he hearing words of praise and thanks? Cries for help, based in faith? A longing to know him more? May each of us be encouraged and cautioned as we contemplate the truth that God hears us.

Why Go to Church?

Why do we go to church services? Do we go out of habit, or because we think it is expected of us? Do we go to visit with friends or to present an image? Are we drawn by a longing for acceptance, a need to belong? Why do we go? The joy of reuniting with friends, the sense of belonging, the comfort of habit are all benefits that a church family enjoys. None of these, however, is an adequate reason to go to church. Attending for these reasons alone would be like choosing a used car based on the color and the stereo system, never noticing there is no engine under the hood. Some factors are significantly more important than others in decision-making.

The primary reason for attending weekly services is to worship God. To worship is to focus our thoughts on how wonderful God is, and to express our love for him. God delights in our worship, but he does not need our worship. The need is on our part. We are made with a need to worship him, and weekly services are a great place to start. It is possible to worship God apart from a formal church service. In fact, each of us needs to spend time alone in personal worship if we are to grow spiritually. Many claim that to be alone with nature takes the place of attending church. God does make himself known through his creation (Romans 1:20), but just being in the great outdoors does not constitute worship. Worship requires a heart and mind totally focused on God. Whether a person is sitting in a church or alone in the woods, there is no worship unless his/her heart and mind are delighting in the Savior. A heart that is truly seeking God may occasionally miss a service in favor of solitude in creation, but the regular practice of that person will be to join together with other believers. The writer of Hebrews instructs Christians, "Let us not give up meeting together, as some are in the habit of doing, but let us encourage one another – and all the more as you see the day approaching" (Hebrews 10:25).

There are other reasons for attending church that cannot be met alone in the woods. When God's people come together in worship, they receive instruction from God's Word. The Holy Spirit applies that Word individually to each heart, calling all who are willing to take a step closer to him. Studying the Word together stretches our thinking and helps to keep us focused. "As iron sharpens iron, so one man sharpens another" (Proverbs 27:17).

Those who attend a given church regularly form a family. The children of God are to work in harmony as parts of one body (Romans 12:4-5, 1 Corinthians 12:12-30). In order for us to work together as God intended, we must know the members of our family. "If one part suffers, every part suffers with it; if one part is honored, every part rejoices with it" (1 Corinthians 12:26). This cannot happen unless we take the time to build relationships and really know one another. We are created to need each other and support each other. We are to "Encourage one another daily, as long as it is called Today, so that none of you may be hardened by sin's deceitfulness" (Hebrews 3:13).

I hope that you are part of a church family. I hope that you attend regularly and truly worship the Lord with all of your heart and mind. I hope that you have healthy relationships within the church that provide support and encouragement to both parties. Let us not only attend services faithfully, but honor God with our lives every day.

Lessons in Suffering

The Apostle Paul boldly said, "I want to know Christ and the power of his resurrection and the fellowship of sharing in his sufferings, becoming like him in his death, and so, somehow, to attain to the resurrection from the dead" (Philippians 3:10-11). Believers today can readily agree with the sentiments about wanting to know Christ, and his power, and attain resurrection from the dead. The other parts of the verse are far less palatable. Do we truly want to know the fellowship of sharing in his sufferings? What does it mean to become like him in his death?

Notice that for Christ, both the suffering and the death preceded the powerful resurrection. The same is true in our lives. Although we do not want to hear it, suffering is a part of life. The verse does not say "I want to suffer" but rather, I want to know the fellowship of sharing in his sufferings. The experience of suffering can draw us close to Jesus and help us to really learn that he is everything we need if we choose to face it with a Christ-like attitude. Peter said, "Dear friends, do not be surprised at the painful trial you are suffering, as though something strange were happening to you. But rejoice that you participate in the sufferings of Christ, so that you may be overjoyed when his glory is revealed" (1 Peter 4:12-13). The question is not, "How can I avoid suffering?" All of us will face difficult struggles. The question is, "Will our suffering help us to draw near to God, or fill us with bitterness and self-pity?"

What did Paul mean when he said "becoming like him in his death"? Paul had many near-death experiences, but he continued to faithfully preach the message of salvation. This phrase was not a death wish, but a determination to imitate Jesus' example. When Jesus was in the garden facing arrest, a mock trial, and cruel crucifixion, he prayed these heartfelt words, "Father, if you are willing, take this cup from me; yet not my will, but yours be done" (Luke 22:42). When we face trials and persecution and suffering, we long for God to take them away. God did not choose to keep Jesus from those awful final hours. He will not always choose to prevent our problems either. When those hard times come, we must learn to trust him enough to say, "Lord, not my will, but yours be done." We do not understand the things God does. He said, "For my thoughts are not your thoughts, neither are your ways my ways . . . as the heavens are higher than the earth, so are my ways higher than your ways and my thoughts than your thoughts" (Isaiah 55:8,9). He knows what he is doing, and we can trust him.

We long to jump straight to the part of the verse about knowing the power of his resurrection, and attaining that resurrection from the dead. God longs for us to learn to know him deeply and walk with him in faith through the mountains and valleys of life. Friends, only through the trials of life do we truly learn to trust God. The more we trust him the more we come to know him and discover his trustworthiness. The more we know him and trust him, the more his mighty power can be displayed through our lives for his glory. If you are suffering today, no matter what the struggle is, the only solution is to choose to become like Christ in his death. Each of us must choose an attitude of "Not my will, but yours be done." As we choose to trust and obey, we learn to really know him.

A Place of Worship

The church building of today, like the tabernacle and the temple in the Old Testament, is intended to be a place where people meet with God and bring to him sacrificial obedience. The first known structure built specifically for meeting with Almighty God was called a tent of meeting (Exodus 33:7). Moses would go there to receive instructions from the Lord. God gave Moses detailed instructions for building the tabernacle, using wood and animal skins, along with some precious stones and metal (Exodus 26). The people brought the best that they had, until there was more than the workers needed. The people had to be ordered to stop bringing their offerings for the sanctuary (Exodus 36:6,7). After the tabernacle was completed and all its contents were dedicated to the Lord, the glory of the Lord covered the tent so that no one could enter.

After the people had settled in the Promised Land, King David began making plans to build a more permanent structure. 1 Kings 6 describes the beautiful temple which was built by David's son, King Solomon. The whole interior was overlaid with gold. When the Ark of the Covenant was brought into the Holy Place, the glory of the Lord filled the place with a cloud (1 Kings, chapter 8). After Solomon prayed a prayer of dedication, the Lord answered him, saying, "I have heard the prayer and plea you have made before me; I have consecrated this temple, which you have built, by putting my Name there forever. My eyes and my heart will always be there" (1 Kings 9:3). Then he warned the people that if they did not observe his commands, but turned to serve other gods, then Israel would be cut off and God would reject the temple. Many years later this beautiful structure was, in fact, destroyed because of the unfaithfulness of the Jews (2 Chronicles 36).

When the temple was rebuilt, in the days of Ezra, the people were returning from seventy years of exile. They did not have expensive building materials. They used what they had available to them. All three of these structures for worship were built with the best materials that were available to the people. It was not the specific materials that mattered, but rather the heart of the people longing to give their best to their Lord. The same is true for our houses of worship today. God is worthy of the very best that we can give him. We are required to be good stewards of what God has provided, including finances, the church building and its furnishings.

Far more important than a building is the attitude of the people. God met with his people in the tabernacle covered with animal skins, in the temple overlaid with gold, and in the re-built temple of stone. He still meets with his people today, in all types of buildings, or with no building at all. If we are whole-heartedly seeking to worship God and draw near to him, he will draw near to us. However, if we turn away to worship other things, even the approval of men, we will lose God's favor.

The Apostle Paul refers to our bodies as the temple of the Holy Spirit (1 Corinthians 6:19). What is true for the church building is true for our bodies. We are to be good stewards of them. Gluttony is still idolatry. Lack of sleep is not healthy. As we draw near to God, we should bring our best by being alert and ready to focus on him. Most important, let us keep our hearts free of unconfessed sin. Let us be sure to keep our consciences clear and our relationship with God ever growing, no matter what excuses we can come up with to stay away from corporate worship.

All on the Altar

What does it mean to give God your all? During a severe famine, God sent Elijah to a widow in Zarephath, in the country of Sidon. When he arrived, this woman was gathering sticks in order to bake one small loaf of bread with the last of her oil and flour. After that she and her son would both starve to death. Elijah asked her for water and a piece of bread. Upon hearing her plight, he said to her, "Don't be afraid. Go home and do as you have said. But first make a small cake of bread for me from what you have and bring it to me, and then make something for yourself and your son. For this is what the Lord, the God of Israel, says: 'The jar of flour will not be used up and the jug of oil will not run dry until the day the Lord gives rain on the land'" (1 Kings 17:13,14). She had almost nothing left to feed herself and her son, yet Elijah asked her to make a cake of bread for him before her family. This woman chose to believe. She did as Elijah instructed, and God fulfilled the prophecy. The tiny amount of oil and flour she had left did not run out. Both her family and Elijah had enough to eat every day. Their faith in God resulted in the provision of their needs.

There is another widow noted in Scripture who gave unto God all that she had. Mark 12:41-44 describes the scene. Jesus and his disciples were near the entrance to the temple. People were bringing their offerings to the Lord, placing them into the temple treasury. Some brought large amounts, but one poor widow put in two small copper coins (worth less than a penny). Jesus told his disciples, "I tell you the truth, this poor widow has put more into the treasury than all the others. They all gave out of their wealth; but she, out of her poverty, put in everything – all she had to live on" (Mark 12:43-44).

Friends, do we have that kind of faith? Not everyone is called to give everything he/she owns to ministry, but all of us are to live with the attitude that everything we have belongs to God. He should be free to do with it as he chooses. Sending our precious children off to school or college or the military is an act of faith. Leaving a comfortable job in order to follow God's call to ministry is an act of faith. Selling a large home and/or toys in faith frees an individual or a couple to give generously to people in need. We must ask ourselves some tough questions: What am I holding on to? Where is my trust? Are my comfort, my pleasure, and the illusion of security, my primary goals? Do I trust God enough to give him all? This is not simply a question of tithing (although Scripture teaches in Malachi 3 that failure to tithe is robbing God). It is a far deeper question of Lordship. If I am truly surrendered and trusting in him, God should be free to put his hand on anything I have, and know I will give it willingly to him. He alone is my trust. This teaching is one of the reasons it is hard for rich people (like Americans) to enter the kingdom of heaven. We tend to put our security in our possessions.

In 1905, Elisha A. Hoffman wrote these words which are still applicable to us today: "You have longed for sweet peace, and for faith to increase, and have earnestly, fervently prayed; but you cannot have rest or be perfectly blest, until all on the altar is laid. Is your all on the altar of sacrifice laid? Your heart does the Spirit control? You can only be blest and have peace and sweet rest as you yield him your body and soul."[22] God through His Holy Spirit is inviting us again to place on the altar all that we have, all that we are or ever will be. Is your all on the altar?

God Will Come Through

A songwriter once wrote, "God will make a way where there seems to be no way. He works in ways we cannot see and he will make a way. He will make a way."[23] Throughout Scripture individuals or nations faced insurmountable struggles. Again and again God answered in powerful, unique ways. The Israelites in the wilderness saw him make a path through the sea, and ate the manna and quail he miraculously provided. Elijah was fed by ravens during a famine (1 Kings 17). The entire Aramean army was blinded and surrounded by God's invisible army (2 Kings 6,7). In the following chapter a huge army ran away in fear when they heard the sound of God's horses and chariots coming after them. Years later, three young man who took a stand before King Nebuchadnezzar found themselves thrown into a furnace, only to be welcomed to the party by the Son of God (Daniel 3).

Friend, what problem are you facing today? Financial pressures or health struggles? Loneliness or an uncertain future? Broken relationships? Unfulfilling work? Whatever the problem, God has a solution. He has not asked you to figure it out. When the problem seems larger than life – like a huge army surrounding you and no way out – God is more than able. He can meet your need in ways he alone knows. He asks you to wait and to trust.

For the greatest need of your whole life God has already provided a solution. Compared to your need for forgiveness from sins, any problem you are facing is small. Have you received the Savior? If not, your problems are far more serious than you realize. If you have given your life to him, the One who met your greatest need is more than able to meet any other issue in your life. Ephesians 3:20,21 says, "Now to him who is able to do immeasurably more than all we ask or imagine according to his power that is at work within us, to him be glory in the church and in Christ Jesus throughout all generations, for ever and ever! Amen."

If your sins have been forgiven and you are a part of God's family, then his power is at work within you. Wait in faith, believing that the God who is "able to do immeasurably more than all we ask or imagine" will come through for you. Like the persistent widow Jesus described in Luke 18:1-8 keep asking in faith until the answer comes. He probably won't use ravens or an invisible army, but God will make a way for you. Trust in him.

Prayer Closet

Matthew 22 relates a parable Jesus told. He said, "The kingdom of heaven is like a king who prepared a wedding banquet for his son. He sent his servants to those who had been invited to the banquet to tell them to come, but they refused to come." Rather than coming to the banquet, each one went about his business. The feast was ready and waiting for them, but they had no time for it. So others, strangers off the streets, were invited to enjoy the banquet instead. In this passage Jesus describes how others (Gentiles) were invited in place of those (Jews) who declined to enter the kingdom of heaven. We Gentiles are greatly blessed to have been given the opportunity to enter into a relationship with

Almighty God. Still, I believe there is another principle in this parable for us. Friends, do we identify with those who were too busy to attend the banquet? Most of us would agree that "too busy" describes our lives, not just occasionally, but year after year. Are we missing out on blessings God has prepared for us because of busy schedules?

Long ago a dark, smelly stable was transformed into a place where those who heard and believed the message met with the Savior of all mankind. Many heard and had opportunity. Only a few shepherds came. In God's presence there is a feast for the soul prepared at any hour of any day. All are invited. Why then, do we go on day after day, busy, weary, hungry for meaning? Are we rejecting his invitation to draw near?

It is important that each one of us have a quiet place where we regularly get alone with God and quiet our hearts to hear his voice. Matthew 6:6 tells us "But when you pray, go into your room, close the door and pray to your Father, who is unseen. Then your Father, who sees what is done in secret, will reward you." The King James Version uses the term "prayer closet." Following in the example of Christ, we need to make time to be alone with God on a very regular basis. How else are we to hear his voice, so that the Holy Spirit can direct our days? How long has it been since you were quiet and awake long enough to hear him speak directly to your heart?

I am compelled to share with you the good news and invite you to come apart from the world and draw near to God. Deliberately set a time and place like you do for other important events in life. Time spent in his presence will be among the richest times you have ever known.

Interruptions

The day started with the usual To Do List and plans for things to be accomplished throughout the week. Then came the phone call, asking my husband to travel to South Dakota in order to help prepare housing for Native Americans before winter. Three days later, he boarded a plane, setting off to help those in need even though details were sketchy and many questions remained unanswered. God interrupted and revised Bart's schedule as he desired.

The Apostle Paul was a man familiar with interrupted plans. His story throughout the book of Acts includes many times when he was re-directed by the Holy Spirit. In Acts 9 Paul was zealously working for God against those he thought were misrepresenting him. Jesus appeared to him in a blinding light and invited Paul to join those whom he had been persecuting. Paul started in a new direction, traveling from place to place telling people the good news of salvation through Jesus Christ. He planned his route, but didn't always follow it. "Paul and his companions traveled throughout the region of Phrygia and Galatia; having been kept by the Holy Spirit from preaching the word in the province of Asia. When they came to the border of Mysia, they tried to enter Bithynia, but the Spirit of Jesus would not allow them to. So they passed by Mysia and went down to Troas. During the night Paul had a vision of a man of Macedonia standing and begging him, 'Come over to Macedonia and help us.' After Paul had seen the vision, we got ready at once to leave for Macedonia, concluding that God had called us to preach the gospel to them" (Acts 16:6-10). He planned several times in his travels to visit Rome, but was prevented from doing so (Romans 1:13). By the time he eventually reached Rome he was in custody, awaiting trial. During his years in prison the Holy Spirit led him to compose letters which comprise much of our New Testament. Because he was willing to be directed and re-directed by the Spirit, Paul preached to far more people through his letters (written while imprisoned) than through visiting new cities and planting churches. The Kingdom grew through his obedience to plans that were very different from his own ideas.

Some of the interruptions God allows in our lives are more painful and difficult than others. Going on a domestic missions trip with a couple of days notice is a walk in the park compared to the long-term interruption of losing a job, or worse yet a friend or loved one. Sometimes the things that come and change our plans include an element of choice – like Paul going in a different direction. Other interruptions come unannounced and our only choice is how to react. The question facing us is this: Are you willing to have your life and your plans interrupted by the Holy

Spirit? Are you available to go in an unexpected direction at a moment's notice, in order to accomplish the purposes of God? Are you living in tune with the Spirit, able to hear his voice showing you the way he would have you go? God can be trusted, even when we do not understand his plans. May each one of us walk in step with him daily, allowing him to guide our steps. I encourage you to meditate on Scripture references related to being led by God (Psalm 37:23-24, Isaiah 42:16, Romans 12:1,2). Learning to follow the Spirit leads to blessings as it brings him glory.

Know the Enemy

On Veteran's Day we take time to honor and thank all the veterans of the USA military. May those who love this country always remember to say "Thank you" to those who serve and to their families who pay such a high price for our continued freedom. A veteran has been described as someone who at one point in his/her life, wrote a blank check payable to the United States of America for an amount up to, and including, his/her life. A pastor friend applied this definition to soldiers in the Lord's Army, pondering "I wonder how many followers of Christ truly are willing to write that same blank check payable to Christ?" (Paul Holcroft, Marquette Miss. Church).

According to the Word of God, all of his children (those who have believed, confessed, and received salvation) are members of his army. We teach children in Sunday School to sing, "I'm in the Lord's army." But what does it mean to be a part of an army led by the Prince of Peace? As soldiers, we are instructed to be equipped and actively engaged in the battle. In order to be prepared to fight, we must be able to identify the enemy and understand his tactics. The Apostle Paul instructed the believers in Ephesus to be strong in the Lord, and to put on the armor of God in order to resist the spiritual forces of evil (Ephesians 6).

The pieces of armor listed here are not standard issue of the US military. In fact, the belt of truth, the breastplate of righteousness, sandals of the gospel of peace, the shield of faith, the helmet of Salvation, the Sword which is the Bible, and prayer are suited for an entirely different type of warfare. Notice in the passage above that our struggle is not against flesh and blood.

Rather, we fight against the prince of darkness, the enemy of our souls. Fighting against the wrong enemy weakens an army needlessly and accomplishes very little.

One of the tactics our enemy, the devil, loves to use is deceit. Jesus said about him, "When he lies he speaks his native language, for he is a liar and the father of lies" (John 8:44). The father of lies is always trying to get us to struggle against flesh and blood. He will make the ruthless boss seem like the enemy, or maybe the malicious neighbor, the uncommunicative spouse, or the government. He will even try to get us squabbling with others in God's army. When we use our mental and emotional energy against flesh and blood (whether we are on the offensive or the defensive) we stop fighting against the devil. In order to avoid this all-too-common pitfall, we must heed the final instruction in Ephesians 6:18, to pray in the Spirit in every situation and to faithfully pray for other believers. As we pray in the Spirit, he shows us the hand of the enemy in a given circumstance and reminds us who we are actually fighting against. The enemy knows each one of us and learns our weaknesses.

Although we want to keep our focus on Jesus, wise soldiers in his army will study what he has told us about the enemy. The truth, salvation through Jesus Christ, righteousness and peace, the Word of God, and prayer will help us to ultimately be victorious in our fight against evil in our own lives, in our families, and in our community. So, whether you ever enlist to fight for our beloved country or not, I exhort you to live as a soldier of the Lord's Army. Keep in mind who you are really fighting against, and never give up!

Given Much

The third week of November is the one week of the year that we consciously remember to give thanks. Believers must acknowledge that all we have received has come as a gift from the Giver of all good things (James 1:17). We ought to give him thanks sincerely and continually, but words are not enough. True thankfulness produces actions in keeping with gratitude. The concept of "pay it forward" did not originate with a movie made in 2000. A couple thousand years earlier Jesus had told his disciples,

"Freely you have received, freely give" (Matthew 10:8b). In fact, the more we receive from God, the more we ought to give.

There are some Bible verses that inspire and encourage and bless me abundantly. There are some that challenge or confuse me. Then, there are those that trouble me. One verse that really bothers me is found in Luke 12:48. "From everyone who has been given much, much will be demanded; and from the one who has been entrusted with much, much more will be asked." Beloved, you and I are among those who have been given much. Therefore, much will be demanded from us. I wish it said "expected" rather than "demanded." Those who have more than two outfits of clothing and enough to eat have been given more than most of the world's occupants. Therefore, much will be demanded from us. Furthermore, we are also among those who have been entrusted with much. There are still people groups who have never heard the gospel. In some areas, Christians risk their lives for a single page of Scripture, which they treasure and commit to memory. In contrast, most of us have multiple copies of the whole recorded Word of God. Talk about being entrusted with much! Beyond that, we have had years of access to Bible teaching, books, and music to help us grow as disciples. So, the question is, what are we doing with all that we have been given?

As we remember to give God thanks for all he has given to us, and especially for the priceless gift of salvation in Jesus Christ, let that thankfulness produce actions. All of us have freely received abundant blessings – material and otherwise – that we could and should be sharing with others. May we not store up things for ourselves without being rich toward God. May none of us ever have to hear from God those gut-wrenching words, "You fool!" (See Jesus' parable in Luke 12:20.) May you be blessed with gratitude that overflows and enriches all those around you.

Too Much To Do

There are so many good, Biblical things that God's people should be doing that it can feel overwhelming at times. For example, each of us should spend time daily in Bible study and in prayer for our families, the sick, the lost, our nation, etc. We should deliberately train up our children to know and love the

Lord. Each of us is to use our Spiritual gifts in serving the church, and to visit those who are sick and/or in prison. We should build relationships with unbelievers and share our faith with them. We should help those who are younger or weaker in their faith to grow as disciples. In addition we need to nurture our marriages and work to grow in our personal faith.

Friend, how are you going to do all those things with excellence as you work to fulfill your regular responsibilities each week? Just reading over the list is almost paralyzing to my brain. We want to honor God with our lives, but sometimes it seems insurmountable.

The answer to this dilemma is not to try harder, but to listen harder. It is the work of the Holy Spirit to counsel and direct us. Our job is to hear his voice, and to follow where he leads. Only through total surrender of my life and my will can I continually be filled with the Holy Spirit. He is the one who guides me and empowers me to do what God would have me to do at any given time. He prompts my heart to turn off the TV and spend time with my Lord. He tells me at just the right time to call or visit someone who is hurting. He shows me the place in the church body where he would have me serve for his glory. He enables me to recognize opportunities to show my children what love for God looks like in real life. The Spirit will guide me in doing all the things God has for me to do in a given day (and also in what things to leave undone) if only I will listen to him.

The Spirit's guiding is always personal. He may lead one person to spend hours poring over the Word and study guides, while prompting someone else to reach out to a hurting friend, and telling someone else to come apart and just worship him in creation. Therefore, if others are not as passionate as I am about a particular area of their Christian lives, that is okay. Our prayer is not that we would all be the same, but that each of us would hear and follow the voice of the Holy Spirit. That is the only path to abundant life, peace, and contentment.

Let each one of us surrender anew to the one who created us and who knows the very best path for us. In that way we can honor him and grow in him, and complete all that he has for us to do without succumbing to guilt or giving up in frustration. "His divine power has given us everything we need for life and godliness through our knowledge of him who called us by his own glory and goodness" (2 Peter 1:3).

Lessons from Jonah

In the familiar story of Jonah, God told (not "invited," not "asked," but told) Jonah, "Go to the great city of Ninevah and preach against it, because its wickedness has come up before me" (Jonah 1:2). Jonah chose to take a spontaneous trip in the opposite direction. As we know, however, God's commands are not optional or multiple choice. God never blesses disobedience. Nowhere is this clearer than in the story of Jonah. God chose to intervene and adjust Jonah's trip itinerary. As it turns out, he was better off in the damp, smelly fish than he was sleeping in the comfortable boat. Trying to live outside of the known will of God is always dangerous, even if it seems comfortable for a while. If you are living today in disobedience, beware!

My Mom, in teaching this story, has noted the use of the word "provided" in this book. When Jonah was drowning, "the Lord provided a great fish to swallow" him (Jonah 1:17). God provided a way out, a path back to obedience, even before Jonah's prayer of repentance. After God had gotten his attention, Jonah went to Ninevah and preached powerfully. The people listened and responded with humble repentance. Jonah was still hoping God would wipe out the city. (Notice that although he obeyed, he still did not exhibit the heart of Christ.) When Jonah was watching to see what would happen to Ninevah after he had preached, "The Lord God provided a vine and made it grow up over Jonah to give shade for his head and ease his discomfort, and Jonah was very happy about the vine" (4:6). "But at dawn the next day God provided a worm, which chewed the vine so that it withered" (4:7). "When the sun rose, God provided a scorching east wind, and the sun blazed on Jonah's head so that he grew faint" (4:8).

God will provide what we need. But God provides what is needed to reach his goals for our lives. He is far more interested in making us holy than in making us happy. Too much comfort tends to get in the way of the development of holiness. The time for comfort and freedom from problems is in the new life in Heaven, not in this one.

Friend, God is unchanging. Although he works differently in each life, his goal remains the same – transformed lives. What will God need to provide in your life to help you become more like him? Will it take rescue from a near-drowning in order to get your attention and help you choose obedience? Does God need to provide you with comfort in waiting on him? Or does he need to provide a worm and/or scorching wind to help break you out of self-pity or self-righteousness so that you can receive his heart of compassion for the world?

God will provide what you need and what I need. The harder our hearts, the stronger the message needs to be in order to get through. For Balaam it was a talking donkey (Numbers 22). For Saul it was a light that left him blind for three days (Acts 9). Will you and I be wise enough to heed the still small voice and do what he tells us to do without extreme measures? God always blesses obedience. God never blesses disobedience. May each of us learn from Jonah and allow God to make us all that he desires us to be.

Orbit around Christ

In describing what it means to "accept Christ" A.W. Tozer writes that a believer's attachment to Christ is both all-inclusive (accepting Christ for all he is) and all-exclusive (no other priority comes close). "The Lord becomes to him not one of several rival interests, but the one exclusive attraction forever. He orbits around Christ as the earth around the sun, held in thrall by the magnetism of his love, drawing all his life and light and warmth from him. In this happy state he is given other interests, it is true, but these are all determined by his relation to his Lord." [24] In a culture that orbits around personal comfort and success, those whose lives are centered on Christ will never really fit. At times those orbits collide, bringing criticism to those who refuse to conform.

True surrender to God will interrupt your life. Following God's leading will take you places you never would have considered going. A life that is orbiting around him cannot simultaneously be centered on something besides him. Scripture and history and modern day life are all resplendent with examples of people whose lives were turned on end when they followed Christ. Many, if not most, of these people were misunderstood.

They endured sharp criticism even from family and fellow believers. Think about Noah, for example. His bizarre behavior probably had tongues wagging for miles around. Or imagine Mary trying to convince her family that she was still a virgin, impregnated by God. Several of the prophets did strange things as commanded by God, in attempts to get people to listen and turn from their sin. Hosea is a vivid example. If you have not read this short book recently, I encourage you to do so. As a picture of God's relationship with the Israelites, Hosea was commanded "Go, take to yourself an adulterous wife and children of unfaithfulness, because the land is guilty of the vilest adultery in departing from the Lord" (Hosea 1:2). In obedience, he married Gomer. She was unfaithful to him. God instructed Hosea to go and reclaim her, even though she was an adulterous, and loved by another man. So he went and bought her back, as a picture of God's desire to redeem unfaithful Israel. Following God determined the steps of Hosea's life, taking him in a very different direction than he probably would have chosen on his own. God did not just call him to prophesy with words, but with his whole life.

Some have been called to leave loved ones and the comforts of home in order to serve as missionaries to people who do not yet know about Jesus. Some, in obedience to God's call, left lucrative, successful careers in order to be trained as pastors. Some have been called to trust God with determining how many children they should have, rather than planning their families themselves. Some who are very introverted have left their comfort zone and learned to speak publically about God's faithfulness. Many have chosen to live without some of the comforts available to them in order to give generously to those who have less. Some have been willing to be made a public spectacle rather than compromise their devotion to their Savior.

Reading through the book of Hosea clearly teaches that true, whole-hearted service to God will always interfere with my personal life. It will determine who I marry, how I treat my spouse, the kind of things I spend money on, the type and frequency of things I do to help others, and the types of entertainment I watch and/or listen to. Friend, has the Son of God become the Sun around which your life continually orbits? Does love and devotion to him supersede all other interests and activities in your life? That is my earnest prayer, for your life and for my own. That is what a transformed life looks like.

What is Your Egypt?

One day while driving home, I found myself mentally planning what to say on Facebook.com about the event I had just left. I realized I was in danger of allowing a computer program to become overly important in my life. I need to be ever vigilant to guard my priorities or unimportant things will take valuable time that should be devoted to my family or ministry.

The story of the Israelites in the Old Testament has many parallels with the believer's walk of faith. Israel's relationship with the nation of Egypt shows their habit of continually returning to something that could not help them solve their problems. Egypt was, for the Israelites, like an addiction. At first (in the days of Joseph's father and brothers during the famine, Genesis 46) it was a place of relief and security. Then it enslaved their descendants and brought them misery. The people were eventually set free from Egypt (Exodus 5-14), but when troubles came, they were tempted to return slavery (Numbers 11:18, 14:4, Jeremiah 42). Egypt was an outright enemy at times, attacking the Israelites (1 Kings 14:25, 2 Chronicles 12:9, 36:4). At other times the Pharaohs would promise to help in return for payment, but trusting in Egypt was like leaning on a "splintered reed of a staff, which pierces a man's hand and wounds him if he leans on it" (2 Kings 18:21). In the end, after the people of Israel had been carried into exile by Assyria, and the people of Judah had been taken to Babylon, a small remnant remained. Rather than stay in the land as God instructed, they fled to Egypt and it resulted in their death (Jeremiah 44).

When stress and troubles came, the people of Israel repeatedly looked to Egypt, even though it never brought the help they needed. They didn't learn much from their own history. Are we any different? What is the Egypt in your life? When stress and troubles come, where do you usually turn? Addictions to food, tobacco, alcohol, or pornography are common ways to try to ease the pains of life. For some, the first response is to call friends in order to complain or gossip. Others respond by thinking of something to post on social networks, venting frustration to a large audience. Some turn to exercise or entertainment to help them forget about their problems. Ask yourself, after a tough day at work, or a disagreement with a spouse, or a dreaded diagnosis, or even after receiving good news, where does your mind turn first? You think, "As soon as I get home (or even before that) I'm going to _____." That is probably your Egypt.

There is nothing wrong with calling a friend for comfort, or with exercise, or entertainment, or the computer. These things have their place, but just as Egypt never came through with the help and power the Israelites needed, so these other sources can never provide the help and guidance we need. There is only One who can help with every problem. There is only One who knows the best response in every situation, and has the power to help his people with every problem and heartache life brings. Why don't we run to him first? Why is he an afterthought rather than the default? It is my prayer, for myself and for you, that we will train our minds to turn first to the One who truly loves us and helps us.

It is Not Easy

"Jesus wants to be your best friend." "God has good plans for your life." "Jesus brings forgiveness and eternal life in paradise." Christians receive peace, joy, and protection from God." These types of statements are commonly used today in attempts to encourage people to become Christians. Although they are all true, the message is incomplete. We do people a terrible injustice when we share the blessings of being a Christian without clearly stating the cost.

Jesus said, "Come to me, all you who are weary and burdened, and I will give you rest. Take my yoke upon you and learn from me, for I am gentle and humble in heart, and you will find rest for your souls. For my yoke is easy and my burden is light" (Matthew 11:28-30). Notice that he doesn't say "Drop your burdens and be on your merry way." There is still a yoke and a burden. He invites us to step into the yoke with him, allowing him to steer and to shoulder the majority of the weight. I am still supposed to work as I walk in step with him. Compared to the burdens of guilt and shame and fear – not to mention eternal damnation – his burdens are light, but they are still burdens we are called to bear. Remember, the same Jesus who invited us to bring our burdens to him also said, "If anyone would come after me, he must deny himself and take up his cross daily and follow me. For whoever wants to save his life will lose it, but whoever loses his life for me will save it" (see Luke 9:23-24, Matthew 10:38 and 16:24, Mark 8:34). The life of the believer was never intended to be a life of ease and comfort. That idea, although common in some circles today, is never taught in Scripture. The life of a true believer is one of devotion, surrender, sacrifice. There is no other path for the follower of Jesus.

The fall of Jerusalem and the exile of its people is described in 2 Chronicles 36 and also Jeremiah 39. Jeremiah had faithfully proclaimed God's coming judgment on the people because of their sin and idolatry. Jeremiah's obedience to God resulted in his being put in the stocks, imprisoned, dumped in a deep cistern, and continually ridiculed. Being God's servant did not assure him a life of ease – quite the opposite, in fact. Ezekiel was an Israelite exile living in Babylon when God called him to be a prophet. God was still trying to get the attention and repentance of his people. He called Ezekiel not only to speak the messages he was given, but also to carry out dramatizations or visual demonstrations, representing God's plans for judgment. God required Ezekiel to lay on his left side (apparently in public) for 390 straight days representing Israel's 390 years of sin, and then to lay on his right side for forty straight days representing Judah's forty years of sin (see Ezekiel 4). God later instructed Ezekiel to shave his head and his beard using a sharp sword, as a demonstration of the ways his people would die – by sword, famine, and fire (Ezekiel 5). From our perspective, these actions seem like a lot for God to ask. God did not even ask: he commanded.

Friend, if we are truly God's disciples, he expects far more from us than regular church attendance. The Apostle Paul urged believers to offer their bodies as living sacrifices (Romans 12:1). God never intended for Christians to just fit in with the world around them, occasionally inviting a neighbor or co-worker to church. True surrender and obedience will at times be very uncomfortable (physically, financially, socially, and emotionally). Young children often expect and believe that every day should be filled with fun. Any expectation to work is taken as an insult and a tremendous imposition. Parents need to help their children realize and accept that work is and always will be a part of daily life. I think many believers, like these children, expect the Christian life to be comfortable and enjoyable. We complain about hardships that we are called to bear, rather than accepting them as a part of life. What is it that God is calling you to do for the glory of His Name? Are you walking humbly and obediently alongside him, or are you struggling to get out of the yoke and put down the cross? If we are to live as children of God, there is a price to pay, but so worth it in light of his grace and mercy and blessings. I encourage you to walk with him, even through the hard times. He will help and comfort, guide and bless.

God laid this message on my heart during my quiet time one Monday. After mulling it over and praying about it, I typed it up on Wednesday morning. Then came Friday – one of the worst days of my life. While attending a funeral for my uncle, we received word that my cousin had just died. On the way home the engine in our van gave out completely on the highway. God reminded me of the truth of this message. He is still good. He can help those who are grieving. Even when life is unbearably hard and we want to hide from the pain, God is still there. He is still good. He still calls us to walk in faith, clinging to his strength and his peace. He is enough – all we will ever need. Let us bring glory to his Name in all things.

Keep It Current

Can a person lose his/her salvation? Many theologians and denominations have very strong, very different views on the topic of eternal security. The question is whether a person who has become a believer forfeits his salvation if he rejects God's ways, or whether he is guaranteed acceptance into heaven no matter how he lives after he becomes a Christian. There are a wide range of interpretations for the various Scripture references that relate to this question, and discussion about what constitutes "a believer." If you have never considered or studied this issue, I encourage you to take the time to search the Scriptures and make up your own mind. For that reason, I am not going to share my opinion, but leave you to study and draw your own conclusions. One day, God will judge each heart, and perhaps we will understand Scripture more clearly then. The Bible tells us that God is more interested in where your relationship with him stands today than where it was in the past. My pastor (who is also my brother) often exhorts us to have a "relationship with Christ that is personal and current." This theme is recurrent in the book of Ezekiel.

I encourage you to read Ezekiel 18. God explains in great detail that if a man is righteous, faithfully keeping God's laws, he will be rewarded. That man's righteousness, however, does not insure equal rewards for his children. If he has a wicked son, the son will not receive rewards even though his father was faithful. Each person is judged for his own actions. The same lesson is explained in Ezekiel 33:12-16.

These passages were written before Christ came to bring salvation. Devotion to God and his Lordship was demonstrated primarily by faithfully following his commands. One of those commands was to "Love the Lord your God with all your heart and soul" (Deuteronomy 6:5, 10:12, 30:6). Although we are no longer under Old Testament law we can learn something from this passage about our God (the God who never changes, according to Malachi 3:6 and Hebrews 13:8). God does not allow our past actions, whether good or bad, to determine the status of our relationship with him today. Living for him today, with sins forgiven through Jesus, leads to abundant life in him even if your past is filled with heinous acts. Even while imprisoned for past actions, a true believer can walk in hope and peace and joy through the Savior. However, the reverse is also true. Growing up in a Christian home, or a history of righteous acts is not enough to shield a person from judgment if he turns from God and walks in wickedness.

God is the God of yesterday, today, and tomorrow. He wants each one of us to be in a healthy, growing relationship with him today and every day of our lives. Those who truly know and love him will always be seeking to draw closer to him, rather than trying to stay as close to the world as possible and still get into heaven. I encourage you to live in a relationship with the Savior that is personal, up-to-date, and growing.

If you have never considered the question of eternal security, I encourage you to study the following passages and do your best to understand what they are saying, based on what you know to be true of God and his character. (Jude 24, John 10:28, Acts 16:31, Romans 8:37-39, 1 Peter 1:5, Hebrews 3:6, 14, John 3:26; 3:16,18; 5:24; 6:40,47, Matthew 26:41, 2 Peter 3:17, 1 Timothy 1:18). After your study, you might want to ask your pastor for information on your denomination's position on this issue.

One final note – although it is good for us to study the Scriptures and seek to understand them, do not be distressed if your conclusions differ from someone else's. Theologians and others who have studied the original texts have reached different conclusions. Time will tell, but the study of God's Word helps us to learn more of his character and draw closer to him. Therefore the process of studying is often more valuable than the conclusions we draw. We can be assured that God will judge justly.

Live in the Moment

"I'm slow, but I'm teachable" is a phrase my husband and I use often as we recognize how slow we are to change and become more Christ-like. God often uses other people to teach me. One such person was my cousin Debbie. I didn't share at her funeral, but this is what I wish I had said, "I am so proud of Deb. Diabetes affected and interfered with every area of her life during every season of her life from age seven to thirty-five. She endured so many health struggles and hospital stays that I lost count. Still, diabetes did not define Deb. Although she had reason to withdraw into a cocoon of self-pity, she chose to go on living life the best way she could. She was an active teenager and graduated high school. She took classes and worked. She had a beautiful ministry of sharing her faith with hurting people. Deb found love and got married and God granted her dream of having a baby. As much as she was able, Deb kept on living and dreaming and experiencing until the day she died. She was not defined by her struggles but by her impact on others. Deb chose to live each day rather than being paralyzed by dread of tomorrow."

God used two friends to reinforce that lesson the same month that Debbie died. In 1999 Mark had been diagnosed with leukemia.

He and Marianne and their loved ones and church family prayed faithfully through the years of treatment and all the ups and downs. Longing and praying for healing, Mark and Marianne watched his health slip away as each new treatment took its toll without buying much time. Mark was not able to hold down a job, but he continued to work and to live. He loved to visit with people and celebrate the beauty of God's creation. Mari walked steadily by his side, even through the darkest of days. With God's help she developed a determination to postpone grieving until grief was all that was left. If she had allowed them to, dread and fear of a future without Mark could have dominated her days and robbed her of the joy those eleven years brought. Instead, she fought back those thieves and took in every blessing of their lives together. When the time for grieving came, Mari had a huge storehouse of rich memories of the time she and Mark spent together. I am so impressed by how these courageous friends chose to live in the face of great heartache.

Let me be clear. I am not saying that Deb or Mark and Marianne achieved perfection. Of course they had their hard days, their battles with self-pity, their negative attitudes. What I am saying is, looking at the big picture, all three of these people chose a life attitude of living rather than an attitude of dying. They learned to live in the moment rather than living in dread of tomorrow.

Friends, I confess that I have a tendency to get so caught up in the problems and responsibilities of the day and the plans we need to make for tomorrow that I miss out on today. I miss the beauty of God's creation. I miss the chance to snuggle with my kids because I am working on the computer or doing household chores. Sometimes I forget what counts most in this life. It is all about relationships – first with God and then with other people. Through the pain of losing both Debbie and Mark in one month, I determined to learn this lesson. I will live in the moment day by day, receiving the gifts and joys God has for me, rather than always trying to figure out tomorrow. I challenge you to do the same. Even if we are slow to learn, let us always be teachable.

Swiss Cheese Church

We used to have a large double pine tree growing close to the side of the house. It provided nice shade, but it was infested with carpenter ants. A representative from the power company came out and looked at it and said he couldn't take it down because it was not a threat to the power lines (because it was more likely to fall on the house). He told us that rain would fill in the cracks where the tree split into two, and then freeze, which would expand the cracks even further.

Like our tree, a church can develop rifts due to personality clashes, disagreements over how to do ministry, how to decorate, and poor communication. Every church is made up of human beings. If we are not careful, Satan can use these little cracks to gain a foothold and weaken the body. I believe that is why Jesus prayed that his followers would be one, just as he and his Father are one (see John 17).

In November 2003, during a storm, that pine tree blew down. Half fell against the house, doing a little damage. A short time later, as Bart and the firefighters watched, the other half fell, taking out the power pole and the electricity for several neighboring houses. It took three days to get it repaired and get the power turned back on. Our inability to take care of those cracks in the tree led to problems and inconvenience for us and also for the people around us.

The burden God laid on my heart through that experience is that we determine not to become a "Swiss-cheese-church" – a church that looks good, but is filled with holes between people. If I just let something go between myself and another person, rather than addressing it, it will never go away. It takes up space between us, like a crack in the base of a pine tree. Every single one of these cracks or issues between people in the body weakens the whole body. Only God knows how many such cracks exist in a particular body of believers, but with a little thought and prayer, you can figure out how many are around you. If each of us takes steps to repair those rifts, the body will be stronger. If we don't, it will eventually cause bigger problems for us, and for those around us.

Let's look at what the Word of God says about resolving issues between believers. "Therefore, if you are offering your gift

195

at the altar and there remember that your brother has something against you, leave your gift there in front of the altar. First go and be reconciled to your brother; then come and offer your gift" (Matthew 5:23,24). "Catch for us the foxes, the little foxes that ruin the vineyards, our vineyards that are in bloom" (Song of Songs 2:15). "For if you forgive men when they sin against you, your heavenly Father will also forgive you. But if you do not forgive men their sins, your Father will not forgive your sins" (Matthew 6:14,15). "Then Peter came to Jesus and asked, 'Lord, how many times shall I forgive my brother when he sins against me? Up to seven times?' Jesus answered, 'I tell you, not seven times, but seventy-seven times'" (Matthew 18:21,22).

Whether you like Swiss cheese or not, I think you will agree that it is not a good model for a church. I ask, I encourage, I challenge each person to take some time to evaluate his/her relationships with other believers and be reconciled for the glory of Almighty God and the health of the church.

Blocked Blessings

Is your relationship with Almighty God healthy and growing? Are you prioritizing time in the Word and prayer? During the time of Haggai, some of the people of Israel had returned to Jerusalem after the exile in Babylon. They were trying to settle back into their lives, but had not rebuilt the temple. It was a frustrating time for the people. They planted a lot, but harvested little. They worked hard and held high expectations, but they harvested barely enough to survive. When the word of the Lord came to Haggai, he said to the people, "Give careful thought to your ways. Go up into the mountains and bring down timber and build the house, so that I may take pleasure in it and be honored, says the Lord. You expected much, but see, it turned out to be little. What you brought home, I blew away. Why? declares the Lord Almighty. Because of my house, which remains a ruin, while each of you is busy with his own house. Therefore, because of you the heavens have withheld their dew and the earth its crops. I called for a drought on the field and the mountains, on the grain, the new wine, the oil and whatever the ground produces, on men and cattle, and on the labor of your hands" (Haggai 1:5-11).

Have you known frustration? Do you know what it is to try and try and try, but never catch up much less get ahead? Does it feel like you are putting your money in a purse with holes in it? These people planned and planted and worked, but never had enough. They tried hard to succeed and held high expectations, but what they brought home God blew away. Friend, I do not claim to understand the reasons for frustrations you may be experiencing, any more than you do. This passage, however, gives us a hint of one issue that may be blocking God's blessings. He allowed great frustration in order to turn the people's attention away from themselves, toward himself. It was an issue of priorities.

The people obeyed and shifted their priorities to line up with God's (Haggai 1:12). They began rebuilding the temple of the Lord. Haggai encouraged the people and told them of God's promised blessings. God promised to fill the house with his glory and grant them peace (Haggai 2:7-9). He even said, "From this day on I will bless you" (Haggai 2:19).

Scripture shows that God delights in blessing his people. If you are experiencing frustration as described in the book of Haggai, there may be many reasons. Ask God to show you anything that is blocking his blessing in your life. First, ask the Holy Spirit to reveal any un-confessed sin (disobedience) in your life. Pray, as David did, "Search me, O God, and know my heart; test me and know my anxious thoughts. See if there is any offensive way in me, and lead me in the way everlasting" (Psalm 139:23,24). Second, ask the Holy Spirit to reveal priorities that are out of line with his, as in this passage in Haggai. God will not bless efforts that lead us further from him rather than closer to him. Third, if the Holy Spirit does not reveal anything in your life that is blocking God's blessing, wait patiently on him (Galatians 6:9). He will never fail. Rest assured that he is working all things for your good.

For Better or Worse

The animated movie *Madagascar 2* includes a mock wedding. In response to the charge, "For better or for worse" the character responded, "for better please." Humorous, but doesn't that sound like the way most of us approach life? We go into marriage

197

expecting good things. We start a family or a new job or a new venture looking for the best. As we go through life, however, we discover that the best and the worst often come hand in hand. Every life is likely to experience both sickness and health, some degree of both richer and poorer, both better and worse. The wedding charge is not multiple choice.

After losing nearly everything, Job said, "The Lord gave and the Lord has taken away; may the name of the Lord be praised" (Job 1:21b). Whether you are living today in sickness or in health, in wealth or in poverty, experiencing the best or the worst, you have reason to give thanks. Even when God has taken away, we need to remember the first part of the verse. God has given. He has given us far greater blessings than we deserve. We need shelter, not big comfortable houses. We need covering, but not a closet full of clothes. We need food, but not three helpings and leftovers to put in the fridge. God has given us so much! Scriptures tell us that "Every good and perfect gift is from above, coming down from the Father of the heavenly lights, who does not change like shifting shadows" (James 1:17). Even in the unspeakable pain of losing a loved one, we can give thanks for the privilege of knowing and loving the one we have lost. We can, in fact, "give thanks in all circumstances" (1Thessalonians 5:18).

How do we shift our hearts and thoughts to an attitude of gratitude? It is a matter of choice and discipline. Whatever is on your heart today, be it grief, or fear for the future, or loneliness, the road toward giving thanks always starts in your mind. Happiness is a feeling that comes and goes faster than the wind. Thankfulness is a mindset that we choose. It takes discipline and determination to shift my focus from the troubles of this life to the goodness of God.

We should give thanks to God for the ways he has provided for and met our needs, and for protection from danger we never recognized. God has answered innumerable prayers for physical healing. He has given each one of us the opportunity to hear the message of the Gospel, and the freedom to worship him. God has given us the Holy Spirit, through whom we receive comfort, counsel, and conviction. There are so many reasons to be thankful!

Choosing to give thanks honors God. It also brings peace to the heart. As we remember how faithful God has been in the past, we are reminded to trust him with the future. Those of us who are not currently experiencing "for worse" will be more effective vessels of light to our neighbors if our hearts are filled with his peace. Let us give thanks today and every day.

A Faithful Servant

In Matthew 25 we find three parables, the second of which is often referred to as the Parable of the Talents. A rich man who was leaving on a long journey called in three servants and gave each of them a sum of money to invest, based on each man's ability. To one the rich master gave five talents, to a second he gave two talents, and to a third he gave one talent. All three were to manage and invest the assets of their master in his absence. The first two did just as they were instructed. By the time the master returned, the man who had received five talents had earned five more and the man given two talents had earned two more. The third man just hid the single talent, and incurred the wrath of his master. In this story, the master says to both of the first two servants, "Well done, good and faithful servant! You have been faithful in a few things; I will put you in charge of many things. Come and share your master's happiness!" (Matthew 25:21,23). The unfaithful servant was rebuked and sent away. The talent which had been entrusted to him was given to the man who had ten. The master said, "For everyone who has will be given more, and he will have an abundance. Whoever does not have, even what he has will be taken from him" (Matthew 25:29).

In 2008 Americans endured a whirlwind of finger pointing as the economy threatened to collapse. Clearly people who were supposed to be experts in financial matters were not wise or responsible in handling money. As I watched our national leaders scramble to throw money at the problem, I marveled at the difference between God's way and man's way. God said those who are faithful with a little will be given more. Our government, in contrast, seemed to reward unfaithful management of money. I do not understand all the ramifications of the situation well enough to conclude whether or not they made a wise decision.

In both the public and private sector, there are those who are striving to make decisions and policies that honor God. Scripture teaches that individuals are always held responsible for their own motives and actions, not for what other people do. Friends, this parable Jesus told in Matthew 25 pertains to more than money. No matter what the balance in our bank account, all of us have been entrusted by God to be managers. He has placed time, money, opportunities, education, and talents in your hands. The question is not, "How much do you have compared to everyone else?" The question is, "Are you being a good and faithful servant?" Notice that the master had the same praise for the man who worked with less and gained less, as he did for the man with more. The amount entrusted to each one was not the big issue. The faithful work of the servant was the focus of the manager. Each was given according to his ability, so the one who did nothing may have assumed that he was unable to accomplish anything. The master disagreed.

What are you doing with that which has been entrusted to you? Do you know your Spiritual gifts (1 Corinthians 12, Ephesians 4)? Are you using them regularly and faithfully to build the body? The abilities and experiences God has given you are unique, and meant to be used in specific ways in the kingdom. Would God say he is first in your time and priorities? Does he receive glory in the way you do your job and the way you raise your children and/or grandchildren? I encourage and challenge you today to be faithful in the things God has placed in your hands (be they many or few). May we one day hear our Master say, "Well done, good and faithful servant."

Pray For This Nation
In the Old Testament, God chose at least sixteen different men to declare his message to Israel and their neighbors, trying to persuade people to turn to God. For the most part, these messages seemed to fall on deaf ears. God also used adverse circumstances to get the attention of his people. He said, "I gave you empty stomachs in every city and lack of bread in every town, yet you have not returned to me," declares the Lord. "I also withheld rain from you when the harvest was still three months away. I sent rain on one town, but withheld it from another. One field had rain; another had none and dried up. People staggered from town to town for water but did not get enough to drink, yet you have not

returned to me," declares the Lord. "Many times I struck your gardens and vineyards, I struck them with blight and mildew. Locusts devoured your fig and olive trees, yet you have not returned to me," declares the Lord (Amos 4:6-9).

Friends, the Scriptures make it clear that God has always wanted people to know him and to come close to him. The same is true today. Although they are not usually called prophets, God has sent leaders in our day who call our beloved USA to repentance. Those who take a public stand for godliness, now as in days of old, are sorely outnumbered and subjected to harsh ridicule. In the passage above (and the verses following) God makes it clear that he allowed adverse circumstances into the lives of people to persuade them to turn to him. Has he allowed adverse circumstances in our land? Clearly, he has. One of the reasons he has permitted these struggles, personally and nationally, is to remind us that we need Almighty God.

In the days of the Minor Prophets, people continued to go their own ways. Some carried on the religious traditions, combined with all sorts of idolatry. Others abandoned the law of Moses altogether. A few remained faithful to God. After years of sending prophets and hard times to call people to him, God apparently stopped. Malachi became a prophet in approximately 430 B.C. From the time of his death until the birth of Christ in approximately 6 B.C. there is no recorded message from God. That period of silence is longer than the history of our nation.

Friends, we live in a remarkable time. Politicians promise "Change" as they have been doing longer than I can remember. There is a strong sense, however, that we as a nation stand at a crossroads bigger than we have faced in many decades. Will we as believers take a public stand for godliness? Will we work to promote morality in our land? I believe that God will not, yea he cannot, bless a nation that destroys babies which God himself knit together in the womb. And that is only one of many areas of godlessness. Broken marriage vows, sexual immorality, and self-absorption seem to define our nation. God has raised up leaders to sound the call. He has allowed hard times to come upon us. Will we turn to him, as he longs for us to do, or will we struggle on in our own strength?

There is no cause for fear. There is, however, grave cause for prayer. Not just fleeting thoughts, "Oh God help our nation," but desperate pleas. We ought to be daily on our knees begging God to have mercy on this country. How many of us care enough to fast – to deprive ourselves of food for a period of time – to show God that our need for him is greater than any other need or desire we have? I believe that if this nation of ours does not humble itself and pray and seek God's face and turn from its wicked ways, then God will not hear from heaven or forgive our sin or heal our land (taken from 2 Chronicles 7:14).

This prayer of humility and repentance starts with individuals. It starts with me and it starts with you. If this nation turns its collective back on God, and he brings the judgment we deserve, there is still hope. Listen to these words in Malachi 3:1-18, "Then those who feared the Lord spoke with each other, and the Lord listened to what they said. In his presence, a scroll of remembrance was written to record the names of those who feared him and loved to think about him. 'They will be my people,' says the Lord Almighty. 'On the day when I act, they will be my own special treasure. I will spare them as a father spares an obedient and dutiful child. Then you will again see the difference between the righteous and the wicked, between those who serve God and those who do not'" (NLT). There is hope. God knows those who are his own. Even though harder times than we have ever known may come upon us, God remembers us. Be of good courage for, "the One who is in you is greater than the one who is in the world" (1 John 4:4b). I ask you to pray – to pray alone, to pray with your family, to gather with other believers and cry out to God for the United States of America.

Is Your Name Written There?

When Barak Obama was first running for president, and even into the beginning of his term, some raised serious questions about whether he was a natural born citizen of the United States of America. This is a non-negotiable requirement for the office of president. Lawsuits were even filed, demanding a legitimate birth certificate. I don't know whether the answer was ever determined beyond a reasonable doubt. Most legal, official birth certificates in this country include information such as the names of the parents, the hospital where the baby was born, and the attending physician, birth time, weight, and length. There is another Documentation-of-live-birth which is far more crucial than a legal birth certificate. It is called The Lamb's Book of Life (Revelation 21:27). A birth certificate is required for things like obtaining a driver's license, or proving your age. Proof of being born into the family of God is required for spending eternity in heaven with the Savior.

President Obama had spent a significant portion of his life in the USA. He dressed American, talked American, acted American. All of those things, however were insufficient to prove his citizenship. Disbelievers demanded firm proof. Likewise, the kingdom of God has many people who consider themselves Christians. They may dress right, talk right, recognize God's hand in creation, maybe even attend church regularly. However, unless a person has become a child of God by believing on Jesus for the forgiveness of sins, all those things are worthless.

Revelation 21 describes the holy city where God is the light. "Nothing impure will ever enter it, nor will anyone who does what is shameful or deceitful, but only those whose names are written in the Lamb's book of life." In the previous chapter, John, under the inspiration of the Holy Spirit, wrote this: "Then I saw a great white throne and him who was seated on it. Earth and sky fled from his presence, and there was no place for them. And I saw the dead, great and small, standing before the throne, and books were opened. Another book was opened which is the book of life. The dead were judged according to what they had done as recorded in the books. The sea gave up the dead that were in it, and death and Hades gave up the dead that were in them, and each person was judged according to what he had done. Then death and Hades were thrown into the lake of fire. The lake of fire is the second death. If anyone's name was not found written in the book of life, he was thrown into the lake of fire" (Revelation 20:11-15).

Friends, one thing matters so much that nothing else in the world even makes the list. The thing that matters more than anything else is the list of names written in the Lamb's Book of Life. Is your name there? The only way to heaven is through Jesus Christ (John 14:6, Acts 4:12) and the work he did for us on the cross. When I came to him in repentance, asking him to be my Savior and Lord, he wrote my name in the Lamb's Book of Life. If you have come to Christ for forgiveness, and given him Lordship over your life, your name is written there too. If you have not come in brokenness, humility, and repentance, to the cross of Jesus, your name is not written there. It is not enough to be a good person, or even just to believe that he is the one and only God. "Even the demons believe that – and shudder" (James 2:19b).

There are those skilled in counterfeit procedures who may be able to produce false documentation, such as a birth certificate. Nobody, however, can circumvent the one and only way to heaven, established by the Father. I encourage each of us to search our own hearts, with the help of the Holy Spirit, and determine whether we have had our names written down. Then, we need to pray earnestly for those who are lost, even those who believe themselves to be found, to come to repentance and forgiveness in Christ. Presidents come and go. Nations rise and fall. But the Word of the Lord is forever. Let's make sure we get the most important question right.

Strong Roots

Along the coast of Lake Superior, near Munising, Michigan, God's amazing handiwork is displayed in Pictured Rocks. There are miles of magnificent rock formations. One of the most memorable for me is a tree growing on top of a tower of rock. Wind and waves have eroded the sandstone, leaving Chapel Rock standing alone on the edge of the lake. This tower of rock provides little or no nourishment for the lone tree perched on its flat top. This remarkable tree continues to thrive primarily because of one particular root. Ten to twelve feet of exposed root bridges the gap from Chapel Rock to the nearby cliffs. That strong root, probably fifteen feet above the current ground level, intertwines with the roots of other trees and takes nourishment from the soil across the span and into the tree. A strong, solid, dependable root makes all the difference for this tree.

In the Scriptures, believers are compared to trees that grow strong and hold fast. "He is like a tree planted by streams of water, which yields its fruit in season and whose leaf does not wither. Whatever he does prospers" (Psalm 1:3). "The righteous will flourish like a palm tree, they will grow like a cedar of Lebanon" (Psalm 92:12). "But blessed is the man who trusts in the Lord, whose confidence is in him. He will be like a tree planted by the water that sends out its roots by the stream. It does not fear when heat comes; its leaves are always green. It has no worries in a year of drought and never fails to bear fruit" (Jeremiah 17:7,8). Are you and I well-rooted trees that have no worries in a year of drought and never fail to bear fruit?

I honor those grandparents who have been faithful to help establish roots of holiness and faith in succeeding generations. Righteous grandparents in every generation have lived out their faith and deliberately helped to lay a foundation in the lives of young children. Not only grandparents, but parents, aunts and uncles, Sunday School teachers, mentors, and others, have tried to teach and show those who are younger what it means to have a personal, intimate relationship with Jesus our Savior. We owe them our thanks. At times most of us feel that our efforts are wasted or ineffective. That is a lie from our enemy the devil who has seen how great an impact just one godly man or woman can have on the life of a child. Although you may never see the fruit, I encourage you to continually work to establish roots of faith. Many believers have testified to turning to Christ as an adult because they remembered the influence of a godly person in their lives when they were young.

The tree on Chapel Rock depends on the nourishment from that important root. Roots from other trees on the cliff top intertwine with that crucial root and help to hold it in place. We as believers fill that role for one another. One of the reasons believers are encouraged to be a part of a church family is so that we might encourage one another as we all follow Christ (Hebrews 10:25). I encourage you to tend to your own roots and to help others establish theirs.

Father Knows Best?

As a soldier was finishing his tour of duty in Iraq, he wrote me a letter stating, "I have seen too many terrible things to believe in God." His words broke my heart. I have thought several times since then, just the opposite should be true. If we are willing to see, there is so much good in the world around us, we can't help but believe in God. We bemoan the accidents that do happen, giving scarcely a thought to those God prevented. We grieve over babies born with severe complications, assuming all should be perfectly healthy. We fuss over the storms that cause destruction. Do we thank God for the storms that don't? Why is it so easy to take the good for granted, but complain about struggles?

Although Scriptures talk a lot about wisdom, it seems difficult to fully grasp. God alone knows the best things to do in every situation. Here is how A.W. Tozer describes God's wisdom: "All God's acts are done in perfect wisdom, first for his own glory, and then for the highest good of the greatest number for the longest time. All his acts are as pure as they are wise, and as good as they are wise and pure. Not only could his acts not be better done; a better way to do them could not be imagined."[25]

Knowing that God knows best is reassuring as we move along the more-or-less level pathways of life. But what does it mean when crises come? When the plant closes and you lose your job; when the bank forecloses and you lose your dream home; when the diagnosis is terminal and you lose your health, it is hard to hold on to faith and believe God knows best. It takes a deliberate act of the will independent of feelings. This blind faith is immeasurably harder when the crisis is bigger. When a storm wipes out your home and all you own, what is God doing? When you lose your only child in an accident, how can God be doing something good? Just saying that to a grieving parent sounds callous and cold. So we don't say it. We don't claim to understand. Rather, we pray earnestly for God to carry them through and draw them near to himself even as he works all things for their good.

Whatever struggle you are facing today, I encourage you to hold on to God in faith. He is good, even when life hurts more than words can express. Chip Ingram said, "And because you are his child, God orchestrates or allows only the best possible results, by the best possible means, to accomplish the highest possible purpose, for the longest time, for the most people in and around your life. Only God can make the wisest choice."[26] Trust in him today.

Tend the Fire

Where do you go when you are empty? There are several Scripture references which exhort us to keep working faithfully, tirelessly, as unto the Lord. (See Galatians 6:9, 1 Corinthians 15:58, Colossians 3:17.) As children of God, we choose to be "crucified with Christ" so that he lives within us (Galatians 2:20). We try to do for those in need as we would do for Jesus (Matthew 25). We try to care for widows and orphans, and to train others to know God. All of us who have received Jesus Christ as Savior, and made him Lord of our lives, are to be ministers. Each one is to be using his gifts for building up the church (Ephesians 4). All of these are very good things and God is honored when we live out our faith in accordance with his Word.

The truth is, though, it can be exhausting. Do you give hard physical labor to help people with home maintenance or other needs? Do you give emotional support and comfort to those who are grieving, or hurting, or in great distress? Do you give of your mental energies helping people to find solutions to problems that plague them? Do you spend time and money calling on the sick, preparing meals or cards or bouquets of flowers to cheer them up? Do you spend untold hours working behind the scenes to keep the church or other ministries running? Do you work a second or third job to support the work of fulfilling the Great Commission? All of these things are good, and can bring God glory if done with the right heart attitude. Each of us has something to give and God expects us to do so.

Giving, whether physically, emotionally, or mentally, is tiring. The Apostle Paul, near the end of his earthly ministry described it as being "poured out like a drink offering" (2 Timothy 4:6). Friend, has your life been poured out like a drink offering? Have you given and given and given until there is nothing left but an empty feeling? Everyone I know who is truly surrendered to God faces this condition periodically. There are times when Kingdom work is invigorating and fulfilling. Then there are those other times. That feeling of emptiness is a clear call from the Savior, "Come away with me and be refreshed." All of us need to follow the example of our Lord. As close as he was to the Father, and as intimately as he knew him, Jesus made time to get alone with the

Father. Saving the world was a full-time job, but Jesus prioritized solitude. Each of us needs to make it a priority to get alone with the Savior in silence on a regular basis. We need to learn to hear his voice, to return to his perspective and priorities, to be renewed. Gail MacDonald, in her book, *High Call, High Privilege*, refers to this as tending to the fire.[27] Like coming and sitting around the bonfire with the Master, each of us needs to get alone with him and ask him, "How are things between you and me?" "What areas do you want me to focus on?" "What do you want to say to me?"

I encourage you, minister in the kingdom, to make time regularly to be alone. When the emptiness comes, make extra time to be alone with the Savior. Read. Worship. Listen. Remember the widow in 2 Kings 4, whose oil did not run out as she filled jar after jar? It did not run out because God was replenishing the oil. He longs to do the same in your heart. I encourage you today with the words of Jesus, "Come to me, all you who are weary and burdened, and I will give you rest" (Matthew 11:28).

A Heavenly Bailout

The threat of economic collapse was the primary news story for several weeks in 2008. Americans had failed to heed Jesus' instruction, "Do not store up for yourselves treasures on earth, where moth and rust destroy, and where thieves break in steal. But store up for yourselves treasures in heaven, where moth and rust do not destroy, and where thieves do not break in and steal. For where your treasure is, there your heart will be also" (Matthew 6:19-21). Like many generations before us, when questions about the future loomed large, the people of God find great peace in the assurance that God is in control. Our Jehovah Jireh will provide all that we need, as he has done for those who have gone before us.

If we knew the troubles that lie ahead, (as individuals, as families, and as a nation) fear and trepidation would render us immobile and useless. It is a blessing that God only gives us one moment at a time to face. Every generation of parents is concerned about the world in which their children will live. God alone knows the times and the ways things will come about. We trust ourselves and our children to him.

Threatened by the possibility of economic collapse, politicians and financial gurus scrambled to find a quick fix for a problem that had been growing for years. Their solution was to give $700 billion (that they didn't have) to bail out failing financial institutions. That amount is a figure our feeble minds cannot begin to grasp. Although the problems we face as individuals are not to that scale, how many of us wish there was a "bail out" plan? We long for a quick and painless fix to our financial problems, our relational problems, our addictions, our grief. The truth is though, that even $700 Billion would not bail us out of our deepest pit.

Can you picture a scene in heaven like the meeting of politicians trying to figure out what to do? What did the heavenly beings think about God's "Bail Out Plan" for mankind? Maybe he didn't even tell them. The price that he was willing to pay in order to dig us out of the mess we had made . . . well, no amount of money in the world could measure. God's love for us is great beyond all description. He gave his only Son. Any parent who has lost a child – imperfect as the child was – will tell you it is a price without measure.

Friend, today I want to remind each of us to put our trust in God. He alone is the Solid Rock. He is immutable – the same yesterday, today, and forever. We thank God for his indescribable gift. Finally, I remind us to pray fervently for this nation. Parents and grandparents, I challenge you to move beyond the easy prayer of "please protect my children" to pray, "Lord, please help my children to draw near to you and to be able to stand strong in the difficult days ahead." Whatever struggles they will face, whenever they come, our God is more than able to meet the needs of his people. It is prayer of investment.

Take This Cup

Country music star Garth Brooks recorded a song with the lyrics, "Sometimes I thank God for unanswered prayer."[28] There is truth in the message that God's answers to our prayers often are not exactly what we expected. After spreading the gospel in many foreign cities, starting churches, and then going back to visit and encourage the believers, Paul wrote to the Christian church in Rome. Believers had traveled there from Jerusalem and other places and started a church. Paul longed to visit that church to celebrate God's grace with them, and to encourage them in their faith. In fact he had tried a number of times to go to Rome, but the Spirit prevented him (Romans 1:13). He wrote the book of Romans as a letter to that church. He asked them to join him in prayer about his upcoming trip to Jerusalem and his plans to travel to Rome. "I urge you, brothers, by our Lord Jesus Christ and by the love of the Spirit, to join me in my struggle by praying to God for me. Pray that I may be rescued from the unbelievers in Judea and that my service in Jerusalem may be acceptable to the saints there, so that by God's will I may come to you with joy and together with you be refreshed. The God of peace be with you all. Amen" (Romans 15:31-33).

Paul had been warned by the Holy Spirit that the Jews in Jerusalem would arrest him (Acts 21:11). Still, he asked the church to pray for him to be rescued from the unbelievers so that he could travel to Rome. Isn't that what we would pray? I think it is. As expected, Paul was not warmly welcomed in Jerusalem. He was arrested on false charges and called to appear before the Sanhedrin. Enemies plotted to take his life, so he was transferred to Caesarea. Over a period of more than two years, he was put on trial before Felix, and then before Festus, and finally, before King Agrippa. As a Roman citizen, Paul eventually appealed to Caesar. He did travel to Rome, but as a prisoner. Along the way he was shipwrecked and then bitten by a poisonous snake. This was not at all the way he had planned to travel to Rome. Did God answer Paul's prayer?

God answers our prayers in the way that brings him the most glory – not us the most comfort. Paul was not, in fact, rescued from the unbelievers in Jerusalem. Yet, because of these troubles he had opportunity to share his faith with many in leadership positions who may not otherwise have heard the Gospel message. On the journey he was a living testimony to unbelieving soldiers and many others. If he had gone to Rome on his own, likely he would have only influenced a small number of people. Going as a prisoner, however, accomplished that and more. He was "allowed to live by himself with a soldier to guard him" (Acts 28:16). The believers were allowed to come and meet with him and care for his needs. He also had opportunity to preach to an assembly of believers on more than one occasion. For two whole years he lived that way, waiting for his trial before Caesar. Many of the New Testament letters were written while he was a prisoner. Even though years of imprisonment were not on Paul's agenda, God answered his prayer in the way that allowed the most people to hear the Gospel message, and that provided the most help to succeeding generations (namely those letters).

Friend, what is the prayer on your heart today? God invites us to come to him in prayer and bring our requests to him. We must recognize, however, that his answer may not be according to our plans or time tables. He is sovereign. Even his own Son Jesus did not get the answer he asked for in the Garden: "Father, if you are willing, take this cup from me" (Luke 22:42), but submitted himself to whatever God saw as best. Some of the things God allows in his sovereignty are painful and hard to understand. When this happens, we must choose to trust that he will carry us through, even as he brings glory to his name and works all things for our good (Romans 8:28). Let us be thankful for all the times God has answered our prayers by not giving us what we asked for. When that happens, he gets the glory.

The Cry of Your Heart

"Now to Him who is able to do immeasurably more than all we ask or imagine, according to his power at work within us, to him be glory in the church and in Christ Jesus throughout all generations for ever and ever" (Ephesians 3:20-21). Friend, what is it that you are asking of God? What is the deep cry of your heart? For more than ten years after high school, the ache in my heart was for a husband and a family. Those were good growing years spiritually and vocationally, but hard years personally. God and I talked about it a lot. He wanted me to wait longer than I wanted to wait. Through the highs and lows of those years God answered the faithful prayers of my parents that I would not settle for less than the best that God had for me. (Parents, never quit praying for your kids and grandkids!) Without those prayers, I'm pretty sure I would have settled for "close enough." In his time, however, he gave me the one that was best for me. Bart's compassion and willingness to help people are a delight to me. His work ethic is a beautiful example to our children. His willingness to use his unique gifts to build up the church is right in line with what the Bible teaches. His friendship and companionship are priceless to me. God gave me a wonderful husband and friend. As if that were not enough, he blessed us with two great children. He did "immeasurably more than all I asked or imagined." The King James Version says, "exceedingly abundantly above all that we ask or think." That is the kind of God we serve. He uses his power in our lives to bring glory to himself.

My friend, God hears the cry of your heart, and he cares deeply for you. In his time he will answer that cry in a way that brings glory to him. Don't miss that second verse. It really is all about bringing glory to God. Although it is unlikely that he will move in the time and in the way you have decided would suit you best, he will answer! Ask yourself: 1. Will I surrender my dreams and my longings to his perfect plan? 2. Rather than pleading for my own way, will I choose to say, "Your will be done"? 3. Am I really looking for that which will bring the most glory to him? May God bless you and stretch you as you wait on "Him who is able to do immeasurably more than all [you] ask or imagine." All glory to His Name.

Keep Your Commitment to God

Have you noticed that when you take a step of faith and commit to rely on God, he often allows the situation to become a little more complicated before it all works out? You commit in faith to tithe ten percent as he commands us, and unexpected bills start coming in. You commit to go where God seems to be leading and hit one road block after another. You commit to let God work his will in a relationship and it immediately gets worse. You turn down a job offer when God doesn't give peace about it, only to wait months for another offer to come along. Can you relate to some of these experiences? Our human response is usually discouragement or even anger. We are tempted to snatch back what we have committed to him and try to handle the situation ourselves (since he doesn't seem to be doing it very well). Times like this are when God takes the little bit of faith we have given him and stretches it to an even larger and stronger faith. Not much fun, but very healthy.

It is right and good to commit to God in faith. Scripture warns, however against making a commitment you are not going to keep. The prophet Jeremiah was repeatedly mistreated and arrested for declaring God's judgment upon Jerusalem. When the Babylonians conquered the city, just as he had prophesied, those who had predicted peace were nowhere to be found. The king, his officials, and most of the Jews were taken as captives to Babylon. A few poor people remained, and a number of fugitives returned from hiding after the soldiers had left. Trying to decide whether to stay in the land or flee to Egypt (out of fear of King Nebuchadnezzar) they asked Jeremiah to consult the Lord for them. They promised to obey whatever God told them to do. "Then they said to Jeremiah, 'May the Lord be a true and faithful witness against us if we do not act in accordance with everything the Lord your God sends you to tell us. Whether it is favorable or unfavorable, we will obey the Lord our God, to whom we are sending you, so that it will go well with us, for we will obey the Lord our God'" (Jeremiah 42:5,6). Ten days after Jeremiah asked, God answered. He instructed the people to stay in their land and he promised to protect them and provide for them. He also gave them stern warning that if they disobeyed and went down to Egypt they would all die there (Jeremiah 42:10-18).

The people had committed to do God's will. When they found out what his will was for them, they reneged on their promise. They accused Jeremiah of lying (although all his predictions had come true so far) and decided to go to Egypt (Jeremiah 43:1-7). They forced Jeremiah to go with them. Jeremiah had warned them, "You made a fatal mistake when you sent me to the Lord your God and said, 'Pray to the Lord our God for us; tell us everything he says and we will do it.' I have told you today, but you still have not obeyed the Lord your God in all he sent me to tell you. So now, be sure of this: You will die by the sword, famine and plague in the place where you want to go to settle'" (Jeremiah 42:20-22). Our God, who cannot lie, kept his Word. Those people never returned from Egypt.

Friends, God wants and instructs us to surrender our lives fully to him. That is the only path to an abundant, fulfilling life, and I pray that you will give yourself totally to him. We must understand, however, that God takes promises very seriously. He always keeps his and expects us to keep ours. If you have made a commitment and have not been keeping it, or if you have never surrendered your life to his Lordship, I urge you to do so today. Commit to follow his will for your life: then keep your commitment. He will see you through.

The Gift of Giving

For several years my family has chosen to exchange home-made gifts at CHRISTmas time. Even though much parental help is required for some, it is worth the trouble. One of the greatest joys of our celebration now is watching how excited each of the kids is about giving away something he/she worked hard to make for a cousin. They have discovered the joy of giving, for which I am very thankful.

Have you discovered the joy of giving to others? If you are a believer, you have already received the greatest gift of all which is Salvation through Jesus Christ. You have also been given some specially selected gifts. 1 Corinthians 12:11 tells us that the Holy Spirit chooses Spiritual gifts to give to each of us. There are a variety of different types of gifts listed or described in Scripture. Some of these include teaching, preaching, evangelism, message of wisdom or knowledge, acts of mercy, faith, and prophecy. All of them, however, have the same goal: "To prepare God's people for works of service, so that the body of Christ may be built up . . ." (Ephesians 4:12). Every single believer is given gifts to help serve and build the body of Christ, which is the Church. The gifts are, in a sense, to be given away.

If you are a believer, but are not actively involved in the church, you are living in disobedience. Sitting in a pew on Sunday morning is not serving. Each of us is a part of the body of Christ and should be involved in Spirit-led ministry (1 Corinthians 12). If you are a believer, you will be held accountable for what you do with the gifts you have been given. Take steps to discover your Spiritual gifts and begin using them today. If you are not sure how to get started, talk to a leader in the church. Remember, after washing the disciples' feet, Jesus instructed them all to be servants

(John 13:14-17). He expects the same from his disciples in every century.

If you are not yet a believer (meaning you have never repented of your sins and asked God's forgiveness through the blood of Jesus) this message does not directly apply to you at this time. Serving others is good, but it will not get you into heaven. On the day when you fall on your knees before Almighty God (as every person will do, according to Isaiah 45:23, Romans 14:11, Philippians 2:10), you will have to answer for how you responded to the message of salvation. Seeking forgiveness of sins through Jesus Christ must be your first step. I pray that you will take that step today and enter into a personal relationship with your Savior.

Let each of us open the gifts God has offered to us. For the unbeliever, the gift is Salvation. For the believer, there are Spiritual gifts to be used in building up the church body. In each case, let us gladly receive the gifts and use them for God's glory.

Join the Battle

"I was pretty frustrated." That sounds far more spiritual than saying, "I was really angry." "Frustrated" is the word I used, but the truth is, I was angry. Both kids had said they wanted to play soccer. If I had known it would cost so much I would never have signed them up to play. By the time teams had played five games, my son had played less than two minutes, half of that in tears. Completely indifferent to the cost I paid, he would sit on the sidelines wanting to be held. He liked to wear the shirt and be included in snack time, even slapped hands with the other players after the game, but he contributed nothing to the goals of the team. As a mom trying to be a good steward, I felt angry when he would cling to me, refusing to join the team.

How often does our Heavenly Parent feel this way toward his children? The price his Son paid for us is beyond all measure. Yet, so many people who decide to join the team, the church, refuse to join the battle. People are happy to be affiliated with the team and to be included in snack time. They even shake hands during greeting time. Still, they do not actively contribute toward the goals. So, what are the goals God has for his church? We have to start with the commandments Jesus said were most important. "Love the Lord your God with all your heart and with all your soul and with all your mind. This is the first and greatest commandment. And the second is like it: Love your neighbor as yourself. All the Law and the Prophets hang on these two commandments" (Matthew 22:37-40). Part of loving our neighbors includes fulfilling the Great Commission "Therefore go and make disciples of all nations, baptizing them in the name of the Father and of the Son and of the Holy Spirit, and teaching them to obey everything I have commanded you. And surely I am with you always, to the very end of the age" (Matthew 28:19-20).

Friends, if we are God's children, a part of his family, we are expected to be working toward the goals he has established for us. It is never about what I feel like doing or what makes me comfortable. It is about becoming all that he desires me to be. A coach's delight is a player who gives his all. God delights when his children give everything they are and everything they have, surrendering their lives to his will. Have we, like Jesus' first disciples, left everything to follow him (see Matthew 4:20-22), or are we sitting on the sidelines expecting to be made comfortable?

Even though I was sure he would really benefit, I did not have words or ways (either threatening or encouraging) to persuade my son to try his best. He had to make that decision for himself. The same is true for you. Our Heavenly Father uses Scripture, prayer time, and messages from other people to remind, encourage, and exhort you. Still, the decision to surrender all to him is yours to make. No one can make it for you. Won't you get off the bench and join the battle today?

Bring Your First Fruits

Harvest Season is a beautiful time in Michigan. All the leaves and fields turn glorious colors as farmers harvest the pumpkins, apples, and other produce. In earlier generations, even more than today, the whole year was centered on preparing and working for the harvest. Even from earliest times it was a time of celebration. In the Old Testament, God gave Moses instructions for three celebrations to be held throughout the year - The Feast of Unleavened Bread, The Feast of the Harvest of First Fruits, and finally, the Feast of Ingathering at the end of the year when all the crops had been gathered (Exodus 23: 14-16). Each was a celebration to help them remember what God had done for them in bringing them out of Egypt, and providing all they needed.

First fruits are the first of something, such as the first child born into a family, or the year's first calf, or the first corn or beans to grow in a garden that season. The Hebrews saw the first fruits as holy. Why? Because the first fruits were a taste of what was to come. Dedicating those first fruits to God was a way of thanking him for providing them. It was also a sign of trust that God would take care of his children.

First fruit offerings included produce in both natural and processed states (e.g., dough, bread, wine, olive oil, and wool). The firstborn son and the firstborn of one's animals were to be treated as belonging to God. Firstborn children and the firstborn of unclean animals were "redeemed" (paid for) with money, and the firstborn of the cows, sheep, and goats were offered in sacrifice to God (Numbers 18:14-17).

In the Old Testament, first fruits were brought as an offering. This was a step of faith, giving God the first of the harvest and trusting him to provide as much as they would need. This compares to the tithe which you and I are commanded to give, the first ten percent of all we earn goes to God. It is an act of obedience and trust. If we choose to disobey, putting our trust in money instead of in God, money will likely be a source of continual worry in our lives.

In the New Testament, the Apostle Paul described receiving the Holy Spirit as the first fruits of the Spirit. Being filled with the Holy Spirit was a guarantee of being adopted as God's child. It represented a faith that God would bring his adopted children home to himself (Romans 8:23-25). The same is true today. Those of us who have received forgiveness of sins through Jesus Christ have been given the Holy Spirit (the first part of dwelling with Almighty God). We trust him to bring us all the way home.

Finally, in 1 Corinthians 15:20-23, the Apostle Paul describes Christ's resurrection as the first fruits. He was permanently resurrected from the dead. We who are his will also be resurrected . . . the rest of the harvest. What great comfort this brings for all who have believing loved ones who have preceded us in death! We believe that Jesus was raised and we trust God to raise us too to spend eternity with him.

Friend, are you bringing your first fruits to God? Are you giving to him first? Of your money? Of your time? Of your talents, plans, and dreams? You see, it is really a question of trust. Does your personal relationship with God convince you that he is trustworthy? This is a very personal decision. I pray that you will give to him first. He has promised to provide for you, and he will!

Hold On To Him

Carol Kent's book entitled *When I Lay My Isaac Down* is a powerful true account of what happens in the lives of this Christian family when their only son is charged with first degree murder. The subtitle says, "Unshakable Faith in Unthinkable Circumstances." The book is geared to help all of us as we come to places where we have to lay down our own plans, our own dreams, our own way, and cling to God alone as Abraham did when God tested him to see whether he was willing to sacrifice his only son (Genesis 22). At some point in each of our lives we will face a crisis that is larger than life. This will test and refine and strengthen our faith like nothing else is able to do. If you are in the midst of such a trial, God has asked me to encourage you to hold tightly to him. Here are two pictures from Scripture:

1. Carol Kent refers to the story in Luke 5:17-26, where four friends brought a paralyzed man to Jesus. They could not get close to him, so they tore a hole in the roof and lowered him down. Jesus not only healed the man, but forgave his sins (met his deepest needs). She notes several important lessons from the story. Here are three of them. First, friends were close enough to know the need and compassionate enough to care. Are we being that kind of friend to those around us, or are we mostly wrapped up in ourselves? Second, a stretcher cannot be carried by one person alone; it takes a small group of believers working together. And finally, she says, "Sooner or later we will all end up on a stretcher due to the circumstances of life. The question is, who has God provided to lift us, and will we allow them to do it?" Those of us who are not currently on the stretcher ought to be working

diligently, creatively, faithfully, to help carry those who are. That is how the body of Christ works.[29]

2. Exodus 13 and 14 describes the Israelites crossing the Red Sea. As the people were panicking in fear, God sent an east wind (Exodus 14:21). The wind was blowing east to west. The Israelites were on the west bank of the Red Sea. God started sending the solution before they could see it. He was in the process of answering before they could see the answer. In our own lives, God is at work long before we see him working to meet our needs and solve our problems.

Friends, all of us face major struggles at various times in our lives. If you are in the midst of a life-changing crisis, please take heart and cling to The Savior. If you are not currently in the midst of crisis, look around and find someone who is. Grab on to the stretcher and don't let go. Find creative ways to help, support, and encourage day by day and week by week. In either case, keep your eyes fixed on Almighty God and know without a doubt that he is already at work providing the answer to your problems and needs.

Be Baptized

In the book of Acts new believers (both Jews and Gentiles) sought to be baptized immediately after coming to believe the message of salvation, and receiving forgiveness through confession of sins. Some examples include the Ethiopian (Acts 8:30), Saul, later called Paul (Acts 9:18), Cornelius and his family (Acts 10:47). Why do we not see this New Testament pattern today? I think part of the reason is because people may attend church for a long time (even many years) before making a total-life commitment to Christ. Often when this happens, those individuals do not make a public declaration, letting others know what God has done in their hearts. When we as a church do not know where others are spiritually, how can we help one another to move forward? Another possible reason I see is lack of understanding about the purpose and significance of baptism. Let's search the Scriptures to see what they say about baptism (New Living Translation).

Who – All those who have confessed their sins (Matthew 3:6,11). Jesus set the example at the beginning of his earthly ministry (Mark 1:9-11). After his resurrection, he said, "Therefore, go and make disciples of all the nations, baptizing them in the name of the Father and the Son and the Holy Spirit" (Matthew 28:19).

What – Baptized with water (Matthew 3:11) as Jesus was in the Jordan River.

Why – John the Baptist was "preaching that people should be baptized to show that they had turned from their sins and turned to God to be forgiven." Jesus said, "Anyone who believes and is baptized will be saved, but anyone who refuses to believe will be condemned" (Mark 16:16).

When – "When you came to Christ, you were 'circumcised,' but not by a physical procedure. It was a spiritual procedure – the cutting away of your sinful nature. For you were buried with Christ when you were baptized. And with him you were raised to a new life because you trusted the mighty power of God, who raised Christ from the dead." (Colossians 2:11-12). Every example I find in Scripture was right after conversion.

Where – In any body of water (Jesus in the Jordan, most references in Acts just say in water).

How – "Since we have died to sin, how can we continue to live in it? Or have you forgotten that when we became Christians and were baptized to become one with Christ Jesus, we died with him?" Paul's letter to the believers in Rome describes how baptism parallels Jesus' death and resurrection (Romans 6:1-6). Being laid or (momentarily) buried under the water represents his death and is also a picture of the individual's dying to self. Rising up out of the water represents Christ's resurrection, and is also a picture of the believer's new life in him. Some choose sprinkling rather than immersion. What matters most is the motivation of the heart. All who have surrendered their lives to God's plans should make a personal decision to be baptized. Then, live every day in a way that exemplifies a new creation in Christ.

Have you noticed that Jesus did not waste time on fluff and gentle suggestions? He does not say, "You might want to be baptized." He says, "Repent and be baptized." It is a command to every believer. Paul clearly shows in both the Romans and Colossians passages above that baptism symbolizes being united with Jesus Christ in his death, and then being raised to new life in him. Baptism is a public, outward expression of a change that has taken place in the heart.

Those of us who have been baptized are not finished, but have only begun. We should be making disciples, teaching them and encouraging them to be baptized. Furthermore, John the Baptist told the people that the coming Savior would baptize them with the Holy Spirit (Mark 1:8). Jesus later said, "For John baptized with water, but in a few days you will be baptized with the Holy Spirit" (Acts 1:5). The children of God, having gone through the waters of baptism, should be baptized/anointed/filled with the Spirit of God. We should be led by him moment by moment. Only with his help can we truly live as new creations in Christ. Those who are filled with the Spirit exhibit the Fruit of the Spirit. Where are you today on this journey with the Savior?

A Different Perspective

Christians experience many of the same problems as unbelievers do. Whether your stressors are financial or physical, emotional or relational, the Apostle Paul has a suggestion for you – shift your focus. Now, if I tell you to do that, especially when I am not (maybe never have been) facing the problems you face, it would probably sound overly simplified and of little help. Paul, however, could certainly relate to major problems, and this worked for him.

"Therefore we do not lose heart. Though outwardly we are wasting away, yet inwardly we are being renewed day by day. For our light and momentary troubles are achieving for us an eternal glory that far outweighs them all. So we fix our eyes not on what is seen, but on what is unseen. For what is seen is temporary, but what is unseen is eternal" (2 Corinthians 4:16-18). What Paul referred to as "light and momentary troubles" included being imprisoned, flogged, beaten with rods, stoned nearly to death, shipwrecked, persecuted and going hungry (2 Corinthians 11:23-27).

The problems you face are probably different from Paul's list, but his solution will work for you. Laura Story has written a song that asks, "What if your blessings come thru raindrops, What if your healing comes thru tears? What if a thousand sleepless nights are what it takes to know you're near? What if the trials of this life are your mercies in disguise?"[30] If problems are looming like storm clouds blocking out your joy, I urge you to look away from the things that are seen, which are temporary and fix your eyes on God and the things that are eternal. In him alone are true joy, hope, peace, love, and purpose. My hope is that you will receive from him these beautiful gifts he longs to give you.

What Is Your Battle Cry?

"First grade, First grade, don't be shy! Stand and give your battle cry! V-I-C-T-O-R-Y that's the first grade battle cry!" Maybe you are as surprised as I was to discover that first graders have a battle cry, or even that they need one. Most of them can't remember all the letters and aren't sure what it spells, but they still stand up and yell during a pep assembly. Remarkable, isn't it? Issues of peer pressure and following the crowd are suddenly as large as life for parents of a six-year-old. As I helped my daughter learn to spell Victory (very loudly) I was left wondering about battle cries in general. After all, if first graders have one, perhaps the rest of us have one as well. In school, cheerleaders you don't know start teaching you your battle cry long before you have any clue what they are talking about. After school, consciously or subconsciously, you choose your own. I am not talking about a battle cry that you shout at the top of your lungs in a crowded auditorium. Rather, I am thinking about the theme song of your mind. What is the chorus that plays endlessly in your thoughts, and influences how you respond to situations? Do any of these sound familiar?

"Everybody is picking on me." When people disagree with your ideas or ways of doing things (as they inevitably will) do you resort to this "victim" mentality?

"God doesn't really care about me." Maybe it was a prayer that did not receive the answer you desired, or a heartache that God allowed to come into your life. Although you might never say this battle cry aloud, it echoes silently and colors your perceptions of everyday situations.

"I don't have time to reach out to other people." Each of us will be called to give an account one day of how we spent all that God gave to us – talents, money, and time.

"I am just too tired to try anymore." In our own strength, we can accomplish very little, and nothing that lasts. Jesus Himself said, "By myself I can do nothing" (John 5:30). Give your burdens to God and allow him to bring the solutions that only he can bring.

"So-and-so was right, I'll never amount to anything." God made you. He gives you value – worth the life of his Son. Zephaniah 3:17 says, "The Lord your God is with you, he is mighty to save. He will take great delight in you, he will quiet you with his love, he will rejoice over you with singing." Isn't that verse a beautiful gift?

"Nobody is going to tell me what to do." Nothing will lead to misery more quickly than pride and stubborn insistence on having my own way. It is not about my rights. It is about pleasing God and representing him well. "Submit to one another out of reverence for Christ" (Ephesians 5:21). Strangely enough, choosing this attitude actually brings the fulfillment we craved before we agreed to submit.

Maybe none of these fits you, but I am guessing you do have a recurring theme in your thinking. A battle cry is intended to inspire and encourage those going into the conflict. You are a soldier. Let God, not your enemy, choose your battle cry. "Take captive every thought to make it obedient to Christ" (2 Corinthians 10:5). Satan is very proficient at attacking and defeating us in our thoughts. Let's each choose a battle cry befitting someone who is in the Lord's army. Try this one: "P-E-A-C-E, God is in control!"

Then They Will Know

I remember reading one time about a woman who came to a marriage counselor ready to file for divorce. The counselor challenged her to give it just a few more months, making one or two changes, starting with giving her husband sincere compliments every day. She thought this was a very hard assignment, because she could only see the negative, but she agreed to try. Within just a few months she was not even considering divorce. Why? She said it was because she had discovered what a great guy she had

223

married.[31] Looking for the good helps us begin to see the good and bring out the best in another person – and everybody benefits! Deciding to have a heart of gratitude can change my whole outlook on life.

God gave Ezekiel messages about future events not only for Israel, but also for Egypt, Moab, Ammon, Tyre, and Edom. In the first thirty-nine chapters of Ezekiel, God uses the phrase, "Then they/you will know that I am the Lord," at least thirty-nine times. It seems that God really wanted to communicate this message. These words show the deep, passionate desire of God's heart. He wants those he created to know him. Since the dawn of time he has been trying to make himself known through nature, through Scripture, through miracles, and through his Son and his Spirit. Those who have learned to know him have brought him great joy. Genesis 5:24 tells us that "Enoch walked with God; then he was no more, because God took him away." God was so delighted with a man who sought to know him that he let him skip death and go straight to God. Can't you picture God's proud-father expression as he greeted Enoch?

How does a message on being a grateful person line up with living to know God? One of the best ways to get to know someone is to spend time with him/her. As we spend time in God's Word, and in fellowship with him through prayer, we begin to know him. What is God like? He is faithful to complete the work he started in your life (Philippians1:6). He is merciful and forgiving. He is patiently changing us. He is all powerful and nothing is too hard for him (Jeremiah 32:17). He is everywhere, all the time. He is all-knowing, far beyond the limited understanding afforded to mankind.

A heart of gratitude is what we all need. The more we seek to know him, the more we learn what he is like, and the more grateful we should be for all he has done. As we thank him daily for his personal participation in our lives, we grow closer to him. God longs for hearts that know him. Let us seek to express more gratitude in worship and our treatment of others, and to continually know him better through his Word as we discover ever more reasons to be grateful.

Come Alongside

In Jesus' final instructions before he returned to his Father he said, "Therefore, go and make disciples of all nations, baptizing them in the name of the Father and of the Son and of the Holy Spirit" (Matthew 28:19). We have all heard many times about our responsibility to win the world for Christ, based on this Great Commission. Our tendency, however, has been to focus on bringing lost people to a belief in Christ. We're making pretty slow work of it, but that was not even the assignment. Jesus said, "Go and make disciples." What is a disciple? A disciple is a follower, one who walks as Jesus walked. As people come to believe in Jesus as Savior and Lord, it is crucial that stronger believers come alongside them and train them to walk as Jesus did.

How do we make disciples? First, experienced believers need to build relationships with newer believers. Then we spend time showing and teaching them how to read the Bible, and how to pray. We study with them what the Word says about how to relate to others. We teach them what worship means and how to do it. We teach and demonstrate forgiveness and keeping no record of wrongs. Someone needs to explain baptism and communion. It is our responsibility to help each Christian develop a view of himself as a witness to the lost, and a discipler of others. This requires far more than one service on Sunday morning, and the involvement of many more people than just the pastors.

This is our responsibility. New believers, like new babies, need individual care. They need help to understand the Bible. They need help to learn how to hear God and to know his will. They need help to understand the role of the Holy Spirit in their lives. People who are not formally discipled are very unlikely to disciple anyone else. Pretty soon we have a whole church full of spiritually immature people and wonder why we struggle with petty disagreements. What else would you expect from a family of children?

Churches in the USA are closing faster than new ones are being planted. Contrast this to how God is working in other parts of the world. In Africa believers are planting new churches without buildings or projects or dollars from us. They are just disciples making disciples who make disciples. While we American

225

churches ponder new carpet, musical choices, and entertaining services, someone else is fulfilling the Great Commission without us. Researchers estimate that there are nearly one hundred million un-churched people in this country.[32] We aren't making much of a dent in that number.

If you are a believer, it is your responsibility to follow Christ's example of making disciples. If you are not trained and were never discipled, it is still your responsibility. Take whatever steps are needed to equip yourself to obey God. This is more important than breathing and there is no excuse which will sound plausible when God asks what you did to fulfill his great commission. If you are a relatively new believer, and are longing to have someone come alongside you and train you, please seek out someone in whom you see Jesus' love.

A Softened Heart

In his book, *Better Together*, Pastor Rick Warren discussed how Christians should be working to identify unbelievers around us to whom we should witness, or share about our personal faith in Christ. He encouraged us to pray for opportunities and then ask God to prepare the hearts of these people we are trying to reach. "Do you know how God softens hearts? He sends the rain. Anytime you see someone going through a storm in life, you can know God is softening that person's heart."[33] At any given time, many people around us seem to be experiencing the rain of circumstances.

For several years a group of us were praying, "Lord, give us this city. Please show us how to reach out to this community with your love and grace in a relevant way." It took a while for us to realize that God was answering in an unexpected way. He provided opportunities to hold funerals and funeral dinners for dozens of families with no home church. Each year, hundreds of people who do not regularly attend church come to a funeral and hear the message of salvation. We finally came to see that we needed to go beyond a service and luncheon, to minister to hurting people in the weeks and months after the funeral. After people have had a positive, compassionate encounter with the Savior, hearts are more open than they were before. We must show through our actions that God remembers their pain, and he cares. We must show that he is relevant in daily life, not just in a crisis. Anyone can call or send a card. Let's show the love of Christ today to hurting people through our continued presence, caring, and love.

A Life Worthy of the Gospel of Christ

Paul longed to return to the churches he had started in order to visit and encourage those whom he had led to the faith. Not knowing how long it might be before he would be released, he wrote letters to help them continue to grow in their faith. Paul's words to them clearly apply to us today. "Whatever happens, conduct yourselves in a manner worthy of the gospel of Christ" (Philippians 1:27a). Whatever happens, from family gatherings to the way we spend money to the way we drive in heavy traffic, our actions and attitudes should be worthy of the gospel of Christ. What does it mean to "conduct yourselves in a manner worthy of the gospel of Christ" as Paul commanded? A few verses later he stated, "Your attitude should be the same as that of Christ Jesus" (Philippians 2:6). No pressure, but the attitude and the mind of Christ should be evident in us at all times. That is the goal. "Continue to work out your salvation with fear and trembling, for it is God who works in you to will and to act according to his good purpose. Do everything without complaining or arguing so that you may become blameless and pure, children without fault in a crooked and depraved generation, in which you shine like stars in the universe" (Philippians 2:12b-15). It is clear from this passage that the bar is set very high in terms of godly living – too high, in fact, for us to achieve. Notice that it is God who works in you to will and to act according to his good purpose. We need God's help to live with the attitude of Christ Jesus. Paul told the believers in Galatia, "So I say, live by the Spirit, and you will not gratify the desires of the sinful nature. For the sinful nature desires what is contrary to the Spirit, and the Spirit what is contrary to the sinful nature. They are in conflict with each other, so that you do not do what you want" (Galatians 5:16,17). Living a life that honors God is only possible as we learn to let the Spirit direct our attitudes and actions.

227

Conducting ourselves in a manner worthy of the gospel of Christ is a lofty and challenging goal. It involves making conscious choices to honor him. Philippians 4:4-8 gives us some helpful instruction for living out our faith:

- We are to rejoice in our Savior, choosing not to worry.
- We are to approach God with thanksgiving even as we ask him for help.
- We are to receive his peace which defies understanding.
- Finally, we are to continually keep setting and re-setting our minds on those things that are healthy and wholesome and positive.

I encourage you to set your mind on Christ all day every day. That is our only hope for living a life worthy of him, which will allow us to "shine like stars in the universe" in our depraved generation.

As For Me and My House

Near the end of his life, Joshua declared to the people, "As for me and my house, we will serve the Lord" (Joshua 24:15). Notice the sequencing of the verse. "As for me" comes before "and my house." In parenting and discipling and teaching, I think many of us tend to jump right to the second part. We recognize our responsibility to train up our children and others who are younger in their faith to serve the Lord. It seems easy and convenient to forget that it starts with me.

Several years ago a friend told me that she had learned that the woman sets the emotional tone for the whole household. I think she was right, but I didn't like it. If I am positive, upbeat, with my mind set on Christ, my whole household reflects it. If peace reigns in my life, my family will see it and experience some of that peace. Unfortunately, the reverse is also true. When I am stressed, discouraged, and irritable it seems to contaminate the rest of the family. Women, we need to make knowing and serving the Lord our first priority. A dirty house is not nearly as serious as a dirty heart.

Men, you have a crucial role to play as well. The Bible tells us that men are the Spiritual head of the home "Fathers, do not exasperate your children; instead, bring them up in the training and instruction of the Lord" (Ephesians 6:4). Talk about a huge responsibility! Men, the tone of Christ-centeredness in the home depends on you. Things like consistent family devotions with Bible reading and prayer, regular service attendance, and godly priorities for use of time and money all ought to come from your leadership. Dads, your role is absolutely crucial in the spiritual development of your children.

If you do not yet have a family, God has given you this time to draw as close to him as humanly possible. I have found that once you have a family, other demands on your time will make this far more difficult to do. Make the most of your time. If your children are grown and gone, you can still influence them and others God brings across your path through a life and a home fixed firmly upon the Savior.

When we say in the words of Joshua, "As for me and my house, we will serve the Lord" let each of us remember to make serving the Lord the first priority for ourselves and pray for our families to follow our lead.

Forecasted Storms

The past several years have brought multiple major hurricanes, deadly tornadoes, and unusually severe snow storms across the nation. Even more severe disasters have occurred in Japan, Haiti, and elsewhere. It leaves anxious people wondering how many more severe storms we will see in the coming months. The building of stronger levees, and advances in forecasting technology can help citizens to be more prepared, but nothing can be humanly done to prevent these storms.

Forecasters warn of destruction to cities when storms come and levees break. God warns of destruction of lives when deserved judgment comes and there is no wall of prayer protection. "I looked for a man among them who would build up the wall and stand before me in the gap on behalf of the land so I would not have to destroy it, but I found none (Ezekiel 22:30). Throughout the book of Ezekiel our Sovereign Lord repeatedly warned Jerusalem about the coming destruction. Why was God angry with them? He identified at least three major faults. First, giving other things first place in their lives (idolatry); second, failure to observe a Sabbath rest and keep it holy; and third, lack of justice and compassion for the poor. Unfortunately, the first two could also be said of churches and believers in America, even you and me. Many of us struggle to keep God first while giving him smaller and smaller chunks of our time and attention. Sunday for many is spent focused on self (what I want or "need" to do) rather than on God (how he would like to spend this day with me).

The actual judgments prophesied in the book of Ezekiel were specific to those people at that time. Those are not prophesies against America, but our God is unchanging. He is the same yesterday, today, and forever (Hebrews 13:8). The things he hated in the days of the Old Testament are the same things he hates today.

The natural disasters we are experiencing may or may not be a form of judgment on an increasingly evil nation. I don't know. What I do know is that they should serve as a wake-up call to those of us who call ourselves believers in Christ. Today is the day to make deliberate changes in our lives. Each of us could and should take steps to get rid of things in our lives that compete with God for our attention and affection. Most of us could do better to keep the Sabbath holy. We don't often see this as very important, but God does. Five times in Ezekiel 20 he mentions desecration of the Sabbath as a reason for judgment. Woe to us if we heed not his warnings.

Finally, we need to stand in the gap through prayer. Faithful, earnest, concentrated prayer is the hardest discipline in the world to cultivate because it is the most powerful. My brother has shared a quote he learned in college that goes something like this, "I don't have a gun, I don't have a knife or a spear, I don't have a bow and arrow, all I have is this nuclear weapon." We tend to think of prayer as a last resort when we can't really do anything. Actually, prayer is the single most powerful action any human being can ever take. Let each of us begin today to purge our lives of evil and stand in the gap for this great nation of ours.

A Warm Welcome

Once upon a time there was a family of five. Like most families they were very busy, with two girls in college and a son in high school. They weren't perfect, but they loved each other and laughed a lot. There came a day when they felt God leading them to open their hearts and their home to three young foster boys in need of a family. They chose to allow God to completely change their future, from looking toward an empty nest and freedom to travel, to starting over with changing diapers.

Paul tells believers, "Do not conform any longer to the pattern of this world, but be transformed by the renewing of your mind. Then you will be able to test and approve what God's will is – his good, pleasing, and perfect will" (Romans 12:2). This family allowed their minds to be transformed and their lives to be turned topsy turvy, as they began making plans to be approved as foster parents looking toward adoption. They grew to know and love the three boys, choosing to obey Scripture's instruction to care for the fatherless. This family of five waited months for paperwork to be processed, all the while growing more and more excited about the hope of becoming a family of eight. One thing was clear – if God opened the doors for these boys to be placed in this family, they would be received with open arms and open hearts.

Friends, you and I are like those foster children. We are battered and scarred. We've known rejection and heartache and loss. Tragedies happen. The world can be a scary, confusing place. We long to be free from all this pain, and go to a home where we'll be loved unconditionally. Did you know that Jesus our Savior, in a far greater way than the parents described above, is excited for us to come and live with him? He told his disciples that he was going to prepare a place for them. John 17 records Jesus' prayer just before he was arrested. He said, "Father, I want those you have given me to be with me where I am, and to see my glory, the glory you have given me because you loved me before the creation of the world" (John 17:24). Jesus wants those who believe in him to be with him and to see his glory. He longs to bring us to a home that will be immeasurably better than we have known before. He waits with great anticipation for the day when you and I will move in to be with him forever. This thought blesses my heart beyond words.

When they look at those little boys, the foster family doesn't see all the work, the messes, the arguing, the expense. They see people made and loved by God. In the same way, when our Heavenly Father looks at us, he sees beyond our failures, our selfish immaturity, and our scars. He sees his precious children, and he loves us. What a beautiful picture.

My sister and brother-in-law, described above, are not God, and their home is not heaven. They are just people choosing to walk in obedience, whatever the cost. Over a period of months, as they prepared their hearts, their minds, and their home for this monumental shift, they learned of another sibling not-yet-born, that would also need a home. Against all logical sense, they once again placed themselves in God's hands, saying, "Lord if you see this as the best place for that new little one to grow up, we trust you and we are available." They got the call late Tuesday night: "Your foster care license has been approved. By the way, that new baby was born today. Can you pick him up on Thursday? The other three boys will be moved in next week." Most of us, myself included, cannot even imagine such upheaval in our lives. But God always has enough love for one more, and he has given this family enough love for one more. In his beautiful way, our loving Heavenly Father will also welcome home those who are yet to be born into his family. As you contemplate what obedience to God will look like in your own life, I encourage you to let your wounded heart be warmed by thoughts of the warm welcome that awaits believers in heaven.

Veterans of the Faith

Veterans' Day brings a sense of pride and gratitude as we remember generations of people who have served in America's armed forces. Soldiers have fought and worked hard, yearned for victory over the enemy, but many have returned home from the battlefield without seeing that victory. Some have been wounded. Others served their allotted time and were re-assigned state-side. Some never came home at all. Weary, lonely soldiers labored and longed for an end to the war. They endured harsh conditions and all types of struggles. Yet when the end came, even when victory was won, most did not get to witness the peace agreement directly.

Hebrews 11 provides a list of some of the veterans of the Christian faith who were waiting and longing for victory. Some are very familiar like Abraham and Moses. Others are less known, like Enoch and Barak. Some are not named at all, and yet they were faithful to their God. Many of these heroes of the faith faced terrible persecution, poverty, and isolation (Hebrews 11:34-38). "These were all commended for their faith, yet none of them received what had been promised. God planned something better for us so that only together with us would they be made perfect. Therefore since we are surrounded by such a great cloud of witnesses, let us throw off everything that hinders and the sin that so easily entangles, and let us run with perseverance the race marked out for us" (Hebrews 11:39-12:1).

Like soldiers who never got to witness the victory, men and women of God in the Old Testament were waiting for the promised Messiah, but died before they got to see him. After Jesus had returned to heaven, a new generation of heroes of the faith rose up. The apostles of the first century were followed by countless other men and women of God, veterans of a great war in the spiritual realm. Even down to this very day, people of God are living faithful, godly lives and pointing others toward the Savior. The writer of Hebrews described those heroes of the faith who had gone on before as "a great cloud of witnesses" that surrounds us. Their example challenges us to live every day as soldiers of the cross.

While members of our military fight, here at home life goes on more or less as usual. They risk their lives while we focus on grocery shopping and kids' homework. Some of us go days and even weeks without giving any thought to the battles being waged around the globe. In the same way, some people who consider themselves Christians go days or weeks at a time without thinking about God or about the continual attacks of the enemy. Although all believers in Christ Jesus are to be trained, prepared, and equipped to take a stand against the enemy of our souls (Galatians 6), many spend no time at all in studying the Word of God or seeking his face.

Brothers and sisters, we are to be the heroes, veterans of the faith for this generation. Since we are God's plan for reaching the world with the good news of Salvation in Jesus Christ, "Let us throw off everything that hinders and the sin that so easily entangles, and let us run with perseverance the race marked out for us." Let us not be the generation that drops the baton, lest our children grow up without knowing God or all that he has done for his people (Judges 2).

One day evil will lose its grip on the people of God. One day we will see the victory for which soldiers of the cross are longing. On that day, will you be listed as active-duty, serving the Commander of the Universe with total abandonment? I am sure that on that day every one of us will wish that he/she had done more and sacrificed more for him. Let's live that way today and every day. Veterans of the faith, I exhort you to keep fighting.

Who is Missing?

In my teens and throughout my twenties I had a close friend named Tara. Although we were two years apart in age, we attended the same youth group at church, were part of the same Bible quiz team, and spent a lot of time together in a group of friends. We ended up attending the same college. Over the years we grew in our faith and shared with one another the things God was teaching us. She was a joy to me. After we both got married we moved apart and lost touch. I haven't heard from Tara in years. My spirit misses her.

Friends, that is the way it should be among Christians. All of us together form the bride of Christ. Groups of believers that worship together as a church or a family of faith form a body. 1 Corinthians 12 describes how individuals within a church are to relate to one another as parts that together make up one body. Each part exists in relationship to the other parts and all are to work together cohesively, led by the Holy Spirit. In the body, we should care deeply about what is happening in one another's lives. "If one part suffers, every part suffers with it; if one part is honored, every part rejoices with it" (1 Corinthians 12:26). We cannot support each other the way this Scripture teaches if we are so absorbed in our own lives that we are oblivious to the suffering – or the rejoicing – of other members of the body.

In the decade that we have been in church ministry, one of the things I have found most difficult is figuring out how to respond to people who stop attending the church. Most of us have left a particular church at one time or another, often with valid reason, but we all handle it differently. Some people start missing Sundays occasionally, and then gradually miss more often than they attend. Others stop suddenly. Those of us left should ask ourselves how we should respond to those who left. Some of them want to be left alone and interpret any questions as a guilt trip. Some people are at the opposite end of the spectrum – wondering why nobody cares enough to even ask where they have been. The problem is that there is no way to tell which response a person wants. Somehow, we are just supposed to know.

Imagine a person facing the probable amputation of a limb. A person in that situation would pursue every possible alternative treatment, seeing amputation as an extreme last resort. People within the church are to be connected to one another like parts of a body. Losing a part of the church body is therefore like an amputation. It is not the sole responsibility of the church leaders to keep track of every single person who attends the church, and try to chase down every person whose attendance is sporadic. That responsibility and privilege is shared by every member of the faith family. All of us need to move beyond our comfortable, established relationships within the body and reach out to begin to know others who are somewhat on the fringe of the family. On the other hand, those on the edges of the congregation who long to be a part of the body carry the responsibility of reaching out to build connections. Everybody needs to know that he/she is a valued part of the family.

Let all of us reach out to some others within the church, learning to know them so that we know when somebody is suffering or somebody is rejoicing. This will not insure that nobody will ever leave the church again. They will. But those who leave will know that the church family cares about them. The body will be a healthy unit, pleasing to our God. That is my prayer for my own church and for the greater Christian church across the globe – that we will glorify our God.

A Treasure I Can't Lose

Somehow I lost my diamond engagement ring. Just a few weeks later my wedding band slipped off my finger and I never felt it. I was certain it couldn't slide off. It had never come close before. It makes me feel a little sick every time I think about it.

235

Thoughts of losing some of my greatest material treasures led me to be even more thankful for the eternal treasures that I can never lose. A wedding ring is a symbol of a covenant relationship between husband and wife. Similarly, in the covenant relationship between God and each Christian, the Holy Spirit is the seal that marks that relationship. Consider the following passages:

- "And you also were included in Christ when you heard the word of truth, the gospel of your salvation. Having believed, you were marked in him with a seal, the promised Holy Spirit, who is a deposit guaranteeing our inheritance until the redemption of those who are God's possession – to the praise of his glory" (Ephesians 1:13, 14).
- "Now it is God who makes both us and you stand firm in Christ. He anointed us, set his seal of ownership on us, and put his Spirit in our hearts as a deposit, guaranteeing what is to come" (2 Corinthians 1:21, 22).

God has given us the Holy Spirit as a deposit, guaranteeing what is to come. Although no human can see the Holy Spirit, his work is clearly evident in the lives of believers. Through his ministries of giving counsel and comfort, as well as bringing conviction, he makes himself known to believers. As we live every day according to his leading, the fruit of the Spirit becomes evident in our lives: love, joy, peace, patience, kindness, goodness, faithfulness, gentleness, and self-control. The evidence of the Holy Spirit in the life of a believer is the clear mark of our relationship with Almighty God. Unlike a wedding ring, it can never be unintentionally lost. The Holy Spirit in our hearts helps us know God and he will never take back that which he has given to us.

As I have been reminded that the treasures of this world are temporary, I give thanks all the more fervently for the treasure of the Holy Spirit whom I cannot lose. He is working in my life and he serves as God's guarantee of that which is to come – an eternity more rich, more sweet, more filled with delight than anything I can imagine. Thank You, Dear God.

Be a Stump Nursery

When my husband and I visited the Grass River Natural Area we saw several examples of a Stump Nursery. Within the stumps of White Pine Trees, new seedlings had begun to grow. Some have grown into mature trees by now. The decaying stump produces rich nutrients in the soil that nourish the young tree and give it a strong start to life. I am not sure if the seedlings were direct descendants of the older tree, or were from seeds dropped by a nearby tree. This is a beautiful picture of the opportunity we have to create an environment that will bless and help those who follow – even those outside our own families, and those we may never meet.

Consider Benjamin Rush. He was one of the founding fathers of this nation, who not only signed the constitution, but had a lot of input in its development. Benjamin Rush started the Sunday School movement in this new country, and also established the Bible Society.[34] Many of us have never studied this man, yet he has had an influence on our lives. Like a stump nursery, he helped to create an environment that would foster healthy growth beyond his lifespan. One important difference is that he did it intentionally, whereas with trees it happens naturally by God's design.

Teachers, neighbors, coaches, extended family members and others can have a powerful influence on future generations. What can we be doing to create an environment that will benefit others, now and in the years to come? I believe we, like Benjamin Rush of a previous generation, must fix our eyes on the goal rather than on our own comfort. We tend to allow the "crises" of life to so consume our time and energy that we rarely give any thought to the kind of legacy we want to leave behind. How do you want to be remembered by your co-workers, your neighbors, those with whom you have served on various committees? I'm afraid we're content to think that people would remember us as nice people. What good is it to be thought of as a nice person? What does that even mean? I want so much more! I want to be seen as a person who reflects Jesus! I want to be a person with whom God speaks, as Moses was (Numbers 12:8) or a person after God's own heart as David was (1 Samuel 13:14). I want to create an environment where nobody wonders where my allegiance lies – not because I shove it down people's throats, but because his joy and love and peace are evident in every area of my life. I want to give myself completely, like the apostles of the first century, to making disciples and teaching them how to know God personally, as we have been invited to do. I would far rather do that than to pile up money or earthly treasures for my children. What about you? What goals are you striving to reach? What kind of message does your life send to those who interact with you on a regular basis? I pray that your desire is to honor God with every deed, every word, every thought for as long as you live. What greater legacy could we hope to leave?

A Lame Offering

When God gave Moses instructions about sacrifices that the Hebrew people were to bring, he specified that they must be male animals without defect (Leviticus 1:3,10). By the time of Malachi the prophet, however, people brought lame and blind animals to offer. The Jews had returned to their homeland after the exile and finished rebuilding the wall and the temple, with God's help. The people observed the laws and rituals given by Moses, but in a half-hearted way. Their hearts were not devoted to God. Malachi wrote in a question-and-answer format, suggesting that the people did not even see anything wrong with what they were doing. The problem with offering defective sacrifices wasn't so much about the offerings themselves as it was about hearts that dishonored God. Like tossing him their worthless scraps, they were showing utter contempt for His Name while still going through the motions of obedience. God said he would rather have them just close the temple doors and sacrifice nothing at all (Malachi 1:6, 10).

Friends, what is the message here for us? We are not bringing animals to be sacrificed, but are we truly giving to God our very best, our all? Or are we, like the Jews of old, just tossing him scraps we don't need? What kind of things do we bring to his altar? Let's ask ourselves some honest questions about that which we offer to God:

- Time – is he first and allowed to direct the activities of my days, or does he just get a few minutes of prayer when I need something, and a couple hours on Sunday if I'm not too busy? Jesus said to do the will of God was his very food for the day (John 4:34).

- Bible study – am I satisfied with just going to church, and listening to praise music or am I actually seeking, studying, and working toward knowing him more intimately?
- Witness – do I just try to be a nice person or do I look and listen for opportunities to share with others what God has done for me?
- Treasures - have I truly placed on the altar that which I value most – my family, my dreams and goals, my earthly treasures, my priorities?

If we are only giving him what we can afford to do without, we are offering blind and lame sacrifices. He would rather we didn't even go through the motions because it shows such contempt for the One whom we call our Lord and our King. Sacrifice involves death and blood and pain and loss. The sacrifices offered in the Old Testament were to be perfect and without blemish because they were a symbol of the perfect Lamb of God who was to be sacrificed for the sins of mankind. To offer a defective animal not only showed great disrespect for the One to whom the offering was made, but it also devalued the representation of the Messiah. This was no trivial matter to God.

On this side of the cross, to offer God our leftover time, energy, money, and treasures indicates how little we value that Lamb of God who died for us. If we truly knew God, truly understood how indescribably awesome and holy and powerful he is, we would worship him with every cell we possess. To offer less would indeed be a lame sacrifice.

Experts estimate that Malachi, the last book of our modern Bible, was written in 430 B.C. After that it was more than four hundred years until the Messiah was born, 400 years without a recorded message from Jehovah. I wonder if God had nothing more to say to people who valued him so little. So we have to ask ourselves, are we hearing from him? How much do we value him, as reflected by that which we offer to him? Let each one of us echo King David, refusing to offer to the Lord that which costs us little or nothing (2 Samuel 24:24).

Transformers

My son enjoys playing with Transformers, little plastic toys with moving parts that can be re-arranged to look like either a vehicle or a robot. As I try to make the transformation, I am impressed by the minds who imagine and make such toys. But, so much more impressive than a toy maker, is the One who can transform a person's life.

A dear friend shared her story of how God forgave her sins and completely transformed her life thirty-five years ago. Within the space of three months God had helped to reconcile her marriage, and drawn her family of three unto himself. From that time forward everything changed and they went in a totally different direction than they had been headed.

Friends, that kind of transformation is what the Christian life is supposed to be. The book of Acts records some of the ways the Holy Spirit worked in the lives of the apostles after Jesus ascended to heaven. These same men who had deserted and/or denied Jesus when he was arrested became powerful evangelists. After Jesus had been crucified, and rose from the dead, "He showed himself to these men and gave many convincing proofs that he was alive. He appeared to them over a period of forty days and spoke about the kingdom of God. On one occasion, while he was eating with them, he gave them this command: 'Do not leave Jerusalem, but wait for the gift my Father promised, which you have heard me speak about. For John baptized with water, but in a few days you will be baptized with the Holy Spirit'" (Acts 1:3-5). This second baptism happened on the day of Pentecost (Acts 2). After the Holy Spirit had come upon the believers, they began to speak boldly, in many languages, explaining the good news of Salvation through Jesus. Peter preached to a crowd and about 3,000 were added to the number of believers that day. Later, Peter and John spoke boldly to the ruling council about Jesus and his power (Acts 2). Believers who had been forgiven and filled with the Holy Spirit, shared their possessions and gave what they had to help those in need (Acts 2). When the apostles were arrested, they were miraculously released from jail, and then spoke again before the council. The disciples were flogged for preaching about Jesus. Rather than feeling sorry for themselves, they left "rejoicing because they had been counted worthy of suffering disgrace for the Name" (Acts 5:41). Stephen, a disciple about whom we had previously heard very little, became a powerful orator. "All who were sitting in the Sanhedrin looked intently at Stephen, and they saw that his face was like the face of an angel" (Acts 6:15). When he was subsequently stoned to death, he asked God not to hold the sin against his accusers (Acts 7:60). Later on, Saul, the persecutor-of-Christians, had an encounter with Jesus through the Spirit and became an international church planter and eventually wrote much of the New Testament. These men's lives were completely and powerfully changed by the work of the Holy Spirit.

Brothers and sisters, we who have repented of our sins and received forgiveness in Jesus have that same powerful Holy Spirit. Are our lives being transformed like the apostles of the first century? If so, we ought to be giving public testimony, sharing with others what God has done for us. If no change is evident, we need to prayerfully search our hearts and ask why not? "Therefore, if anyone is in Christ, he is a new creation; the old has gone, the new has come!" (2 Corinthians 5:17). If I am not a new creation, is it possible that I am not really in Christ? If you and I are truly surrendered, and Jesus is really Lord, we should be living transformed lives. Let us be seeking him always, and allowing him to do all that he desires in us.

There is a Limit

In September 2011 Hurricane Irene was blamed for at least forty-six deaths in thirteen states. Some 9.6 million customers lost power due to the storm. Still, it was not as destructive as it could have been. Of the millions of people in the effected area, most experienced nothing more severe than the inconvenience of a few days without electricity. Some people suffered major damage to homes and businesses, but escaped with their lives and their loved ones. Even a storm as powerful as a hurricane has limits it cannot surpass. One remarkable photograph captured the very distinct line of clouds marking the edge of the storm. The storm had to stay within distinct boundaries.

In the book of Job, God describes his great power over his creation. He "shut up the sea behind doors" (Job 38:8). He "fixed limits for it and set its doors and bars in place." He said, "This far you may come and no farther; here is where your proud waves halt" (Job 38:10,11). God also mentioned his storehouses for snow and hail (Job 38:22). God sets limits that his creation cannot cross. Even though storms and floods seem massive from our perspective, God is immeasurably bigger and stronger. Our hope is in him.

The prophet Jeremiah spent many years warning the Jews of impending disaster because of their unfaithfulness to God. The national leaders and the common folks alike rejected his message, but the prophecies were fulfilled. The army of Babylon swept through the land. The walls were torn down, buildings were burned, citizens were put to death or dragged away as captives. The entire nation was in shambles. Only the poorest of the poor were left in land. Jeremiah witnessed the terrible wrath of God upon his beloved homeland, and he was devastated. The book of Lamentations records Jeremiah's cries of grief for the nation which had been all but annihilated. His people were starving, overcome with despair. Even though there was no flicker of hope, nothing positive to cling to, Jeremiah set his hope on God. In the midst of lamenting the destruction of Jerusalem, he said, "Yet this I call to mind and therefore I have hope: Because of the Lord's great love we are not consumed, for his compassions never fail. They are new every morning; great is your faithfulness. I say to myself, 'The Lord is my portion; therefore I will wait for him.' The Lord is good to those whose hope is in him, to the one who seeks him; it is good to wait quietly for the salvation of the Lord" (Lamentations 3:21-26).

Sometimes God allows storms of unimaginable severity in our lives. Not all of them are storms of nature that wipe out homes and neighborhoods. There are storms of depression and loneliness, painful betrayals in relationships, insurmountable financial woes, incurable diseases, and so many more. In the storms of life we sometimes feel nearly overwhelmed by circumstances. When life seems to be out of control, and the floods threaten to sweep us away, we must remember that our God is far more powerful than our crisis. The same God who sets limits on the waves, sets limits on the storms in our lives too. No storm ever gets out of control for him. When there is nothing else to do, and we are tempted to despair, that is the time to "wait quietly for the salvation of the Lord." If you are facing an overwhelming storm today, choose faith, my friend. God's compassions never fail. Truly, they are new every morning. He is faithful. He is utterly incapable of being less than faithful. He is more powerful than the storm, and he cares for his own. May God Bless you as you walk with him.

Put on the Brakes

My husband is a very good driver. The problem is, he doesn't drive like me. Of course he doesn't see that as a problem. He is more trusting than I am that slower vehicles ahead of us will move out of the way before we get there. There are times that I wish I had a brake pedal on the passenger side. I am sure that when my kids are learning to drive I'll really wish for that extra brake pedal.

In life, even more than in travel, we often wish for a way to slow things down. In the spring we look forward to the slower, more relaxed pace of summer. In the summer we are so busy that we look forward to the slower, fixed routine of fall. In the fall as we prepare for the holidays, we talk about how things will settle down after the first of the year. I have concluded that life is not going to slow down any time soon. When it does, it seems to come to a screeching halt rather than a gradual deceleration. If life is not going to slow down (as we somehow keep expecting) then we are going to have to find ways to prioritize that which is – or should be – most important. It turns out, when it comes to life, you do have a brake pedal on your side. You choose to use it when you say "no" to excess activity.

When we reach our final destination what will God say about the way we have lived our lives? Are we spending our time doing the things he has commanded us to do, or are we filling our moments, hours, and days with things of temporary worth? As I look back at a very long week, filled with an overabundance of activities, what have I accomplished that is of eternal value? Is even one person closer to my beloved Jesus because of the way I've spent my 168-hour week? In all honestly, I am not sure and it troubles me deeply.

Some of us, myself included, need to re-evaluate the activities to which we are giving ourselves and realign our schedules according to that which we believe is most important. Each of us has the right and the responsibility to determine how we will spend our time. Each of us has a brake pedal. Each of us will be called to account for the way we have used these hours. We must choose to slow down and clear out our schedules when our days get too busy.

Just doing less, however, will not bring joy and fulfillment, nor will it bring glory to the Savior. So what will bring him honor? What does God want us to be doing any way? Reverend Steve Jones said, "What do you give the God who has everything? You give him what he asks for. He asked for disciples." Are we living in obedience? Are we spending ourselves to help others to know him personally? God longs for his children to seek his face. He longs for us to be still, to focus our hearts on him in worship. He calls us to be still and to wait on him. When we take the time to hear his heart, he brings our hearts into line with his. Let us ask God to teach us to spend our days as Jesus did, led every moment by God's plans. "Those who live in accordance with the Spirit have their minds set on what the Spirit desires" (Romans 8:5b).

What's Your Name?

As my nieces and nephews were being born, I gave each one a unique nickname. These were names used only by me, signifying a special relationship with each one. Some of those names stuck, and others I never use any more. Such is the nature of nicknames.

The last chapters of Ezekiel (given while the Jews were still in exile) describe a vision of a new temple in a restored land. The new city is not called Jerusalem, but rather, "The name of the city from that time on will be: The LORD is There" (Ezekiel 48:35). What a great name. The very next chapter is the beginning of Daniel, and gives the account of God allowing Nebuchadnezzer to conquer Judah and take Jews into exile. He enrolled some of the most promising young men into a training school in order to raise them up in the culture and thinking of Babylon. As part of this indoctrination, their names were changed. These new names were intended to help create a new identity, encouraging them to leave behind the traditions and beliefs of their homeland. Hananiah meant, "whom Jehovah hath favored." His name was changed to Shadrach, to reflect the sun-god. Mishael meant "who is comparable to God?" but his name was changed to Meshach, in reference to the Babylonian goddess, Sheshach. Azariah meant, "whom Jehovah helps." His new name, Abednego identified him as a servant of the fire god.[35]

The young Hebrew men were given names to honor the idols of Babylon, but they did not allow the culture to define their identity. These young men maintained their devotion to the God of Israel. Our culture, like ancient Babylon, is one of self-indulgence.Christians have been given names like Irrelevant, Inconsistent, Judgmental, and Intolerant. We, like those men of long ago, must decide whether we will allow those names to define us.

One day, God will give each of his children a new name, known only to us (Revelation 2:17). For now, however, maybe he has temporary nicknames. God described Job as "blameless and upright" (1:8). When Jesus met Nathaniel he said, "Here is a true Israelite in whom there is nothing false" (John 1:47). Perhaps he would call you "faithful in affliction" or "an unflickering flame in the darkness." Maybe God calls you "a man after his own heart" or maybe he just calls you "Friend."

Both the world and our God desire to define our identity. Each of us surrenders to one or the other. Who is defining your life? Personally, I long to be known by the description of that great city called, "The Lord is there." I long for my life to be so consumed with love for Jesus that people see him in me. I don't want a nickname of Bible Thumper, or "Holier than thou." I just want to be known as a girl who loves Jesus and shows his love to everyone around me. Oh to have the words, The Lord is There, describe Lynn Adams! That is the nickname I am striving to live up to, in honor of my Savior.

Winter

In this part of the country winter is breath-taking both in beauty and in temperature. Special care is needed to keep things functioning properly. Bodies need extra layers. Icy surfaces need salt or sand. Roads, driveways, and sometimes roofs need snow removal. Travel requires caution and extra time. With the proper precautions, however, it can be a delightful season. Walking, sledding, skiing, snowmobiling, snow-shoeing, and ice-fishing are some of the ways people enjoy the wonder of winter.

Seasons that require extra time and effort sometimes occur in our Spiritual lives as well. When the storms of life blow, or when the heart feels cold and empty, it is time to pull back and re-group. It may mean taking a break from some commitments in order to make time for quiet, personal reflection. Whatever the temperature outside, seeking intimacy with the Savior brings warmth and refreshing to the soul. It also brings a renewed sense of direction and purpose. These times of slowing down can be among the richest experiences in the life of a Christian.

Snow On The Branches

The beauty of winter in northern Michigan is breath-taking. I continually marvel at how the Ultimate Artist decorates every tree limb so perfectly. If man were trying to blanket the world in white, it would look quite different. In his endless quest for efficiency, he would dump large blobs in strategic areas. God, on the other hand, patiently works flake by flake, hours on end, to create his masterpiece.

The Bible tells us that God makes himself known through his creation (Romans 1:20). The way he patiently clothes each branch in snow parallels the way he patiently clothes each area of a Christian's life in righteousness. Isaiah said, "I delight greatly in the Lord; my soul rejoices in my God. For he has clothed me with garments of salvation and arrayed me in a robe of righteousness, as a bridegroom adorns his head like a priest, and as a bride adorns herself with her jewels" (Isaiah 61:10). From the day a person gives God control of his life until the day he dies, God is doing the work of sanctification – making him holy.

He desires to have every area of my life be a reflection of him . . . the thoughts I dwell on, the way I speak, the way I spend time and money, the way I act when things go wrong, everything. Philippians 1:6 tells us that "He who began a good work in you will be faithful to complete it." There is, however, a catch. God will only clothe in righteousness those branches of my life that have been wholly submitted to him. Some of us who are new to the faith have a light dusting of snow. Others should have a much thicker blanket. As we grow in him, he reveals areas of our lives which need to be surrendered. If we refuse, that area will not reflect him. Like one bare branch on a tree otherwise blanketed in snow, so one un-surrendered area of life is very obvious to people nearby.

Let each of us go to the Savior and ask him, "What do you see in my life? A tendency to worry? Unresolved anger? Misuse of finances? Pride? Self-pity? An ungrateful attitude?" As we choose to surrender, he will begin to work, bringing healing, wholeness, and righteousness – for his glory.

The Count Date

When I was working in the public schools, there was significant emphasis on the "Fourth Friday Count." The state would determine financial disbursements to each school district based on the total attendance for that particular day. Some schools provided pizza parties and other incentives to make sure kids came on the fourth Friday of September. This count had major ramifications, and was taken very seriously. In Special Education, similar importance was placed on the first of December. Reimbursement for the extra cost of educating students with special needs was based on the number of such students with up-to-date paperwork by this date. The last week of November was always filled with meetings regarding children who might qualify for services.

Educators take these count dates very seriously, and plan for them continually but there is a far more important count date. Those of us who have read our Bibles know that there will come a day when God will take a roll call. Those who have made him Lord of their lives, and have had their sins forgiven will be invited to spend eternity with him. Since none of us knows when that date will be (Acts 1:7) we must always be waiting and watching, ready for his return (Luke 12:37). One day each one of us will be called to give an account of the way we have lived. May the number of those around the world who are ready and looking forward to that day be continually growing. I urge you to be sure, above all else, that your sins are forgiven and you are in right standing with God.

Getting Ready

Picture this scene. It is Sunday morning. The children are fed and dressed. The living room is a mess. Hair and teeth are brushed. Squabbles and tattling steadily increase in volume and urgency. A parent rushes about finalizing preparations, telling kids to be kind to one another. Upon command the dour-faced parade traipses slowly to the family vehicle. At last everyone is ready to go to church and worship God. This scenario may not exactly fit the routine at your house, but unless you live alone I am guessing it is somewhat familiar. On any given Sunday, how many families growl at each other all the way to church and then put on happy faces as they walk in to worship?

Part of my preparation for worship service should include examining my heart to make sure things between God and me are as they should be. Psalm 139:23-24 says, "Search me, O God, and know my heart; test me and know my anxious thoughts. See if there is any offensive way in me, and lead me in the way everlasting." A heart that is not right with God cannot really worship. One difficult Sunday morning, God reminded me of Matthew 5:23-24, "Therefore, if you are offering your gift at the altar and there remember that your brother has something against you, leave your gift there in front of the altar. First go and be reconciled to your brother; then come and offer your gift." I sat my children down and explained this principle to them. I told them that we must repent of the way we treated each other before we could go to worship God. How much more effective and blessed would our worship be if we did that every Sunday?

The Body of Christ

When was the last time you stubbed your toe? Or cut your finger? Or maybe pulled a muscle? When one part of our body, however small, is wounded we notice it. We feel pain when the injury occurs, and are reminded of it for days afterward every time we move wrong. Some of those injuries heal quickly. Some never heal completely, giving us trouble for years.

Scripture teaches that believers together form the body of Christ. Each member performs different functions in the body, but all are important. "In fact God has arranged the parts in the body, every one of them, just as he wanted them to be" (1 Corinthians 12:18). The relationship between believers is supposed to look like this: "If one part suffers, every part suffers with it; if one part is honored, every part rejoices with it" (1 Corinthians 12:26). Is this verse a good description of your church family? The responsibility begins with me and it begins with you. Even more than focusing on an injury to our physical bodies, we should be tuned in to those in our church who are wounded. Some wounds of the heart and spirit heal fairly quickly, some take years. It is our responsibility to care for those among us who are hurting, either physically or emotionally. Every believer ought to be in relationship with other members of the body. If a part of the body is missing for a week or two or three, other members should notice the absence and make the effort to reach out and check on the missing individual or family. If one part is suffering, other parts should be close enough to know that and to suffer with him or her. This is not the responsibility of church leaders alone. In fact, as a church grows it becomes impossible for a few to keep track of all the members of the body. It is all the parts of the body who have been given the responsibility to care for all the other parts.

I encourage you to build relationships with people within your church that you do not really know. I also implore you to be careful how you talk about other members of the body. Saying things that are critical or complaining about someone else is detrimental to the body. It also damages our Christian witness. Let us truly learn to live as the body of Christ. This is good for the body, and is also a beautiful testimony to the world around us.

Jesus said, "By this all men will know that you are my disciples, if you love one another" (John 13:35).

Beyond reaching out to those within the church who are hurting, we have a responsibility to show the love of Christ to those outside the body. Jesus took time to touch hurting people. We are to do the same. I challenge each of us to prioritize those things which have value for all eternity.

Why Me Lord?

Most of us have asked this question from time to time. It is usually associated with painful circumstances which God has allowed to come into our lives . . . illness, loss of job, broken relationships, family crises, accidents, and so forth. If I get into a car accident, I may be quick to ask, "Why did you let this happen to me?" Yet, in all the hundreds of miles I have driven safely without an accident, do I ever ask, "Why did you not let anything happen to me?" How often do we ask, "Why Me?" about the blessings in our lives?

In 2006 a church about three hours south of our home invited our family for an evening service. After learning about us and God's work in our lives, they invited us to a time of fellowship and snacks. Then they gave us gifts . . . abundantly! We went there expecting nothing but to make some new friends in the family of God. We left there with gifts, gift cards, groceries, and money. During the three-hour trip home the only response we could come up with was, "Wow!" The blessing was so generous, so unexpected, so surprising, that it left me wavering all week between feeling thankful and feeling guilty. After all, there are many with far greater needs than ours. I do not know why they chose our family. I do not know why God chose to pour out such blessing on us. "Why us, Lord?"

More than 2,000 years ago, a gift was given. It was unexpected. It was undeserved. It was extravagant beyond words. Why was this gift given to me? There are others who deserve it much more. There are those who (through human eyes) appear to need it much more. Still, God chose to give the gift of Salvation through Jesus to Lynn. "Why me, Lord?" Because I needed him more than I ever could have realized.

I often find it hard to conjure up the strong feelings I think I should have in response to all that God has given to me. My mind chooses to be thankful, but it is hard to make my heart get excited about a message it has been hearing for more than forty years now. That particular year, for whatever reason, God chose to bring it home to me in a very real way. He also provided multiple opportunities to help our children understand a little more of God's extravagant gift of grace.

Let us train ourselves to stop and ask, "Why me?" Here is a part of my list: "Why have You given me a loving family, and the privilege of living close enough to spend time with them?" "Why have You blessed me so much?" "Why have You never let me go hungry?" Most of all, "Why did You love me enough to send Your Son to be my Savior?" I encourage you to make your own list, enumerating the wonderful things God has done in your life.

Enter With Thanksgiving

Isn't it interesting that the holiday called Thanksgiving comes just a few weeks before the holiday called CHRISTmas? We fill the intervening weeks so full with gatherings and preparations that sometimes it feels like the two holidays are too close together. I think, however, that the timing is just right for our spirits. We need the clear reminder to choose to give thanks as we enter into the busiest time of the year. If we are to come close to the precious Christ child, we need to come with thanksgiving.

"Open for me the gates of righteousness; I will enter and give thanks to the Lord. This is the gate of the Lord through which the righteous may enter" (Psalm 118:19, 20). "Enter his gates with thanksgiving and his courts with praise; give thanks to him and praise his name" (Psalm 100: 4).

Giving thanks is a crucial part of entering in. "This is the gate of the Lord through which the righteous may enter." If we are going to do more than just pass by the stable and nod at the Christ child, we need to come with hearts of thanksgiving. No other offering will do.

Thinking of those without a home reminds us to give thanks for our own homes. Giving food to the hungry reminds us to be thankful for the food God has provided. In the same way, taking a few minutes to think about what it would be like to live without the Savior helps us to give sincere thanks for the gift of salvation. If Christ had never come, there would be no Christianity. There would be no government based upon Christian principles. There would be only lies and selfish ambition. There would be no hope for the future. God would still be God, but probably nobody would know him except a few devout Jews. We would have no source of hope, no guidance for life beyond our own consciences. The highest goal in life would be to get all you can for yourself and your children before you die. Our lives are so richly blessed because the Savior came. Only because of him can we have hope, peace, joy, purpose, and fulfillment, not to mention a glorious eternity. We have countless reasons to give thanks.

Psalm 50:14 tells us, "Sacrifice thank offerings to God, fulfill your vows to the Most High." Every day, let us draw near to God by bringing an offering of thanks and praise. There is no other way to draw near to him, but in humility and gratitude. If we neglect to come to him with thanksgiving, we will go through our CHRISTmas celebrations tired and spiritually empty. What a waste. I challenge you, as I have been challenged myself, to choose to continually give thanks to the Giver of all good things.

Precious Treasure

One December we were privileged to attend a live nativity called Journey to Bethlehem. Being a part of the CHRISTmas story as it was played out helped to keep the wonder of this story fresh and new. One of the most beautiful parts of the experience was the delightful celebration of the angels as they shared the good news of the Savior's birth. The most poignant part for me, however, was seeing the baby lying in the manger while his parents sat nearby. As a mother, my thoughts shifted to the sacrifice of this couple, giving up hours of their time in December to share their baby in the reenactment of the birth of Christ. It seems like a lot to give in this day and age, but it is next to nothing compared to what Mary and Joseph gave. Their precious first-born son was not theirs alone to cherish. From the first hours of his life, they had to share him with strangers. Even more mind-boggling is the extravagance of Almighty God sharing his precious Son with humans.

Luke 2 relates the unique story of the birth of Christ. The shepherds in the field were astounded by the appearance of an angel who came to announce the most important event since the creation of the world. Then a whole host of angels appeared confirming and celebrating this amazing news. The angel said to the shepherds, "Do not be afraid. I bring you good news of great joy that will be for all the people. Today in the town of David a Savior has been born to you; he is Christ the Lord. This will be a sign to you: You will find a baby wrapped in cloths and lying in a manger" (Luke 2:10-12). Note again what the angel said, "A Savior has been born to *you*" (emphasis mine). This was a personal message of a personal gift, personal for each shepherd and personal for each of us. Jesus did not come just for the world. He came specifically for you. He came to meet the deepest need of your heart. That is the message of CHRISTmas. It is not like going to a concert and being part of a crowd of thousands listening to the artist. No, Jesus comes right into your home, your heart, your life and invites you to be with him all day every day as long as you live.

Years later, Jesus told his followers, as he sent them out to proclaim the gospel message, "Freely you have received, freely give" (Matthew 10:8b). Scripture also teaches that "It is more blessed to give than to receive" (Acts 10:35b). This refers to something far deeper than giving CHRISTmas presents. It is about giving of yourself and that which is most precious to you.

What is your most precious treasure? God shared his. Joseph and Mary shared theirs. What do you have to share with others? Parents can share their children today by "adopting a grandparent" who can become like part of the family, enjoying the joy and laughter kids bring. Maybe you have a beautiful home or other material blessing you could use to show hospitality. Perhaps you are part of a warm family that could invite someone who is lonely this holiday season to join in the fun. For many of us, the most precious commodity we have to share with others is our time. How can we use it to bless someone? Perhaps we could help with a chore like shoveling snow, or provide a listening ear to someone who is struggling. Far more important than what you give is the motivation of your heart in giving freely to others as you have freely received the gift of Salvation and forgiveness of sins. Not just at CHRISTmas, but all year round, let us give generously of ourselves, following the perfect example of Jesus.

Every Knee Will Bow

As we ponder and celebrate the birth of the Christ Child so many years ago, let's look at how this miracle was announced. An angel came quietly to Mary and then to Joseph to let them know what was about to happen. A new star appeared in the sky, silently moving toward the Savior. The only loud announcement was made to some shepherds on a hillside in the dark of night. There was no loud earth-shaking, undeniable, un-ignorable proclamation to the world. Instead, there was a quiet, gentle call to any who were willing to hear. I am sure Joseph and Mary's family members were told about the angel's message, but there is no indication that they were there, supporting and encouraging the new parents. In a culture centered on extended family, they are conspicuously absent in the gospel accounts. The shepherds, after hearing the excited rejoicing of the angels, hurried to Bethlehem. The angels had told them they would find the baby wrapped in cloths and lying in a manger (Luke 2:12). Note that they were not given an address. They went on the earth's greatest Treasure hunt that night. They searched hurriedly until they found him, and then spread the word to everyone they saw about the angels' announcement and the new Savior. I don't know how many people were told by the shepherds, but there is no indication that anyone listened and went looking for the One for whom Israel had waited so long. People were told, given an opportunity to welcome him, but they did not listen to the invitation. The only other recorded visitors were astrologers from eastern lands. They saw the star, studied its significance and set out to find the newborn king. How many other people saw the bright new star in the sky, but did nothing? How many people, besides Herod's court, did they meet along the way and talk to about the brilliant, silent invitation in the sky? And yet, once again, there is no indication that anyone else responded to the quiet invitation to greet and honor the Son of God. The birth of Christ was announced quietly to those who were willing to hear the good news. Only a handful responded to the invitation.

The same is true today. God does not thunder your name from heaven insisting that you come to know His Son and receive forgiveness of your sins. Rather, through the Holy Spirit, he quietly calls to anyone willing to listen and respond. Patiently, for months or even years, he calls. Many hear. Some respond and find life abundant. So many others ignore or deny the call, going on about their lives as if they never heard. Even as God allowed people to ignore or reject his Son as a baby in Bethlehem, still today he allows people the freedom to choose whether or not to respond to his invitation.

But that will not always be true. Jesus' birth was announced softly, but his death was proclaimed loudly, undeniably. Matthew 27 tells us that the land became dark for three hours in the middle of the day when Jesus was on the cross. The great curtain in the temple, separating the holiest place (where God's presence dwelt) from the more common areas, was torn in two from top to bottom without human hands. The earth shook and rocks split. Tombs broke open and many holy people who had been buried there were raised to life and appeared to people. Even the centurion standing by the cross was convinced that Jesus was the Son of God.

Our God is all-powerful. Nothing is too hard for him. Men, however, have the power to fool themselves into seeing only what they want to be true. There were those who denied that Jesus was God, even in the face of amazing miracles. There were those who rejected or ignored Jesus' birth and his death. However, Jesus Christ will come again and in that day, no man will be able to ignore or deny him. "At that time the sign of the Son of Man will appear in the sky, and all the nations of the earth will mourn. They will see the Son of Man coming on the clouds of the sky, with power and great glory. And he will send his angels with a loud trumpet call, and they will gather his elect from the four winds, from one end of the heavens to the other" (Matthew 24:30,31). Scripture tells us in three places that the day is coming when "every knee will bow" before Jesus (Isaiah 45:23, Romans 14:11, Philippians 2:10).

Eventually, every human being will be forced to acknowledge Jesus as God. For many, though, it will be too late. The question for each of us is not whether we will honor him and submit to him, but when we will do it. At this point in time, God is gently calling each of us through the Holy Spirit to draw near to him. Will you come of your own free will, rather than waiting until you are forced to bow? If you have already come, the Holy Spirit still calls to your heart to come apart from the hustle and bustle of the world, to be still and deepen your relationship with him. Are you listening to his call like those who came to him so many years ago?

Don't Leave Him In The Manger

The preschoolers had finished their short CHRISTmas program, and the pastor was preaching his message. As he spoke, little Emily sat in the pew, staring at her favorite baby doll, lying alone in the manger up on stage. As Reverend Matteson concluded his remarks and the congregation began to sing the Doxology, the preschooler could stand it no longer. She bolted up onto the platform to retrieve "Baby Jesus" and hold him in her arms.

The wise minister (who happened to be Emily's proud Grandpa) recognized the significance of her actions. He left his congregation with this clear thought: As the CHRISTmas season and all the celebrations draw to a close, do not leave the Christ child in the manger.

Jesus, our beloved Savior, did not come just to be remembered as a cute baby born in very unusual circumstances. He came to change the lives of every human being on the planet for all time and eternity. He came to bring forgiveness of our sins so that we might live in sweet harmony with Almighty God (John 3:17, John 14:6). He came to show us the way to live and the way to walk with God. He came to dwell in our hearts, enabling us to love others (John 13:35).

Friend, I encourage you to take a lesson from little Emily. Do not leave Jesus in the manger of Bethlehem. Take him with you day by day, hour by hour, for as long as you live. That is the only way to truly honor and celebrate his birth.

Prioritize Your Mind

In his *Financial Peace University* materials, Dave Ramsey talks about the need to have an emergency fund for all the expected and unexpected expenses that we face. In one session he said something like this: "Oh no! Christmas is on December 25 this year! We have to buy gifts. It's an emergency!" [36] It is true. CHRISTmas will be on December 25 again this year. Let us be prepared so it is not an emergency – in terms of the time and money and work required. It is, first of all, a season to celebrate the Savior.

The early chapters of Revelation contain letters to seven churches. Dictated by the Holy Spirit and written by John, these letters contain words of conviction and encouragement for those in the Christian church. I think the words to the church in Ephesus are appropriate for us at this time. He talks about their hard work and perseverance, then he puts his finger on the heart of the problem. "These of the words of him who holds the seven stars in his right hand and walks among the seven golden lamp stands: I know your deeds, your hard work and your perseverance. I know that you cannot tolerate wicked men, that you have tested those who claim to be apostles but are not, and have found them false. You have persevered and have endured hardships for my name, and have not grown weary. Yet I hold this against you: You have forsaken your first love. Remember the height from which you have fallen! Repent and do the things you did at first. If you do not repent, I will come to you and remove your lamp stand from its place (Revelation 2:1-5).

I believe the lamp stand in this passage refers to the abiding presence of the Holy Spirit. The young church at Ephesus was working hard to do what was right. They were holding fast to the truth and standing strong in times of trouble. But, in the midst of their hard work and good intentions, their hearts had grown cold. They were doing the right things, but it was no longer as an outflow of hearts in love with the Savior. It was just "doing."

This word of caution is applicable to us busy Americans. Is your mind and your heart filled with thanksgiving to God for the gift of his Son and his many other blessings, or are you overwhelmed with thoughts of things to be done?

The letter to the church at Ephesus clearly stated that the lamp stand, the Holy Spirit, would be removed if love for the Savior was not the central theme and motivation for all they were doing. Friends, to lose the help and presence of the Holy Spirit in our lives or our church would be a great tragedy. Far worse would be to lose him and never even notice as we go on our way.

I challenge you today, even as I remind myself, to be a good steward of time over the coming weeks, and to keep love for Jesus as a raging fire in our hearts that guides our every step. There is no better way to honor him.

What kind of Man is this?

Isaiah chapter 9 foretold that a child would be born, a Wonderful Counselor, Mighty God, Everlasting Father, Prince of Peace, whose kingdom will never end. Clearly the Messiah would be mighty and wonderful. Later the same prophet penned chapter 53, which described a man of sorrows, despised and afflicted, familiar with suffering. How do all these descriptions fit together? What kind of Savior could this be?

Mary received a startling message from the angel Gabriel (Luke 1). Soon after that her fiancé Joseph received a similar angelic visit (Matthew 1). Hearing the puzzling and amazing words from the angel, both Joseph and Mary had to be thinking, "What in the world is God doing? We are not the kind of people to whom a mighty warrior, Savior of his people, would be born." On the night the Holy Child was born, the first ones invited to celebrate his arrival were a bunch of unrelated shepherds. Seeing and hearing an unimaginable angel choir had to leave them totally befuddled – what kind of baby gets an announcement like this? Why is he in a stable?

The magi, or astrologers, from the East were apparently expecting the appearance of a special star announcing the birth of a new king. Nobly, they packed up and set out on a long journey to greet him, but what they found was confusing. The present king, Herod, didn't even know about this event, the birth of a newborn king, yet the baby merited his own star in the heavens. What kind of royalty could this be?

Members of Jesus own family and residents of his home town found it nearly impossible to see him as more than a strange kid with strange ideas (John 7:5, Matthew 13:54-58). His disciples were quicker to recognize him as somebody special and powerful, but they too had difficulty figuring out who he really was. In the boat, as he calmed the furious storm, they asked, "What kind of man is this? Even the winds and the waves obey him!" (Matthew 8:27). The Jewish people in general were divided. Their respected synagogue rulers didn't like him, yet he taught as one who had authority (Mark 1:22) and performed great miracles. Many followed him, at least out of curiosity, asking themselves, "What kind of man is this?"

People today are still asking the same question. What is the big deal about some baby born into poverty more than 2,000 years ago? The Apostle Paul described it this way, "Beyond all question, the mystery of godliness is great:

He appeared in a body,
Was vindicated by the Spirit,
Was seen by angels,
Was preached among the nations,
Was believed on in the world,
Was taken up in glory" (1 Timothy 3:16).

I encourage you to ponder the question, "What kind of man is this Jesus?" Study his Word. Read Psalm 72 for another prophecy about his life and work. Get to know him. Study his character and the ways he has worked in the lives of people throughout the generations. The more you know him and know of him, the more your heart will long for eternity with him.

Prepare Him Room

I have a sister-in-law and two nieces who love CHRISTmas carols so much that they start listening to them several months before December rolls around. I am not quite such a diehard, but I do enjoy hearing songs about the birth of the Christ child being played in stores and other public places during the holidays. One phrase from *Joy To The World* repeatedly catches my attention "Let every heart prepare him room, and heaven and nature sing."[37]

How do we "prepare him room"? At CHRISTmas time we are very busy making room.

- We make room in the house for the tree and other decorations
- We make room in the cupboard for all the ingredients for special CHRISTmas baking, and in the freezer for all those goodies
- We make room in the budget for buying gifts
- We make room in the schedule for programs and parties and time with family

We work hard in December making room for traditions and activities that are important to us. The most important preparation is also the most difficult. Each of us must make room in our heart and mind if we are to receive our King. Without this deliberate choice, the busy holiday season will just leave us feeling tired and empty.

Think about another favorite CHRISTmas carol – *Silent Night*. The angelic announcement was not made to the bustling crowds in Jerusalem, or even in the overcrowded village of Bethlehem. It came instead to calm, quiet shepherds on a hillside. They were awake and listening – ready to hear if a predator came after their sheep. Rather than a predator, they heard about the Lamb of the World. Only a quieted heart can really hear and see and celebrate this priceless gift. The joy that has come to the world can only be received by those who set aside all else and set their hearts on welcoming their king. Let us take to heart the words of God recorded by the Psalmist, "Be still and know that I am God; I will be exalted among the nations, I will be exalted in the earth" (Psalm 46:10). I remind you, as I remind myself, to find quiet stillness and delight in the Savior. Choose today to prepare him room in your heart and mind.

That Beautiful Star

If you have never watched Louie Giglio's presentation of *How Great Is Our God* – I strongly encourage you to see it.[38] He describes the sizes of the largest stars discovered so far, as compared to the size of our sun and solar system. The greatness of the known universe is both humbling and mindboggling. Yet God created these huge objects with just a word from his mouth (Psalm 33:6). Though there are billions upon billions of stars, he calls them all by name (Psalm 147:4). "When I consider your heavens, the work of your fingers, the moon and the stars, which you have set in place, what is man that you are mindful of him, the son of man that you care for him?" (Psalm 8:3-4). All of God's creation, including sun, moon, and stars, bring glory to him (Psalm 148:3). Even after he had created such an amazing universe of stars, God wanted one more for a special occasion. Our Awesome God chose to create a special, brilliant star as his own birth announcement to the world. In the CHRISTmas story we read an account of the magi who traveled far to greet the newborn king. "After they had heard the king (Herod), they went on their way, and the star they had seen in the east went ahead of them until it stopped over the place where the child was. When they saw the star, they were overjoyed. On coming to the house, they saw the child with his mother Mary, and they bowed down and worshiped him. Then they opened their treasures and presented him with gifts of gold and of incense and of myrrh" (parenthetical insert above, mine, Matthew 2:9-11). The star led them all the way to the Holy and Righteous Son of God. God knows his stars and uses them to do his bidding.

So, when that same Awesome Creator commands his people to "shine like stars in the universe" (Philippians 2:15) it is no empty command. We are to "become blameless and pure, children of God without fault in a crooked and depraved generation." That is how we shine like stars. "Those who are wise will shine like the brightness of the heavens, and those who lead many to righteousness, like the stars for ever and ever" (Daniel 12:3). The lives of God's people should be always be shining brightly in this dark world, and leading many people to righteousness – which is only possible through a personal relationship with Jesus Christ.

Just as that bright star led the magi to the Righteous One, so you and I are to lead many to righteousness. We will not become bright burning balls of gas in our next life. We are to "shine like stars" in the way our lives stand out from the darkness around us. This is not just a general instruction for God's people, but a personal command to each of us. "The Lord knows those who are his" (2 Timothy 2:19). God knows your name, your history, your personality, your dreams. He knows you better than you know yourself, and he has asked you to shine for him. If your light is the only star announcing to those around you that there is a Savior, is it shining brightly enough for people to follow and find him? The most sincere prayer of my heart is that I may "lead many to righteousness." That is my prayer for you too.

Perseverance in Suffering

At any given time, there are many people even within the church experiencing loneliness and heartache. Our hearts go out to them, for as Christians we rejoice with those who rejoice and mourn with those who mourn (Romans 12:15). Pain is a part of life that each one must endure. Some, however, through no apparent fault of their own, seem to have life harder than the rest of us do. There are individuals and families who (from my limited perspective) experience far more than their fair share of suffering and struggles. From major health problems to relational strife, to abuse, to seemingly endless financial pressures, to terrible tragedy, some people just have hard lives. I do not claim to know or understand why the apparent discrepancy. Sometimes I feel guilty about how easy my life is in comparison, but I too will have to experience grief and loss.

The question of why God allows so much suffering has been addressed by many authors with wisdom far greater than mine. I would like us to look at the question of how we are to live during these times of struggle and difficulty. The early Christian churches, those established in the decades after Jesus returned to heaven, experienced terrible persecution for their faith. The Hebrew writer describes some being tortured, facing jeers and flogging, others being imprisoned or stoned or sawed in two. Some were killed with the sword. Many lived in poverty, destitute and persecuted (Hebrews 11:35-37). Letters written by apostles Paul, James, and Peter to some of these early believers often contained encouragement to persevere in the face of suffering and persecution. The book of 1 Peter includes many such words of encouragement. He instructs believers to choose to live in joy, to be holy and mentally prepared for action at all times (1 Peter 1:13). Salvation is guaranteed through Jesus Christ. "In this you greatly rejoice, though now for a little while you may have had to suffer grief in all kinds of trials. These have come so that your faith – of greater worth than gold, which perishes even though refined by fire – may be proved genuine and may result in praise, glory and honor when Jesus Christ is revealed" (1 Peter 1:6-9). Believers are to keep living for God even in the face of suffering (1 Peter 4:12-14, 19). Suffering produces perseverance, which develops godly character and hope (Romans 5:3,4). Those not currently in crisis have a responsibility to intercede faithfully for those in trouble. We are to "encourage one another daily" (Hebrews 3:13) and to carry one another's burdens (Galatians 6:2).

Although none of us wants to go through hard times, it is often those very experiences which provide the most powerful opportunities for giving testimony to people around us. When your co-workers and friends see you go through trials, they watch to see how you will respond. Does your relationship with God surround you with peace and hope and even joy in the middle of a crisis? That may be the clearest testimony you ever give of what your faith means. If you are suffering today, you are likely praying for relief from the pain. There is nothing wrong with such a prayer, but I encourage you also to pray for strength to shine his light in the midst of your trouble. Ask God to help you be a clear and positive ambassador for him to the unbelievers in your life.

Come To Adore Him

The angel who appeared to Joseph told him that the baby born to Mary would be called "Immanuel" which means "God with us" (Matthew 1:23). The all-powerful creator and ruler of all universes came to earth to dwell with people. Although the story is old and familiar to us, may we never cease to wonder at the kind of love that birthed CHRISTmas. The people of Israel did not recognize the Savior when he came. He was not what they expected. Apparently those who studied the prophesies expected the Messiah to come as a powerful king and free them from the rule of the Roman Empire.

When an earthly king is born, the heir to the throne, it is a big deal for the whole nation. Detailed, elaborate celebrations and ceremonies are planned. Countless people are expected to join in the celebrations. It is in the news and on the lips of everyone. The citizens, even those attending the events, may or may not truly care about the king or any of the royal family. I don't believe that type of celebration was what God wanted for His Son.

My limited human mind cannot understand all the reasons God does things. I think, in part, that Christ came in humble circumstances to show that he was the Savior of everyone, not just the wealthy or the poor or one culture or race. I also think, however, that God wanted the celebration of his birth to include only those who sincerely rejoiced in him. The shepherds were invited, and received the news with glad hearts. They went straight away to the stable and worshiped the new King. Then, they told everyone they met the good news (see Luke 2:8-20). The only other recorded visitors were so sincere that they traveled many miles from a distant land to meet him. There were no bright, elaborate parties when Jesus was born. Nobody came out of sense of duty. The only people who celebrated were those who were sincerely glad to see the fulfillment of the promise.

Friends, God never changes. He is the same yesterday, today, and forever (Hebrews 13:8). God did not want people pretending to celebrate the birth of the King so many years ago. The same is true today. Just dressing up nice and attending a service or humming a few carols or even mailing out cards depicting a manger scene is not what he expects of us at CHRISTmas. If we do not come in sincerity, each one recognizing how desperately he needs a Savior, we might as well not come at all. God is not to be mocked. He detests hypocrisy. I invite you today to lay aside the distractions in your heart and mind (whether it is a whirlwind of commitments and details, or feelings of loneliness and self-pity, or painful depression, or fear, or whatever) and come to worship. When we are truly grateful for the gift of salvation, then God is honored by our celebration. Oh come, brothers and sisters, let us adore him.

One Powerful Baby

One year the kids at church sang a song with the lyrics, "You wrapped your power in sweet simplicity. Lord Jesus, I thank you for coming as a child like me." I am so glad that he came as one who was approachable to old and young, to weak and strong, to brave and timid, to me.

The line of the song recited above is so much more meaningful when you read in Scripture how much power he actually had to wrap up in simplicity in order to come as a child like you and me. Revelation chapter 5 describes a scene in heaven in which Almighty God, seated on the throne, is holding a scroll. No one in all of heaven or earth or under the earth was found worthy to break the seals on the scroll and unroll it. The Savior, the Lamb that had been killed and had risen victorious: he alone was found to be worthy to open the scroll. "And as he took the scroll, the four living beings and the twenty-four elders fell down before the Lamb. Each one had a harp, and they held gold bowls filled with incense—the prayers of God's people! And they sang a new song with these words: 'You are worthy to take the scroll and break its seals and open it. For you were killed, and your blood has ransomed people for God from every tribe and language and people and nation. And you have caused them to become God's Kingdom and his priests. And they will reign on the earth'" (Revelation 8-10 NLT). Then thousands, yea millions of angels began to sing, "Worthy is the Lamb!" Then every creature in heaven, and on earth, and under the earth joined in the song.

Friends, that is the kind of power Jesus had. That is the power he laid aside to come as a humble child to save you from your sins and save me from mine. That is the power he has today to guide you and help you and empower you to walk in godliness. It is far more than sufficient to meet your need. I pray that the greatest desire of your heart is to know him more and love him more. His immeasurable power is available to you as you walk in step with him.

The Only Appropriate Response

The second chapter of Luke describes how the shepherds heard the news, hurried to the stable, and then spread the word as they praised the Lord. In the second chapter of Matthew we see that the wise men who had traveled from afar were "overjoyed" to find the Savior. They bowed down and worshipped him before giving their gifts. Have you noticed that in most of our nativity sets and CHRISTmas pageants, those who come near to the Son of God fall to their knees? This is the only appropriate and natural response for those who come near to the Savior of the world. In Scripture we are told no less than three times that "Every knee will bow." Isaiah 45:23b says, "Before me every knee will bow; by me every tongue will swear." Romans 14:11 tells us, "As surely as I live" says the Lord, "every knee will bow before me; every tongue will confess to God." And in Philippians 2:10,11 it says, "that at the name of Jesus every knee should bow, in heaven and on earth and under the earth, and every tongue confess that Jesus Christ is Lord, to the glory of God the Father." Clearly, God tells us he is worthy, and the only way to come to him is in humility. In the Old Testament, when an individual encountered God or one of his messengers, his immediate response was to drop to the ground in reverence and fear. Moses (Exodus 34:8), Joshua (Joshua 3:14), and Abraham (Genesis 18) are a few examples.

Some of our favorite CHRISTmas carols remind us to come humbly and bow before him:

- In *Angels We Have Heard on High*, "Come adore on bended knee."
- *O Holy Night*, "Fall on your knees!"
- *The First Noel*, "Full reverently upon the knee."

This year, my friends, let us not just sing the words, but follow through with our actions. I invite you to take time often to come and kneel in reverent awe at God's amazing gift. This one small act will truly help you to keep focused on the Christ. And after CHRISTmas is over and the decorations packed away, I encourage you to keep coming and kneeling both in worship service and in private.

Responding to the Call

Hasn't God been good to us? His faithfulness defies comprehension. What a privilege it is to know him, to call him Father and to worship him. Let's look at the primary characters in the beloved CHRISTmas story. Zechariah and Elizabeth waited years for a child. In their old age they were given a son whom the angel compared to Elijah – one who would "make ready a people prepared for the Lord" (Luke 1:17). Mary was told she would bear the Christ-child. Joseph was instructed to marry her and to act as a father to the Son of God. Shepherds were invited to go see, and greet the Christ-child. All of these received part of their instructions from angels. I don't understand the call upon the hearts of the magi, but they too came to worship the new king. Have you noticed that the angelic messengers God sends do not give suggestions? Mary was not asked to weigh her options and consider this rewarding, but difficult, new position. Each one was given an assignment, a part to play. God expected each one to do his/her part to the glory of God. None of us will ever be asked to fill the roles they filled, but God will assign tasks to each of us. Our response ought to be the same as Mary's: "I am the Lord's servant. May it be to me as you have said" (Luke 1:38).

Friend, perhaps the role you have been asked to play for this season of your life is not one you would have chosen, be it lonely widow, single parent, unemployed/underemployed consumer, childless, or other. I encourage you to do whatever it is that God has assigned to you in the very best ways you can, for his Glory.

What is CHRISTmas About?

Many young children think CHRISTmas is about Santa Claus and reindeer and getting presents. Those who are a little older often say that CHRISTmas is about giving, about thinking of others rather than yourself. We tend to think of CHRISTmas as being a time of joy and celebration. We want it to be a time when the whole family gathers together and everybody gets along. Every year, however, CHRISTmas fails to live up to those expectations. Some families are separated by too many miles to get together. Some families gather, but spend their time bickering. For some, old traditions are just a painful reminder of loved ones who have passed away. This season of celebration is always brighter for some folks than for others, but never all that we long for it to be.

One year we had three funerals in our community in mid-December. Somehow, decorations seemed out of place in the midst of so much mourning. Celebrations and desperate grief don't really go together. Although we want to think of Christmas as a time of parties and fun, actually the darkness of grief and despair is more of what Christmas is all about. Jesus didn't come to bring a party.

Jesus came because the world is full of pain and brokenness and despair – in desperate need of a Savior. In coming to Earth, Jesus introduced a better hope, by which every human being can draw near to God (Hebrews 7:19). In the midst of the mourning and the yearning and the questions without answer, God is near. Believers are exhorted to "Hold unswervingly to the hope we profess, for he who promised is faithful" (Hebrews 10:23).

One of the greatest sources of hope in dark times is the certain promise that Jesus Christ will come again, and take his people to be with him forever. (See John 14, and 1 Thessalonians 4:13-24.) Jesus will come again to bring a great victory over evil. That will be cause for unparalleled celebration for those who have received him as Savior. "He will wipe every tear from their eyes. There will be no more death or mourning or crying or pain, for the old order of things has passed away" (Revelation 21:4). Beth Moore said it like this, "In this land of Evermore, part of its most exquisite beauty will be found in the "never more."[39] The worst experiences of this life will be no more.

So, if Christmas is about the darkness, should we stop celebrating? No. Emphatically No! Jesus' coming, and the free gift of salvation that he brought are worthy of humble, thankful, exuberant celebration. We must remember, however, that Christmas observances in this life will always be tinged with sorrow, with disappointment, with a sense of something missing. The celebration will never be all that our souls long for until he comes again to conquer evil and death for the last time. May the difficulties and pain of this life help us to rejoice all the more fervently in the gift of the Christ-child born in Bethlehem on that night so long ago. May it stir our yearning for his triumphant return.

God's Tools

Several years ago I was living outside Grand Rapids, working at my first professional job. My roommate Terri and I decided to get a Christmas tree. So the two of us and another friend drove to a tree lot and selected a beautiful tree. (Have you noticed that a tree that looks small outside and surrounded by other trees looks much bigger inside a small living room?) We huffed and puffed and finally got our tree on top of Terri's Ford Escort and tied it down the best we could. About half-way home it slid down onto the windshield and the hood, so we had to stop and re-tie it, much to the amusement of some kids playing outside in a nearby yard. When we got back to the apartment, we dragged the tree inside. It hardly fit through the door. We soon discovered that the base of our tree was bigger than our tree stand. We decided to taper the end of the trunk so it would fit. Unfortunately, the only tools we had for this job were kitchen knives and scissors. As you can imagine, there was far more laughter than progress.

God doesn't always use conventional tools in our lives either. In my Christmas tree story, it was just poor planning, but God deliberately chooses to use a wide variety of tools to accomplish his good plans. The prophet Jeremiah records a picture God had shown him in which God was a Potter and the lump of clay in his hands was the nation of Israel. God explained to Jeremiah that he was the one to choose how to shape the nation (Jeremiah 18). In the same way, God deliberately shapes his people even today.

Looking back I can see that God has used a wide variety of tools on the lump of clay named Lynn. He used a stable Christian family to give me a solid foundation of Bible knowledge. He used friendships all along the way to bring laughter and remind me to find joy in the journey. He also used some harder tools, like loneliness to teach me intimacy with my Savior. Car repairs are complicated for a single person, and my cars needed frequent repairs. It wasn't fun, but my faith grew as I saw God meet my needs. As I watched all my siblings and most of my friends get married while I remained single, I bought Satan's lie that I was unlovable. God chiseled and chiseled to remove that lie. He taught me to really receive his love and he gave me the gift of self-acceptance. God consistently made things happen in ways that were different than my plans, in order to teach me to stop advising him on how things should work out. God uses my children to show me what discipleship is all about. God has also used grief and loss in my life to give me a heart for hurting people.

All of these tools and many more have helped to shape me into the woman of God that he created me to be. That process is on-going. My job is to submit to his methods. Rather than asking

44444444

him to remove or fix situations I don't like, I need to ask him to teach me to know him better through these circumstances. I want to be all that he wants me to be.

In the Christmas tree story above, my friends and I ended up going shopping at midnight for a bigger tree stand and more decorations. Our tools and lack of expertise were no match for the job at hand. That never happens with God. He will continue and complete the work he has started (Philippians 1:6) if we will submit to his working. Friend, what tools has God been using in your life? Are you surrendered to his will, or are you resisting, asking him to take away the difficulties? Will you allow him to carry out his work in you?

Too High a Standard?

One Sunday while driving to church, my young daughter and I had a brief but profound conversation. It went something like this:

"Mommy?""Yes?"

"How come me and Sarah had to help carry stuff to Aunt Lee's garage yesterday?"

"Well, because it needed to be done. I think Jesus would have gladly done such a small thing. Don't you?"

"You mean we are supposed to try to be like Jesus EVERY DAY?"

"Hmmm, well, yes... That is the goal."

"Aye-aye-aye! That is a lot! I think we need to take a day off sometimes to rest. Don't you?"

I love the way kids put into words what I feel but am "too spiritual" to say! Living like Jesus every day sounds like a pretty tall order. The message of continually striving to follow Christ's example is a recurring theme in Paul's New Testament letters: "So whether you eat or drink or whatever you do, do it all for the glory of God" (1 Corinthians 10:31). "Let us not become weary in doing good, for at the proper time we will reap a harvest if we do not give up" (Galatians 6:9). "Be imitators of God, therefore, as dearly loved children and live a life of love, just as Christ loved us and gave Himself up for us as a fragrant offering and sacrifice to God" (Ephesians 5:1-2). "And we pray this in order that you may live a life worthy of the Lord and may please him in every way:

bearing fruit in every good work, growing in the knowledge of God, being strengthened with all power . . ." (Colossians 1:10-11a). "Whatever you do, work at it with all your heart, as working for the Lord, not for men" (Colossians 3:23). "And as for you, brothers, never tire of doing what is right" (2 Thessalonians 3:13).

Clearly, the bar is set very high. None of us can, in our own strength, live every day doing as he would do. Even our best attempts fall flat pretty quickly, leaving us with a desire to take a day off . . . maybe even a whole weekend, or even longer. Friend, if you are discouraged in trying to follow Jesus' example, you can probably relate to my daughter's questions. Trying to "be holy as he is holy" (1 Peter 1:16) is exhausting! In fact, it is impossible. Continually trying and failing is very discouraging, and causes some to turn from the faith.

The issue is in the relationship. When we truly know God and love him and thrive on being close to him, living every day for him does not seem like such a monumental task. Although we still fail, as we grow more deeply in love with him, his desires become our desires. Beloved, if you have "become weary in doing good" I urge you to deliberately shift your focus from "doing" for him to "being near" him. As you draw near to God, he will draw near to you (James 4:8).

I pray that you will grow ever more deeply in love with him. Then a lifetime of walking in his way is a pleasure to seek out rather than an obligation to fulfill. May God bless you with a heart that loves him deeply and continually longs for more of him.

The End Goal

Wise people take stock of their lives and make some mid-course corrections at the start of the new year. We set goals and resolutions by looking at the desired end result, and then planning out steps for achieving that result. We want to have healthy bodies, healthy finances, healthy relationships, healthy minds, and to train our children to be disciples of Jesus, so we resolve to make some changes in order to work toward those goals. Far more important than New Years resolutions, which are all too quickly forgotten, we should set goals for the very end of life as we know it.

Much of what the Bible teaches about end times is filled with confusing symbolism. God has given some scholars wisdom to understand and explain parts of these prophecies, and I encourage you to study them. There are, however, some very clear teachings that we all need to know. Jesus will lead "justice to victory" (see Matthew 12:22, Isaiah 42:1-4). The book of Revelation describes visions John saw of that process where God's justice is finally victorious over evil. The visions are recorded in past tense. Our God, who has made known the end from the beginning (Isaiah 46:10) has firmly decided how these events will unfold and they are guaranteed to happen as he has said they would.

Those who are whole-heartedly God's will be always longing to know him more. Is that true of you? If you are just going through the motions, doing mostly the right things without a personal relationship with the Savior, you are in danger of hearing him say, "I never knew you" (Matthew 7:23). The thirteenth chapter of Matthew includes several short parables in which Jesus describes the coming process of separating those who are his from those who are not. God sees every heart clearly and there will be no grey area in his decision-making. If the end goal we seek is a wonder-filled eternity with our Savior, what steps do we need to take to move toward that goal? I encourage you to spend some time with God, asking him to show you where your relationship with him really stands. If you are truly his, you will long to grow closer to him. Whatever the specific details, the most important resolution you will ever make is to surrender fully and continually to the Savior. He is life. May each of us resolve, not only at New Years but every day of our lives, to pursue him wholeheartedly.

Whose Plan Was This Anyway?

In Matthew 16 Jesus told his disciples about his plans for the near future. "From that time on Jesus began to explain to his disciples that he must go to Jerusalem and suffer many things at the hands of the elders, chief priests and teachers of the law, and that he must be killed and on the third day be raised to life" (Matthew 16:21). These plans did not sound good to his closest friends, and did not line up at all with their plans and hopes. "Peter took him aside and began to rebuke him. 'Never, Lord!' he said.

'This shall never happen to you!'" (Matthew 16:22). Predictably, the Son of God did not accept correction from man. Peter had the best of intentions from a human perspective. Jesus' response must have caught him totally off guard. "Jesus turned and said to Peter, 'Get behind me, Satan! You are a stumbling block to me; you do not have in mind the things of God, but the things of men'" (Matthew 16:23). Can you imagine having Jesus himself liken you to Satan? Jesus' strong reaction made it very clear that he didn't want his friends trying to derail him from the plans God had for his life. Peter's suggestion was far more comfortable and therefore tempting, but it wasn't God's will. God's best plan for the world required a sacrifice in order that sins might be forgiven.

God's plan for your life requires a sacrifice as well. Jesus went on to say, "If anyone would come after me, he must deny himself and take up his cross and follow me. For whoever wants to save his life will lose it, but whoever loses his life for me will find it. What good will it be for a man if he gains the whole world, yet forfeits his soul? Or what can a man give in exchange for his soul? For the Son of Man is going to come in his Father's glory with his angels, and then he will reward each person according to what he has done" (Matthew 16:24-27).

In the story above, which character do you relate to? Are you, like Jesus, fully surrendered to God's plans even though they may bring difficulty and pain? Or are you more like Peter, seeking the most comfortable path not only for yourself, but also for those you love? Are you seeking your own comfort more earnestly than you are seeking that which will bring glory to God? God does have good plans for our lives, even as he had for the Israelites (see Jeremiah 29:11). We must remember, though, God always plans that which will bring him the most glory. Those who truly love him are abundantly blessed when God is glorified.

I challenge you to seek God's plans for your life. The road will not be easy, but no other plan will ever be more rewarding, more peace-filled, or lead to such abundant life. Follow Jesus. Deny yourself. Take up your cross, and follow him.

What's in a Name?

Do you like your name? Some parents give their children beautiful, unique names. Some choose names in honor of grandparents or other respected relatives. Others stick with more common names. I, for one, have a very ordinary, unremarkable name – which suits my personality. Lynn was derived from the word lake.

The father of the Christian faith had been given the name Abram which means "exalted father" (interesting since he fathered no children at all until the age of eighty-six). When Abram was ninety-nine years old, God Almighty appeared and reaffirmed his covenant. He changed Abram's name, saying, "No longer will you be called Abram; your name will be Abraham, for I have made you a father of many nations. I will make you very fruitful; I will make nations of you, and kings will come from you" (Genesis 17:5,6). Abraham means "father of many." God also changed Sarai's name to Sarah, promising to bless her and make her the mother of nations and kings (Genesis 17:16), although she was still barren at the age of ninety. Two generations later, Jacob (the "heel grabber" who had always been only out for himself) wrestled with an angel through the night and the angel changed his name to "Israel" which means "contended with God" (Genesis 32). That was a defining moment in Jacob's life, when he finally shifted his focus away from himself.

Whatever name your parents may have given you, you've probably had others along the way. Maybe you were called "popular" or "geek" or "jock" in high school. Perhaps you've been labeled "clumsy" or "lazy" or even "stupid." What name describes you, particularly with regard to the way you live as a Christian? There have been times in my spiritual walk when "fickle" or "inconsistent" would have been appropriate names for me. Maybe you could be labeled "doubter" or "critical" or "half-hearted." Many believers have rightly been called "hypocrite" or "phony." What names describe you?

What name would you, as a child of God, like to be called? Barnabas means the "son of encouragement" (Acts 4:36). Enoch means "dedicated." Maybe you long to be described as "faithful" or "evangelist" or "generous" or "compassionate." God's children are to exhibit the fruit of the Spirit (Galatians 5:22). Therefore these words should describe us: loving, joyful, peace-filled, patient, kind, good, gentle, and self-controlled. I long to be known as one who leads many to righteous (Daniel 12:3).

Friend, if you are not yet who you long to be in Christ (or more importantly who he longs for you to be) it is not too late. No matter how old you are, no matter how long you have been walking with the Lord, it is not too late. Abram was ninety-nine and Sarai was ninety. God can give you a new name, a new identity. Jesus changed Simon Peter's name the first time they were introduced (John 1:42), recognizing the potential for who he could become. When he looks at you, he sees who you could/should be. Who is that? Will you become that person?

Walking With a Limp

A friend of mine who lost her husband in a tragic motorcycle accident described the painful road of grief. "I'm trying very hard to absorb this tragedy into my life and learn how to walk with this newfound limp." Some of you can relate to this description far better than I can. Friend, has life left you with a limp that makes your steps painful and difficult?

Jacob once wrestled with an angel (or possibly a pre-incarnate Jesus) all night and ended up walking with a limp for the rest of his life (Genesis 32). I encourage you to read the story of Jacob's son Joseph in Genesis 37-50. Joseph's life was a study in contrasts. He was the favorite son of his father, yet despised by his brothers. He was cursed and mistreated (by his brothers, and then by Potiphar and his wife), yet God blessed his work even while he was a servant and later a prisoner. He was unjustly imprisoned and forgotten there for more than two years, and then he was exalted in a day to second-highest ruler in the whole land of Egypt. Talk about living a roller coaster.

Joseph too had to learn to live and walk with some limps. Although it wasn't a physical disability or grief over losing a loved one, he must have grieved over losing his dreams of what his life could have been like. Sold into slavery, he had to learn to walk with that limp. He chose to work hard rather than allowing anger and bitterness to consume him. God blessed his labor (Genesis 39) and Potiphar elevated him to a position of overseeing his entire household. Then came the heartache of being falsely accused and imprisoned. Joseph once again had to choose how to respond. Would he curl up in a miserable heap of self-pity or would he learn to walk with this new limp life had dealt him? Once again, he learned to walk. He worked and served in the prison and even in that unenviable situation, God blessed him (Genesis 39:21-23). God used him in the prison to minister to others and gave him the chance to interpret some dreams. This was laying groundwork for a future work God had for him to do. Still, it took a full two years before that experience of interpreting a dream was remembered by the cupbearer and became a catalyst for getting Joseph released from prison.

Some limps last even longer than two years, don't they? Grief and heartaches may last a lifetime. Childhood abuse and neglect can effect multiple generations. Healing comes and people learn to walk again, but they are never the same. Many among us are limping or hobbling today.

Yet, the example of Joseph clearly reminds us that God has plans for limping people. In order to become all that he wants us to be, we need to lean on God. Authors Rick Warren and Erik Rees have suggested the acronym S.H.A.P.E. to describe how God uses every part of who we are (Spiritual gifts, Heart, Abilities, Personality, Experiences) to uniquely shape us for the specific ministries to which he calls us.[40] God uses our experiences, both good and painful, to equip us for specific areas of ministry. Beloved, wounded friend, I encourage you today to take another step. Seek God earnestly. Let him lead you, and be the crutch you lean on. There is still life in him, even for we who limp.

God On Your Side

There are several passages of Scripture which always bother me a little bit when I read them. One of those is Matthew 27:41-43 "In the same way the chief priests, the teachers of the law and the elders mocked him. 'He saved others,' they said, 'but he can't save himself! He's the King of Israel! Let him come down now from the cross, and we will believe in him. He trusts in God. Let God rescue him now if he wants him, for he said, "I am the Son of God."' The sarcasm just grates on me. Don't you wish somebody had come up with an immediate comeback for these mockers? I want to say to them, "Oh yes he *can* save himself!" In Max Lucdo's book, *Next Door Savior*, one little paragraph related to this passage stopped me cold. Here it is:

> And thanks to the Pharisees for the sermon: "He saved others; himself he cannot save." Could words be more dead center? Jesus could not, at the same time, save others and save himself. So he saved others. [41]

Did you ever think about it that way? Here I am wishing for a clever comeback, when all the while the Pharisees were right! Jesus was choosing to save me rather than to win a battle of words. As always, I am thinking immediate, he is thinking eternal.

In this passage, Jesus thought long-term, what will bring the greatest glory to God? I thought only of immediate gratification. How often in our lives as Christians do we beg God for immediate relief from troubles, rather than waiting for God to work the situation out for his glory? Whether it is marital problems, a terminal diagnosis, watching kids make poor choices, financial stress, job uncertainty, or some other crisis, most of us cry out to be rescued. This is human nature, but we are to be governed by the Spiritual nature. "Those who live according to the sinful nature have their minds set on what that nature desires; but those who live in accordance with the Spirit have their minds set on what the Spirit desires" (Romans 8:5).

I see three truths which we need to keep in mind. First, problems are guaranteed to come. Plan on it. You don't get to pick which crisis you'll face, but odds are you'll face one of some kind during the coming year. Second, God is not caught off-guard by my problem, nor is he left scrambling for a solution. He knows what is coming, and he has a plan to work it out for my good and his glory. Third, in every situation, no matter how painful, God has plans to bring glory to himself, and draw people to himself.

Perhaps God allowed you to face this very problem at this very time because it will draw you closer to him, and it will allow you to be a witness to someone else in crisis. I have heard it said that God never wastes pain. He has a purpose in everything he allows in your life. As problems come let us choose to pray for his glory rather than praying for our own relief and comfort.

Know God Through His Word

One day a three-year-old I was babysitting decided to read me a book. The story was not familiar to her, but she looked at the illustrations and "read" each page to me. Some of the words were hard to interpret, but the parts I understood went along with how she saw the picture. The only problem was, she got the story all wrong. At the end, she was quite satisfied, but had not received the message the author had intended to convey.

How many Christians are like that with God's book? It is fine and even healthy for a young child to read like this. It is another thing entirely for mature adults to call this reading. The phrase "a little knowledge is dangerous" seems to describe the problem. Do any of these phrases sound familiar?

- God just wants us to get along with each other
- God wants me to be happy
- God would not expect me to _____
- God is too loving to really send people to hell
- Tithing is for people who make more money
- It's the pastors' job to witness and to visit the sick, not mine

Friends, anyone who has actually read the Word knows that all of those statements are wrong. Scriptures clearly tell us to take a stand for what is right, to do what is holy rather than what is easy, to be men and women of integrity, to repent and seek forgiveness, to tithe, and so much more. If we draw close to him, we'll want to know him more and we will want to do the things that please him. In order to know him more and have a life pleasing to him, we must be in the Word. It is not wise to just blindly follow someone who claims to know the way. Rather, we should be like the church people at Berea who "were of more noble character than the Thessalonians, for they received the message with great eagerness and examined the Scriptures every day to see if what Paul said was true" (Acts 17:11).

When a person comes to repentance, accepting Jesus as Savior, he or she is often encouraged to start reading the four Gospels (Matthew, Mark, Luke, John) and Acts. This is a great place to start learning about Jesus and his example for our lives. It is not, however, all that God wants us to know of him. God does not waste his time or ours. If he didn't think all of it was important, he would not have given it to us. "All Scripture is God-breathed and is useful for teaching, rebuking, correcting and training in righteousness, so that the man of God may be thoroughly equipped for every good work" (2 Timothy 3:16-17). Every single book of the Bible, all sixty-six of them, has something to teach us about who God is and how he relates to his creation. I encourage you to read them all, so that you may be thoroughly equipped for every good work.

I encourage you once again to commit to reading through the Bible. Whether you have read it cover-to-cover dozens of times, or just once, you will find that God speaks through his Word in different ways at different times. A passage you have glossed over in the past will suddenly strike you in a new, clear way. The writer of Hebrews described this phenomenon this way: "For the word of God is living and active. Sharper than any double-edged sword, it penetrates even to dividing soul and spirit, joints and marrow; it judges the thoughts and attitudes of the heart" (Hebrews 4:12). Even if you fall behind the schedule, just get back on track and keep plugging along. Even if it takes well over a year, keep on keeping on. Each time you open the Word, ask the Holy Spirit to speak to you. God longs to make himself known to you.

A Picture of Trust

Each new year brings a sense of optimism and hope, but also trepidation and questions. Every year brings its share of pain and trouble as well as new joys and victories. There are those who have been so battered by life's circumstances that they face the new year with more fear than hope. Some are expecting a job lay-off, or a difficult move, or a scary diagnosis, or the likely loss of a dear loved one in the next twelve months. We cannot stop time – even if we wanted to. Day will follow day until God brings time to a stop. This year will go forward, bringing both joy and hardship. How do we prepare ourselves for the uncertain future? Let us look to the words of our Lord.

"Do not let your hearts be troubled. Trust in God; trust also in me. In my Father's house are many rooms; if it were not so, I would have told you. I am going there to prepare a place for you. And if I go and prepare a place for you, I will come back and take you to be with me that you also may be where I am. You know the way to the place where I am going" (John 14:1-4). As we wait for Jesus to come and gather his Church and take us to the home he has prepared for us, we are to trust. He said, "Do not let your hearts be troubled." Letting our hearts be troubled is a choice. We can choose to allow worry and fears to run rampant in our hearts, or we can choose to trust the One who is ultimately in control.

Author Karen Kingsbury has written a beautiful description of what trust looks like in the life of a believer. Trust, she says, is like riding in the passenger seat of a car while God is driving. Sometimes he chooses a different road than I would have chosen, but God is driving and I can trust him. Sometimes the path leads along a sharp, scary cliff, but God is driving and I can trust him. At times he drives slowly through a dark valley. It is painful and I don't want to be there, but God is driving and I can trust him.[42]

Friend, whatever the coming months hold of joy and of sorrow we are invited to trust the Author and Creator of the universe. He knows the way that is best, the way that will bring him the greatest glory. We can hold fast to him in trust, refusing to let out hearts be troubled. He is more than able to handle every issue that will arise. I pray for you a year in which your heart is filled daily with the peace and hope and joy that can only come through fully trusting in Jesus. I pray his very best for you.

Misfits Like Us

In the book of Exodus, we read of Moses, who was a classic misfit. He was an Israelite who was raised by an Egyptian. The other Israelite baby boys his age had all been murdered in infancy. The Israelites did not see this guy who received such special treatment as one of them. He was the enemy that had enslaved the Hebrews. Although Moses grew up Egyptian, he was not really one of them, and apparently did not see himself as one of them (see Exodus 2:11-14). After murdering an Egyptian who was mistreating a Hebrew, Moses fled across the desert to Midian. He became a shepherd and got married. His identity crisis is evident in

Exodus 2:22 where he said, "I have become an alien in a foreign land." Friend, have you ever felt like an alien in a foreign land?

- The only believer from an un-churched family
- The black sheep of a Christian home
- The employee who has tried many types of jobs without finding one that seems to fit
- A person who has been in the church for some time but is not really connected
- A parent who is trying to raise godly children with a lot of interference from extended family members

In Exodus 3, Moses had a personal encounter with God. As he learned to know God, he became the person God created him to be and so much more than he had ever planned. The same will be true for you. God has a plan for your life. In fact, "all the days ordained for [you] were written in [His] book before one of them came to be" (Psalm 139:16).

Be encouraged, misfit. There is a place in God's family that is a perfect fit for you. Seek to know him and you will find yourself in him. My prayer for myself, for my children, and for you, is that none of us will settle for less than the very best that God has for us.

Though No One Join Me

In case you haven't read the Chronicles of Narnia recently, let me share one of my favorite scenes from *Prince Caspian*. Peter, Edmund, Susan, Lucy, and Trumpkin the Dwarf are trying to find their way to friends in need of help. Lucy sees Aslan (representation of Christ) in the distance and senses him calling her to follow. She tries to get her companions to go in that direction, but they have not seen him and choose to follow an easier route. Miserably, Lucy tags along behind them. Late that night Lucy awakens to see Aslan again, and goes to him. Realizing that he wanted her to come to him earlier, regardless of what the others did, she says, "Oh Aslan . . . How could I - I couldn't have left the others and come up to you alone, how could I? Don't look at me like that . . . oh well, I suppose I could. Yes, and it wouldn't have been alone, I know, not if I was with you. But what would have been the good?"[43]

Friends, you and I are called, as Lucy was, to move toward the Savior. Sometimes we move and grow along with others in the family of God, enjoying rich fellowship all the while. There are times, however, when each of us must stand alone in obedience to God. When conflict comes into a relationship, as it is bound to do from time to time, the children of God are called to walk in holiness and love. When there is trouble in my marriage, I must choose to be godly and change myself rather than trying to make my spouse change. The same is true in relationships with parents or siblings or co-workers. Even between believers each one is responsible for his own attitudes and behaviors. The Apostle Paul said it this way, "If it is possible, as far as it depends on you, live at peace with everyone" (Romans 12:18). If you are in a strained relationship today, I urge you to imitate Christ (Ephesians 5:1-2) no matter what the other party does.

You may be experiencing another type of call to follow Christ alone. Perhaps he has laid a burden on your heart to embark in a new area of ministry, or to get a different degree, or to leave your job, or to go to a foreign mission field. Maybe he is calling you to take a stand for a higher level of holiness, which your friends might take as criticism of their life style. Friend, when God calls you he expects you to come even if nobody understands. I encourage you to live out the verse of *I Have Decided to Follow Jesus* which most all of us have sung, "Though no one join me, still I will follow. No turning back, no turning back."[44] It is my prayer that each one of us, when the call comes, will follow the Savior in complete obedience.

God Knows What We Need

It was Saturday evening and the kids were with relatives. Elizabeth was looking forward to an evening with her husband, eager to get out of the house for a few hours. Unfortunately, car trouble resulted in those plans falling through. As her husband worked on the vehicle, Elizabeth was in the house letting God know how disappointed she was. Many of us can relate.

Joseph was one of several biblical characters who faced disappointment time after time (see Genesis 37, 39). This is a man who understood frustration. After being sold into slavery, he was blessed of God and gained a high position in Potiphar's house. Things seemed to be looking up for Joseph. Then a false accusation landed him in prison. Can you imagine the conversation Joseph may have had with God? "God, I don't understand why You let this happen! I was trying my best to serve You. I don't deserve to be here. Please get me out of this mess."

Let's go back to Elizabeth. Since she and her husband ended up staying home for the evening, they heard and smelled the fire start in the ceiling. They responded quickly – he grabbed the fire extinguisher and she grabbed the phone. They caught it early enough that fire fighters were able to save their home. Our Sovereign God knew what they needed even more than a night out. He graciously gave Elizabeth what she needed rather than what she wanted.

God did the same for Joseph. The time he spent in prison gave him a connection to the Pharaoh. He would have been more comfortable remaining in Potiphar's house – at least for a while, but God saw the famine coming. He gave Joseph what he needed rather than what he must have wanted. Through Joseph God spared the whole nation along with surrounding peoples and even Joseph's own family. God worked all things for his good (Romans 8:28).

Friend, bad things do happen. Hard times do come. Mike and Elizabeth still had the work and trials of trying to provide for their family while repairing their home. God saw them through. Joseph still had to endure the seven years of famine, but God saw him through. If you are struggling with disappointment over a turn for the worse in your life, be of good courage. Choose to have faith, being sure of what you hope for and certain of what you do not see (Hebrews11:1). God knows what you need and he will see you through.

Tithes and Offerings

Have you been reading your Bible daily? I encourage you to keep trying to develop this habit. No matter how many days you have missed in a row, today is a great day to start again.

In the Gospel of Matthew there is a story of a woman who interrupted a meal Jesus was having in the home of a man known as Simon the Leper. This woman came in with an alabaster jar of very expensive perfume, and poured it on Jesus' head as an act of love and devotion. (Lack of water in that day and time made personal hygiene practices far different than they are in modern America.) The disciples were critical, but Jesus received the gift in the spirit in which it was given. He defended the woman, noting that her actions had helped to prepare his body for upcoming burial. He foretold that her actions would be remembered and retold as part of his story (Matthew 26:6-13). When this event is recorded in the book of Mark, chapter 14, it notes that the perfume could have been sold for more than a years wages (Mark 14:5). This is a story about priorities and extravagant love.

Did you notice in the story above that no mention is made of what kind of career would earn that amount in a year? The amount is not the important point in the story. The whole point is the attitude of the heart. There are two kinds of giving described in the Bible, tithes and offerings. Scripture commands us to give a tithe of everything to God. That means ten percent of all I earn or receive. This is not a suggestion. It is a consistent commandment throughout the Bible. Why should I give money to God? Not because he needs it. The Bible tells us that he owns the cattle on a thousand hills (Psalm 50:10). Not to mention the fact that he made the gold and everything else we use for money. Giving to God regularly helps us remember to place our faith in God, rather than in our possessions or bank account. This is the point of tithing.

Refusal to tithe reflects two major problems of the heart. The first is a problem of treating self as more important than God (money for me before money for him). The second is the problem of thinking that money rather than God can take care of my needs. Withholding your tithe is actually called robbing God. "Will a man rob God? Yet you rob me. But you ask, 'How do we rob you?' In tithes and offerings. You are under a curse – the whole nation of you – because you are robbing me. Bring the whole tithe into the storehouse, that there may be food in my house. Test me in this, says the Lord Almighty, and see if I will not throw open the flood gates of heaven and pour out so much blessing that you will not have room enough for it" (Malachi 3:8-10).

Beyond tithes is the matter of offerings. A tithe is a set amount given off the top every time you receive money or something of value, like First Fruits. Offerings, on the other hand, may be in any amount and given at any time as an expression of love and gratitude to the Savior. This is the type of giving described in the story above with the woman giving perfume. She did not just give a couple of dollars left over after the week's expenses. She gave extravagantly, displaying indescribable love for the One who had forgiven her sins. Do we love like that?

One important thing that happens during the month of January each year is that W-2 tax forms are sent to everyone who has received a paycheck during the past year. I don't get paid in money these days, but I remember when I was working full time, I was always surprised at how much money I had earned. Every year I wondered where the money had gone. This year when we receive our W-2 forms, I challenge each of us to look at the gross earnings and consider whether we would give that amount to the One who has saved us from eternal torment. I am not suggesting that everyone should go deeply in debt giving to the church or other ministries. I am not suggesting that everyone or anyone should give an amount equal to their gross income. What I am saying, is that each of us should examine the attitudes of our hearts with regard to the security of money versus faith in God. Do we love him more than our comfort and pleasures? How are we showing that love and devotion? Let's to give unto the Lord not just until it hurts, but beyond that until it feels great!

Trusting the Shepherd

My friend Jenny shared the following story of how God had been working in her life.

"A couple of months ago I was praying about some life decisions and one thing I prayed for was how long I would stay with my roommate, Kelly. I heard the Lord say 'until February.' So I went on with life but still had this month in the back of my mind. Then Christmas time came and I went home for Christmas/New Years and when I got back, my roommate Kelly and I had a talk about our living conditions. She wanted more rent and I didn't feel like it was a good, healthy place to live so I made a decision to move out; the Lord was right on time. February was right around the corner! During this time I asked the Lord where he wanted me to move or with whom. He said 'Wait, Trust and Pack.' So that's what I did. When Saturday, January 30th came, I cried out to the Lord in desperation because I had no place to go. I gave my thoughts of where to move, or with whom, up to the Lord. Sunday came and he made a way for me to live with a Christian widow who I've never met before who lives across the street from the church where I work. He provided what I needed, not what I may have wanted. He came through for me, as he always does, just at the right time! She is a blessing to have in my life. She is like a mom to me and we have many things in common! Praise the Lord, His Love Endures Forever!"

The book of Exodus tells the story of the Israelites leaving Egypt after ten horrific plagues displayed God's power and majesty over the Egyptian gods. It goes on to tell of their wanderings in the wilderness, their victories and their failures. In Exodus 16, the people grumbled against their leaders because they were hungry. Rather than asking God, they complained. (Earnest, wrenching prayer is hard work. Complaining and blaming others is easy.) God provided nutritious manna for them to eat for the next forty years. The manna came with clear instructions. "Each person is to gather as much as he needs. Take an omer for each person you have in your tent . . . No one is to keep any of it until morning (Exodus 16:16,19)." The notes in my Bible estimate an omer to be roughly the equivalent of two quarts. So all the people went out and gathered the flakes of manna and each one ended up having just what he needed (Exodus 16:18). Some of the frugal, thrifty types ignored God's instructions and tried to save some for the next day – just in case. In the morning it was stinky and full of maggots (Exodus 16:20). Five days a week the people were to gather just enough for that day. On the sixth day, they were to gather enough for two days, so that they would not need to gather food on the Sabbath, the day of rest. On that first Sabbath after the manna started appearing with the morning dew, some of the people once again ignored the instructions and went out looking for manna – but found none. Again and again, God's people tried to second guess his instructions, as if their feeble human intellect was on par with his omniscience.

Friends, if we are honest, don't we tend to do the same today? For example, we ignore the command to tithe because we think our budget won't balance. This is in effect allowing our "wisdom" to override his instructions. It is not wrong to be thrifty and to conserve resources, but we must never find our security in our stuff. The Israelites who tried to save manna overnight were, in fact, questioning whether God could be trusted to provide for them tomorrow as well as he had provided today. They were using their own wisdom rather than obediently relying on him. God wanted them to learn that he could be trusted completely to care for them and to meet all their needs. The message is restated elsewhere. "There is a way that seems right to a man, but in the end it leads to death" (Proverbs 14:12). "The Lord knows that the thoughts of the wise are futile" (1 Corinthians 3:20). That lesson is one many of us struggle with today.

It is this same characteristic of God that is described in the beloved 23rd Psalm. In his book, *A Shepherd Looks at Psalm 23*, Phillip Keller wrote this: "'The Lord is my Shepherd – I shall not want.' I am completely satisfied with his management of my life. Why? Because he is the sheepman to whom no trouble is too great as he cares for his flock. He is the rancher who is outstanding because of his fondness for sheep – who loves them for their own sake as well as his personal pleasure in them. He will, if necessary, be on the job twenty-four hours a day to see that they are properly provided for in every detail. Above all, he is very jealous of his name and high reputation as The Good Shepherd" [45]

Friend, have you found peace and contentment in your Good Shepherd? Have you learned to completely trust that he knows what is best and will lead you in the way you should go, or are you still trying to use your own wisdom to find your own way through the struggles of life? I encourage you to put your trust in the One who knows all the ramifications of every decision – the One who cares for you. He can always be trusted.

Hearing and Obeying

Moses is one of my heroes. Born a Hebrew, raised an Egyptian, Moses killed a man and fled to Midian. He became a shepherd in the wilderness (see Exodus chapter 2). Moses may have had some familiarity with the God of the Hebrews, but he did not know him. There came a day when God called to Moses from a bush that was burning but not consumed in the fire. God knew Moses. He called him by name and invited him to come closer. Then God commissioned Moses to be a spokesman and a leader for the whole Hebrew community, and to be a part of God's plan to deliver his people from slavery (Exodus 3). Do you remember how Moses responded to this invitation? He asked God his name. God told Moses to call him "I AM WHO I AM." He provided signs for Moses to perform in front of Pharaoh to demonstrate God's power. Moses, still trying to figure out who this God was that was speaking to him, made excuses. "O Lord, I have never been eloquent, neither in the past nor since you have spoken to your servant. I am slow of speech and tongue" (Exodus 4:10). A few verses later he pleads, "O Lord, please send someone else to do it" (Exodus 4:13). Moses, aware of his inadequacy, did not want to do the work God called him to do. God agreed to have Moses' brother Aaron act as the spokesperson. Together they were used of God to procure release for the Hebrews.

Fast forward a few chapters. God called Moses to go up onto Mount Sinai to meet with him. Moses and Joshua stayed on the mountain with God for forty days. During that time God not only gave them the ten commandments, but also gave long, detailed instructions on how to make the tabernacle, the ark of the covenant, the altars and table, the lamp stands and basins, the special garments and incense. He also listed many laws for how the people were to live (Exodus chapters 19-31). Friends, if ever there was a time to say, "God, I can't do this!" this would be it, wouldn't it? But Moses just accepted all the instructions.

What made such a difference in Moses' response? The second set of commands was, in some ways, more difficult than the first. Making the tabernacle and all the articles that went with it required specialized skills from weaving and sewing to working with gold, silver, and bronze, cutting and setting precious gems, and working with wood. There is no indication that Moses had any of these skills. Still, Scripture doesn't even record so much as a "Yeah, but God . . ." By the time Moses met with God on the mountain, he had been walking with him for a least a period of several weeks, perhaps longer. He had seen God perform the ten miraculous plagues, the parting of the Red Sea, and the provision of food and water for roughly a million people. Moses had begun to know God personally. Knowing God involves seeing him work in the world around you. A personal relationship with God develops trust. The more Moses came to know God, the greater assurance he had that God could and would take care of all he needed. With regard to the instructions for making things, at the end of the detailed directions, God named two men whom he had specifically gifted in the crafts needed for the work to be done (Exodus 31).

Friend, God has work for every one of his children to do, "For we are God's workmanship, created in Christ Jesus to do good works, which God prepared in advance for us to do" (Ephesians 2:10). It should be the goal of each one of us to draw close enough to God to hear his voice. The more intimately we know him, the quicker we are to say, "Yes, Lord, I will do as you have said." It is all about knowing God. My prayer for you and for me is that each of us will be ever learning to know and love him more. Trusting him comes with knowing him. Do you know him and trust him enough to obey whatever he says?

Standing For Him

God sees us as individuals. He doesn't just love "the world," he loves every person he created. That is a beautiful message of hope and blessing, but it is also a caution. God sees us not as a mass of humanity, but as individuals. He also judges us as individuals.

In the book of Numbers, chapters 13 and 14 relate the story of the twelve spies Moses sent to explore the Promised Land of Canaan. Shammua, Shaphat, Caleb, Igal, Hoshea (whom Moses called Joshua), Palti, Gaddiel, Gaddi, Ammiel, Sethur, Nahbi, and Geuel had the honor of being selected to represent their tribes for this mission. They did the assigned work and brought back a report as Moses instructed. They brought good news of the beautiful, abundant land but they also shared their fears about the large, strong inhabitants of the countries. The reports they shared reflected the degree to which each man trusted in God. It wasn't just an issue of majority opinion. The Holy One of Israel heard not one or two points of view, but twelve individual reports. Each man was ultimately held responsible for the report he brought back. Only Joshua and Caleb expressed faith that with God's help they could conquer and possess the land. The community not only rejected their claims, but talked of stoning them (Numbers 14:10). Forty years later, these two men were the only two of their entire generation to live long enough to enter the Promised Land. The other ten spies were struck with a plague and died after they gave their report to the people (Numbers 14:37). The whole generation of Israelites, who were swayed by their report, died in the wilderness as well – not as a big group but as individuals. Each one was held responsible for the choice that he made at this major crossroad.

A person of integrity stands up for what he or she believes, whatever the cost. A good example of this is the men who signed the Declaration of Independence, willing to give their lives for the cause of freedom. Brothers and sisters, none of us has been called to take such a dramatic, historic stand. However, each one of us has been given the honor of being chosen to represent our Heavenly Father in this world. This great privilege brings with it a tremendous responsibility. Like the twelve spies of old, each one of us will be called one day to give an account for the way we lived our lives and represented our Master. No exceptions. None of us knows when that day will come, but it will come. When the Creator and Master of all the universe asks you "What have you done with My Son?" how will you answer? Have you given your plans, your preferences and comfort, your dreams and priorities, your very life, to following wherever he leads and going wherever he sends you? It is not just a choice, but a seemingly endless stream of choices every day, in which we represent Jesus Christ. Choosing to honor him in the small choices of day-to-day living is training for the big, life-changing decisions that each of us will face. May we be so fully devoted to the Savior that we are willing to stand strong for him no matter what kind of opposition may come against us. That is my prayer for you and for me. God bless you as you stand for him.

Peace That Defies Understanding

What role does faith play when we face uncertain circumstances? What does it mean to have peace in times of trouble? In Scripture "peace" often means not the absence of war, but the absence of worry, fear, and internal strife. "And the peace of God, which transcends all understanding, will guard your hearts and your minds in Christ Jesus" (Philippians 4:7). What does peace that transcends understanding look like? Here are several examples.

- A parent putting her five-year-old on the school bus for the first time, without having a panic attack
- The couple watching their first born leave to start college, assured that God goes with him/her
- A man facing a terminal diagnosis, yet finding the strength to face each new day without paralyzing fear
- The family breadwinner faced with an unexpected layoff, choosing to believe God will provide
- A family sending a loved one off to serve in a foreign country, refusing to dwell on questions of whether this precious one will ever return to them
- A retired couple facing a total life change, yet not feeling worried about income, or purpose, or health, or their role in a new community
- The tired saint facing his last days without fear of what follows death

Do you know this peace that defies logic? The gospel account shows that Jesus came to bring peace on earth (Luke 2:14), but not peace between people (Matthew 10:34). Jesus came to bring inner peace, independent of external circumstances. He is the Prince of Peace (Isaiah 9:6). Peace is the goal of people the world over. Some think the perfect job, or a higher income will free them from worry. Some try desperately to protect their loved ones and belongings through things like antitheft devices and insurance. Others try meditation or other religious experiences to find peace.

In reality, however, true peace can only come from the Savior, the Prince of Peace (John 16:33). He left his peace with his followers (John 14:27). Peace is really a demonstration of faith. It is a belief that God is in control of every circumstance, and I can trust him to do what is best. Peace involves making a conscious choice to trust and not fear. Worry and fear are from the enemy. They serve to paralyze us and make us useless in the

291

kingdom. I encourage you to accept this peace, which "will guard your hearts and your minds in Christ Jesus." Learning to trust and not fear is a habit that takes time to develop. Start today and practice throughout each day. God is faithful. Accept the peace He offers.

The Altar

Although some denominations have moved away from the practice, evangelical services have traditionally ended with an invitation for people to come forward and kneel at an altar to pray. Why should a person do that when we can meet with God anywhere and anytime? What is the significance of a bench or railing at the front of a sanctuary? The word "altar" was used in both the Old and New Testaments. Although we still use the same term, the altar of today is very different from those mentioned in the Bible, in both structure and practice. I believe, however, that it is still just as vital for the person devoted to pleasing the Lord.

In the Old Testament, altars were used as symbols of remembrance (Noah, Jacob, etc.) and also as places of sacrifice (Abraham, Moses). People who were trying to serve God brought valued possession such as animals and harvested grains to the temple, "the place where God dwells." For many who lived far from Jerusalem, this required a long, difficult journey. It was not so much about the actual value of the sacrifice as much as the act of putting God first. In the New Testament Christian Churches the altar is mentioned less, but people still brought offerings to God. Animal sacrifices for the forgiveness of sins were no longer required, because Jesus came as the sacrificial Lamb once for all. When he returned to heaven, he left the Holy Spirit to counsel, convict, and comfort each believer.

Today, as in the days of the early church, we can interact with God anywhere, as the Holy Spirit guides. The altar we use is a wooden rail with no ashes, no animals, no fire. Why then do people at times feel a strong pull to kneel at the altar? Why would God ask me to do that, when the price has already been paid for my sins through the death of Jesus Christ, my Savior? Although we no longer bring animals or produce to the temple, there are still sacrifices we owe him. A true sacrifice is not just a discomfort or an inconvenience. Sacrifice requires a death. What kinds of things does our Holy God ask us to put to death?

- A destructive habit
- An unhealthy relationship
- My right to spend my time and money as I choose
- Refusal to obey what God is telling me to do
- A grudge against someone who has hurt me
- My plans for my life

While all these decisions can be made anywhere, there is something powerful about sacrificing my comfort, my privacy, my image, in a public way that shows that I am placing God above all these things. Even though we don't have to walk days on end over rough terrain to get to the temple, the walk to the front of the sanctuary can feel just as long. The altar is often located as far away as possible from the entrance, forcing us to remove ourselves from the cares of the world in order to draw nearer to him. Kneeling at the altar is really all about surrender. It is a matter of caring more about what God thinks than about what anyone else thinks.

God's Big Plans

God had much bigger plans for Moses than Moses had for himself. Ordered by Pharaoh to be murdered at birth (Exodus2) he was, instead, raised in Pharaoh's palace. Later he was guilty of murder, and hid out in a remote area called Midian. Moses apparently planned to spend his life as a shepherd in Midian.

Have you been there? Has a poor choice, sin, a broken relationship, a tarnished reputation, left you feeling like you just want to blend in to the wallpaper and get by? God had much bigger plans for Moses (as he does for you), but it took quite a bit of convincing. God called Moses to surrender his life to God's use. Have you heard God calling you to come closer to him? Perhaps you can relate to Moses' impassioned plea in Exodus 4:13, "Lord, Please! Send someone else!"

Total surrender to God is scary and difficult, for us as it was for Moses. In order to follow God's plan for your life, you have to let go of your own plans. Often, our plans center around our own personal comfort. For some it is a steady job and good income. For others it may be living close to family, or good health and security. Letting go of your own plans in order to embrace God's plan is a difficult test of faith. These tests come along periodically in different forms throughout our Christian journey. It seems that after we pass that hard test and choose to obey his calling, things should just fall right into place. It does not take long to discover, however, that is not reality. More often the sequence goes Call - Obedience - Problems - Blessings. After I finally surrender my will and have peace about doing what God is telling me to do, I run into problems.

After Moses agreed to obey God's call, with Aaron's help, he went to the Israelite leaders. God showed his power, the leaders believed and worshipped God for sending deliverance from slavery to Pharaoh (Exodus 4:29-31). Next they went to the Pharaoh. His harsh response was to require the slaves to work harder with less. In the face of this big problem, the Israelite leaders turned on Moses (Exodus 5:19). Moses in turn went to God asking why he had not delivered his people as he had said he would. God gave Moses reassurance of long-term victory, but the leaders were too discouraged to listen. For five long chapters (Exodus 7-11) God showed his total power through the plagues he sent to wipe out the land of Egypt. Only then did God lead his people out of the land victoriously. After Moses had agreed to obey, there were many obstacles and set-backs before the blessing came. Still, imagine what Moses would have missed experiencing if he had refused God's call altogether. God would have accomplished his will in another way, but Moses would have missed a tremendous blessing. When God calls you to follow his dreams for your life, it is always worth the fight.

I want to encourage you.

- First, if you have not yet experienced God's call to follow his dreams, you must start by submitting yourself totally to him. Humbly ask him to lead you into whatever he wants you to do and be.
- Second, if you have felt God's call upon your heart, but have not been willing to let go of your own dreams, your own comfort, I encourage you to trust him. Nothing else in life will ever be meaningful if you try to live outside the center of his will. Remember, his plans for you are much

bigger and richer than any plans you have for your own life.

- Finally, if you have chosen to obey, it is likely that are facing obstacles of some kind. Do not be discouraged. God makes himself known to you and to others as he works through those problems. Hang on tightly to him. He will not – he can not – fail you. As problems come, they drive us to deeper dependence and a deeper relationship with God. Stand firm.

Remember, Jesus did say, "If anyone would come after me, he must deny himself, take up his cross, and follow me" (Matthew 16:24). Your cross is hard to bear, but not as hard as his was. Stand firm. Victory is assured!

Fragrance Of God

"But thanks be to God, who made us his captives and leads us along in Christ's triumphal procession. <u>Now wherever we go he uses us to tell others about the Lord and to spread the Good News like a sweet perfume. Our lives are a fragrance presented by Christ to God</u>. But this fragrance is perceived differently by those being saved and by those perishing. To those who are perishing we are a fearful smell of death and doom. But to those who are being saved we are a life-giving perfume. And who is adequate for such a task as this?"(2 Corinthians 2:14-16 NLT).

So, how do you smell? Does your life give off a fragrance that attracts people to God and a life of forgiveness? Does the purity of your life remind those who have rejected God of their impending, fearful death? What have your co-workers smelled this past week? What have others in the community smelled through your words and actions? What kind of fragrance have you given off to your spouse and to your children?

The Holy Spirit has repeatedly had to remind me to listen to the words coming out of my mouth. You would think any intelligent parent would realize that sarcastic responses are not an effective way to train up my children to use words that build others up (as instructed in Ephesians 4:29). If my children base their decisions about Christianity in part on how I live out my faith, I must do better. Your children, your unsaved loved ones, your neighbors and co-workers, also make decisions about Christianity in part based on how you live as a representative of Christ. What does the fragrance of your life say to them? Mother Theresa put things so clearly in perspective.

People are often unreasonable and self-centered.
Forgive them anyway.
If you are kind, people may accuse you of ulterior motives.
Be kind anyway.
If you find happiness, people may be jealous.
Be happy anyway.
The good you do today may be forgotten tomorrow.
Do good anyway.
Give the world the best you have, and it may never be enough.
Give your best anyway.
For you see, in the end, it is between you and God.
It never was between you and them anyway.[46]

Running the Race

Although I have never been an athlete, and I don't watch many sporting events, I thoroughly enjoy watching the Olympics. I am always touched by the emotional aspect of the various competitions. These people put the rest of their lives on hold for years just to concentrate on training. Some see their dreams materialize but many face the heartbreak of falling or being disqualified, or just not being as strong as the other competitors. They put in countless hours of training and self-denial with no reward in the end. How discouraging! This has me thinking about another race each one of us runs.

The Apostle Paul told the Christians in Corinth, "Remember that in a race everyone runs, but only one person gets the prize. You also must run in such a way that you will win. All athletes practice strict self-control. They do it to win a prize that will fade away, but we do it for an eternal prize. So I run straight to the goal with purpose in every step. I am not like a boxer who misses his punches. I discipline my body like an athlete, training it to do what it should. Otherwise, I fear that after preaching to others I myself might be disqualified" (1 Corinthians 9:24-27 NLT).

There are three clear messages in this passage. First, Paul talks about running purposefully toward the prize. Is Christianity just a part of my life, or is every step aimed at pleasing Christ and drawing closer to him? Goals of professional success, a nice home and car, personal beauty, education, or comfortable living are often incompatible with running toward the prize. All my efforts toward self-improvement should be focused on becoming a more effective tool in the Master's hand. After all, it is not about me.

The second lesson in this passage is the possibility of failure. An athlete who fails to win or even finish his Olympic race can either go back determined to train harder and succeed next time, or he can leave competition and enter the world the rest of us live in. Either can be a good choice. In the race of life, however, failure is eternal. The author of this passage, the Apostle Paul himself, took nothing for granted. He said that he must be careful always to practice what he was preaching or be disqualified for the prize. The prize of eternity with Jesus is worth so much more than a medal made from heaven's pavement (gold).

Finally, the passage tells us to give our all. Picture a downhill skier who stops every hundred yards or so to take a rest, or enjoy the view, or have a snack. That is not racing, but it is how many of us run the race of life. We get wounded or discouraged or tired as we try to serve Christ. Sometimes we stumble back into sin. Other times we get pushed down by others. In either case, the temptation comes to just lie down and lick our wounds for a while. We don't renounce our faith, we just stop working at it. We stop trying to draw near to God. We stop serving in his kingdom. We stop running the race. Just like Olympic athletes, we must get up and continue on toward the prize. God has given us all we need, but we must choose to use it and keep on keeping on. If you find yourself spiritually on the sidelines, Friend, I encourage you today to get up and resume the race . . . not because it doesn't hurt, but because the Savior is calling. "His divine power has given us everything we need for life and godliness through our knowledge of him who called us by his own glory and goodness" (2 Peter 1:3).

A Growing Disciple

Over the years we have lived in our home, most rooms have undergone some remodeling. Through every project since my son learned to walk, he has clearly demonstrated to me what discipleship is all about. Any time his Daddy was home, Hunter would be right there working hard. In the beginning he was not skilled in using power tools, and didn't even understand the big plan, but he would give his all every day. When Bart wasn't working on the project, his young disciple would still think about it and talk about it all day long.

After an exhausting week of construction, my tired little builder snuggled on my lap telling me he would always stay three years old and always stay with Mommy. I had the (unusual for me) wisdom to leave the floors dirty and just rock him and pray for him. What a beautiful hour!

As I rocked my little builder, God reminded me of a passage of Scripture that compares new Christians to newborn babies. Despite Hunter's words that day, he has continued to grow and mature, and eventually he will leave home. That is the way we are made. The same should be true for believers in Christ, but some do not want to grow. The writer of Hebrews addressed this issue, "In fact, though by this time you ought to be teachers, you need someone to teach you the elementary truths of God's word all over again. You need milk, not solid food! Anyone who lives on milk, being still an infant, is not acquainted with the teaching about righteousness. But solid food is for the mature, who by constant use have trained themselves to distinguish good from evil" (Hebrews 5:12-14).

Some of us have been Christians for a year or two, even five or ten, but still act like infants. We come to church to have someone feed us the Word, but make no effort to feed ourselves on the Word at home. Some of us read the Bible, but do not put into practice what it says. Too many believers want to sit on the Father's lap and bask in his peace, but don't want to get down to the work of teaching and serving others. This is not natural, or healthy, or pleasing to God. Each of us is called to be a disciple, following daily in the steps of the Savior. We need to do the work he has given us to do, and make time to climb into his lap.

Holy Conversation

Before I got married, I lived and worked several hours drive from my family. I spent a lot of time with a group of Christian singles from the large church I attended. One night we were all gathered at the town house I was renting with two friends. People started telling jokes and someone said he knew one, but he wasn't sure if he should share it. I suggested that if it was questionable he probably shouldn't. A few minutes later, he started telling it any way. Having already spoken up once, I didn't want to seem judgmental or "holier than thou" so I just went upstairs. Not long after that, as I was praying for my friends to want to be more Christ-like, I heard a mocking voice say, "She's probably upstairs praying for us right now." Even though it was true, the comment hurt my feelings. These people called themselves Christians, and they were, but some were mocking me for trying to be holy. (Years later the joke-teller apologized to me.) Maybe something like this has happened to you.

Scripture has some pretty stern things to say about our speech. Here are a couple of examples:

- "Do not let any unwholesome talk come out of your mouths, but only what is helpful for building others up according to their needs, that it may benefit those who listen" (Ephesians 4:29).
- "May the words of my mouth and the meditation of my heart be pleasing in your sight, O Lord, my Rock, and my Redeemer" (Psalm 19:14).
- "Nor should there be obscenity, foolish talk, or coarse joking, which are out of place, but rather, thanksgiving" (Ephesians 5:4).
- "But the things that come out of the mouth come from the heart, and these make a man unclean" (Matthew 15:18).

In light of these passages, what are we to do? I believe there are two major areas of responsibility. First, we must guard our own tongues very carefully. Second, we must encourage others to do the same. I have heard it said that my words should be a gift to everyone who hears them. Let's think about the words and tone of voice we have used this past week, this past day, this past hour . . . Were they given as gifts to build others up, and to benefit those who listen? I think most of us don't have to rewind very far to find words we have spoken which do just the opposite.

The second area of responsibility may be even harder for some than the first. Once I begin learning to control what I say, I should become more concerned about what I hear. Obviously, there will be things said in your hearing over which you have no control. There are many times, however, when you can either remove yourself from the situation or ask those speaking to change the topic. Although many of us don't do this for fear of offending, it ought to be our common practice among believers. If you aren't sure what to say, try using my Dad's line, "I'm uncomfortable with this conversation." This statement is non-threatening, nonjudgmental, and yet effective communication. If another believer is using language that tears someone down rather than building him up, I believe we have a responsibility to gently and lovingly rebuke him or her in a way that is beneficial. It is not fun, but it is taking a stand for righteousness and holiness. Remember, you will be held responsible for what you do and say, not for how the other person responds. We need to be more concerned about offending God than we are about offending people. I challenge each of us to invite the Holy Spirit to examine every word we speak, and bring conviction when it is needed. Let us honor him in every word.

State of Your Life Address

Each year in January, our President delivers a State of the Union Address. Where else do government leaders with such divided viewpoints meet together peacefully? Whether you agree with the current President's politics or not, you are obligated to pray for those God has placed in authority over you (Titus 3:1, Romans 13:5-7).

Each year in January our Pastor gives a State of the Church Address at our local conference. We celebrate how God has led and provided so far, and look at where God is leading next. Whether you approve of your pastors' decisions and priorities or not, you are obligated to respect him and pray for him. I admit it seemed strange, six years ago, to look up to my little brother as a spiritual leader. God has made it clear, however, that his hand is on Pastor Jim because he is a man after God's own heart.

January, then, is a good time for each of us to get alone with God and ask him to give us a "State of My life Address." I must warn you, though, if you ask, he will tell you what he sees. One afternoon my son was helping clean the house before a Bible Study. I intended to just straighten things up and sweep the floors. My four-year-old had bigger plans. I swept, and he mopped, then we tackled the mud room, just in case anyone might come in that way. I was just going to have him do the exposed part of the floor. (How clean does a room named "mud" need to be any way?) I explained my plan and left him to finish the job. Moments later I returned to find the rug folded up and all the shoe racks and shelves piled on top. Hunter was attacking the dirty corners with his mop.

Needless to say, the whole room got cleaned that day. As I worked I thought about how God works in our lives. Often we just want to look good to anyone who is watching, but God calls us to be "Holy" which means to be set apart. (See Romans 12:1, 1 Corinthians 1:2, 1 Thessalonians 4:7, 2 Timothy 1:9, 1 Peter 1:16, 2 Peter 3:11.) He wants us to become more and more like him, set apart from all evil. Each of us would do well to periodically get alone with God and let him show us the corners of our hearts which we have not fully surrendered to him. In this way we will draw closer to him and become better reflections of him to those around us.

The people who live in your house (like the people who live in my house) know all about the areas that are cluttered and less than clean. Even worse, these same people know us so well that they see the areas in our lives that are unclean. We are really hiding very little from them, and nothing at all from God. May we have the courage to let him decide what really needs to be cleaned.

Raising Disciples

In his book, *Faith Begins at Home*, Mark Holmen tells about hearing Dr. David Anderson ask a group of parents how many of them desired to see their teens to have a stronger faith. Then he responded by telling them that kids mirror the faith of their parents.[47]

301

Therefore, if we want to see our kids living in faith more fully, we need to live that way ourselves. Where is Christ standing in your life? Is he at the very center of your existence, influencing the decisions you make and the way you live your life? Or is he still outside knocking? Mr. Holmen cites research which clearly shows that mothers and fathers (not church leaders or teachers) are the top influences in the faith development of children. Our children's faith will likely be a reflection of the faith they see in us. What do they see?

"Hear, O Israel: The Lord our God, the Lord is one. Love the Lord your God with all your heart and with all your soul and with all your strength. These commandments that I give you today are to be upon your hearts. Impress them on your children. Talk about them when you sit at home and when you walk along the road, when you lie down and when you get up. Tie them as symbols on your hands and bind them on your foreheads. Write them on the doorframes of your houses and on your gates" (Deuteronomy 6:4-9).

The task of becoming a true disciple seems somewhat daunting to many of us. The task of raising children who are whole-heartedly devoted to God seems well beyond impossible. Where do we start? Clearly, we need to start by looking at our own lives and the level of our own devotion. Do I pray enough with my children that they will know how to pray in any and every situation? Do I model for them how to read the Bible and apply it to daily life? Do we regularly discuss the ways God has made himself known through creation and through daily circumstances? Are we involved together in service to those less fortunate? Do I exhibit the fruit of the Spirit when nobody is home but the family? Parental hypocrisy is a common reason given by college students for deciding not to attend church. We must live what we say we believe. The eternal destiny of those we love most may depend on it.

If you have children at home, I urge you to start asking God regularly to show you how to train them to be disciples. If your children are grown, you still have opportunity to pray with them and talk with them about the things that matter most. This will only be effective if you are honest about your own struggles in the faith. Finally, if you do not have children of your own, society still needs you desperately. Pray, pray, pray for those in your community. Find ways to reach out with the gospel message to some who will not see that example at home. Invite them into your home and live that example before them. Seeing faith in action in the home is far more powerful than hearing about it at church.

One final thought. The cover of the book mentioned above shows a drawing of a young child walking with his feet on the feet of his parent. Where are your feet leading your children/step children /grandchildren?

Prayer Warriors

In one month, three prayer warriors from our church all suffered serious health problems at the same time. A prayer warrior is someone who regularly does battle against the evils of the world through earnest, impassioned prayer. These women of faith have been faithfully on their knees over the years to fight the enemy. Who among us, if anyone, is not here as a result of someone praying for us? The illnesses of these women left me with a very troubling question: Who is going to fill their shoes? One day these faithful warriors will go to receive their reward. If the future strength of the church depends in part on the faithfulness of your prayers and mine, we might be in trouble.

Prayer – earnest, faithful, effective prayer – is the most difficult spiritual discipline to develop. The enemy would far rather have you sing praises, read good books, even serve others than have you pray. Why? Satan doesn't want you to pray, because that is where the power is! In Ezekiel 22:30 God says, "I looked for a man among them who would build up the wall and stand before me in the gap on behalf of the land so I would not have to destroy it, but I found none." What would it mean to "stand in the gap" faithfully for your church? Here are some of the things we ought to be seeking God for:
- Lost souls to come to salvation all around the world
- Unity within the church body
- Wisdom and discernment for church leaders
- More laborers (pastors, missionaries, and lay leaders) to be raised up from this body
- Protection over marriages and families

- Believers to continually go deeper in their spiritual walks

How many of us are praying, even occasionally for these needs? Looking at my own track record, I wonder if even five percent of believers are engaged in the battle. Some of us are too lazy to work that hard. Others are too wrapped up in the so-called crises of daily life. Too many are not yet totally surrendered to the Master. Still others have never been taught the discipline of prayer. Finally, there are those who would deny that we are engaged in spiritual warfare. Can you imagine a Marine sitting on a street corner in Baghdad insisting that there is no war? Ludicrous and foolhardy! Furthermore, because he is not making an effort to protect himself, he is an easy target. If you are a follower of Christ who is not fighting the enemy through prayer, not protecting yourself through studying the Word, "If you think you are standing firm, be careful that you don't fall!" (1 Corinthians 10:12). Each of us is a soldier. In 2 Corinthians 10:4, the Apostle Paul reminds us that "The weapons we fight with are not the weapons of the world. On the contrary, they have divine power to demolish strongholds." A large part of the battle is fought through prayer.

Still, effective prayer is much more than giving God a daily list of concerns even if the things on the list are very important. It is learning to hear the heart of God; to pray in the Spirit; to have a heart that breaks at the things that break the heart of God. It is fervent, urgent. This is not a battle to be fought lying in bed at the end of the day, tossing up requests as I fall asleep. This is blood, sweat, and tears day after day, on my knees, pleading like souls depend on it. Because they do. Remember, "The prayer of a righteous man is powerful and effective" (James 5:16). May those who come behind you and me find us faithful as prayer warriors.

Whom Do You Serve?

For many years I have tried to read through the entire Bible in a year. I try to make it a practice, each day before I read, to ask the Holy Spirit to speak to me through the Word. He is faithful to answer that prayer. Truly "The Word of God is living and active" (Hebrews 4:12) like no other book ever written.

Matthew 19 describes an encounter Jesus had with someone described only as a rich young man. "Now a man came up to Jesus and asked, 'Teacher, what good thing must I do to get eternal life?' 'Why do you ask me about what is good?' Jesus replied. 'There is only One who is good. If you want to enter life, obey the commandments.' 'Which ones?' the man inquired. Jesus replied, 'Do not murder, do not commit adultery, do not steal, do not give false testimony, honor your father and mother,' and 'love your neighbor as yourself.' 'All these I have kept,' the young man said. 'What do I still lack?' Jesus answered, 'If you want to be perfect, go, sell your possessions and give to the poor, and you will have treasure in heaven. Then come, follow me.' When the young man heard this, he went away sad, because he had great wealth" (Matthew 19:16-22). Jesus then told his disciples that it is hard, but not impossible, for rich people to enter the kingdom. Notice how Jesus answered the man's question. He came in sincerity, wanting to know how to earn eternal life. He had apparently spent his life trying to do the right things. Jesus started where the man was, telling him to obey the commandments. The man asked which ones he should obey. I am not sure why he did not assume Jesus meant all of them. Perhaps it was because the religious leaders had added on so many rules to the ones handed down by Moses. Anyway, Jesus gave a surprising answer. I would have expected him to mention the ten written on stone tablets by the hand of God, or to state the two he later identified as being the greatest commands ("Love the Lord your God with all your heart and with all your soul and with all your mind" and, "Love your neighbor as yourself," Matthew 22:37-39). Instead, Jesus listed five from the original ten, and the second-greatest commandment. Why did he choose those six? Why did he skip over all of the commands about how to love God supremely, to have no other gods or idols, to speak His Name with respect and keep the Sabbath, and the command to avoid coveting things that others have? Jesus, knowing the man better than he knew himself, initially mentioned the things this young man was doing. The wealthy young man, stating that he had already been observing these commands, recognized that his good deeds were not enough. He then asked, "What do I still lack?" At this point in the conversation, Jesus went to the matter of the man's heart. Although he did not list any more commandments, he put his finger on that which was most important in the man's life – his wealth. You see four of the remaining five commandments, and the Greatest Commandment all address the heart attitude. Faced with a choice, this sad young man chose to hold onto his money and possessions, placing them before God in his life. For him the cost of following Christ was too high.

Friends, what can we learn from this passage? The Bible does not teach that all believers should sell their possessions and give the money to the poor. The issue is not the money, it is the heart. In order to truly follow Christ, I must die to myself – my goals, my comfort, my desires – and take up my cross daily (Matthew 16:24, Mark 8:34, Luke 9:23). There is no other way. I cannot serve both God and my own pleasure (Matthew 6:24).

How would this conversation read if we replaced "the rich young man" with "an American church member" who encountered Jesus? Friends, we are the rich people whom Jesus said would have difficulty entering the kingdom of heaven. We, like the rich young man, are strongly tempted to find our security in our stuff, to spend our time and energy protecting our stuff and trying to get more stuff.

I believe that every person who sincerely wants to follow Christ will at some point be faced with a choice between serving self or serving God. Will you, like the rich young man, turn away from God in sorrow, or will you let go of the things of this world in order to allow the kingdom of heaven to reign in your heart? The only way to experience fulfilling, abundant life is to fully surrender control to the Savior. This is a daily, hourly choice each of us has to make. Are you ready to do that today?

The Work You've Been Given

Genesis tells the story about a man named Noah. Noah had a relationship with God, and God was pleased with him. When God decided to destroy the earth's population with a flood, only Noah and his family were to be spared, along with enough animals to continue each species. God could easily have provided Noah with an ark full of animals and simply said, "Come aboard!" He could have scooped them all up and placed them on a mountain top and skipped the boat ride altogether. Why didn't he do that? It would have saved Noah a hundred years of hard work, frustration, and ridicule. Instead, he invited Noah to be a part of the plan. He waited for Noah to complete the work he had been given to do.

God did not need Noah's help any more than he needs my help or yours. Any parent can testify that allowing small children to help with a project (vacuuming, washing dishes, shoveling snow, stacking wood, cooking, etc.) usually results in more mess, slower progress, and an end-result of lower quality. Still, we allow and invite our children to be involved in what we are doing because it strengthens the relationship, and fosters an attitude of service to others.

To some extent the same is true with God's children. He invites and expects us to participate in the work he is doing. Not because he needs us, but because it helps us to recognize how much we need him. Working in tandem with God for his glory helps us to keep focused on his goals. It also helps us to be aware of the needs of others, rather than being all wrapped up in ourselves. Doing the work God has given us to do, develops in us a Christ-like character. It isn't the work itself that concerns God, nearly so much as it is our obedience to his leading. When we are surrendered to him, he can win a war or save a nation or change a community or break the cycle of abuse in a family. Nothing is too hard for God (Jeremiah 32:17).

Mordecai told Queen Esther, "For if you remain silent at this time, relief and deliverance for the Jews will arise from another place, but you and your father's family will perish" (Esther 4:14a). Mordecai understood that God was able to bring deliverance with or without Esther. Disobedience would be costly to her and her family, not to God.

Friend, are you doing the work God has called you to do? If you choose to disobey, God will get the work done some other way, but you will pay a price. Your relationship with God can never be as rich and fulfilling and abundant and rewarding as he wants it to be if you live in disobedience. Let each of us ask the Lord today what work he would have us do, and then set out to do that work.

More Than I Can Handle

Are you familiar with the statement, "I know God will never give me more than I can handle, I just wish he didn't trust me so much"? I have concluded that, as clever as this phrase sounds, it is categorically untrue. Anyone who has endured abuse, or received a dreaded diagnosis, or buried a loved one unexpectedly, or been abandoned, can testify that sometimes in life we are given more than we can handle. Prisoners of the holocaust and many more can testify to this. In the midst of a serious crisis, just breathing in and out all day long seems about as much as a person can handle. Many of you know this from personal experience far better than I do.

2 Corinthians 10:13 tells us, "No temptation has seized you except what is common to man. And God is faithful; he will not let you be tempted beyond what you can bear. But when you are tempted, he will also provide a way out so that you can stand up under it." I have found no place in Scripture that says God will not give me more than I can handle. Rather, the Bible is replete with examples of people being given more than they could handle. Think of Moses, leading a million Hebrews out of Egypt with minimal provisions and no itinerary. Trapped between the Red Sea and the chariots of the Egyptian army, caring for the Israelites was far more than Moses could handle (see Exodus 13, 14).

I believe God allows us at times to be given more than we can handle because it forces us to depend upon him. Depending on him when there is no hope of any way out, develops faith in God. He is faithful to lead and to provide and to help us along the way. The Apostle Paul, who endured great hardship, wrote, "But he said to me, 'My grace is sufficient for you, for my power is made perfect in weakness.' Therefore I will boast all the more gladly about my weaknesses, so that Christ's power may rest on me. That is why, for Christ's sake, I delight in weaknesses, in insults, in hardships, in persecutions, in difficulties. For when I am weak, then I am strong" (2 Corinthians 12:10). He also said, "I can do everything through him who gives me strength" (Philippians 4:13). There are many things I cannot do without his strength. With his strength, however, God's children can do whatever he calls them to do. He never expected you to handle those storms on your own. He has no desire to sit in the passenger seat like your driver's training instructor and just watch how you do on your own. Rather, he desires to guide you and to empower you as you allow his strength and discernment to flow through you.

It is the role of the Holy Spirit to help us to know and recognize and follow the example of Christ Jesus our Savior all the days of our lives. Let each of us welcome the Holy Spirit to dwell and to reign in our hearts. In our weakness he is strong. Through his strength we can face each new day, each hour, each moment. When we don't know the words to pray, he intercedes. If the storms of life are more than you can handle today, I invite you to find rest, hope, and renewed strength in the Savior.

Not Nearly Close Enough

Author A. W. Tozer argued there are many riches available to God's people, but some of those riches can only be claimed through earnest effort. He lists eight such blessings. The two that really resonate with me are the riches of "awareness of the presence of God," and "an unbroken spirit of worship."[48] Is it really possible to go through the moments and hours of each day with a continual awareness of his presence and an unbroken spirit of worship? I think this is what is meant by Paul's admonition to "pray without ceasing" (1 Thessalonians 5:17). Praying is communion, interaction with God. The Word tells us to do that constantly. That has not been my experience thus far, but if it is possible, that is what I want. How do I get to that place where my mind is aware of him and praising him no matter what else I am doing? The only way is by allowing the Holy Spirit to help me to "be transformed by the renewing of my mind" (Romans 12:2). Keith Green described this longing beautifully in his song, *Make My Life a Prayer To You*.[49]

Being a "doer" my mind is running almost constantly with things I need to do. In my first professional job as a school psychologist, my daily To Do list was always far longer than I could reasonably accomplish in a day. There were so many files to examine, parents to contact, teachers to touch base with, children to test, tests to score, reports to write, and meetings to schedule . . . I could never catch up. After a couple of years on the job I noticed that I could go through an entire day, actually nearly every day, without giving God more than a passing thought between seven a.m. and four p.m. I started writing "pray" on my list of things to do so that I would remember to include a moment with God in my day. Friends, that is a far cry from living each day in awareness of his presence!

These days I no longer work as a school psychologist. My days are now filled with caring for a family and a home, and ministry to people. Ministry is always on my mind. Sadly, I have discovered that it is possible and even easy to do all kinds of ministry tasks without ever really taking time to focus on being aware of God's presence. I am trying to develop the discipline of training my mind to be continually aware of his presence throughout the day and to choose to praise him with words or songs no matter what else I am doing. For me personally, being a visual learner, I picture in my mind God seated on his throne (as described in Isaiah 6 and Revelation 4). That helps me shift my focus from earthly things to the One I am serving. Even in prayer I am trying to keep my focus on who I'm talking to rather than on my list of people or situations to pray for. I am trying to sing songs of praise, at least in my mind, all throughout the day. The bottom line is an overwhelming desire to be as close to God as he wants me to be, and I have a long way to go.

What about you? Is your heart yearning for the richness of unbroken fellowship with the Savior? Do you desire him more than anything else in all of life? I invite you, I exhort you, I urge you, to seek him more earnestly. Do not be satisfied with where you are spiritually, but always be striving to go deeper in Christ. What could/would God do in our lives if the highest priority each day was to love him more today than yesterday?

Life is Hard, but God is Good

Having been single for so many years, I never liked the excuse-for-a-holiday that is celebrated on February 14. It was just one more occasion when it was painful to be alone. Of course, there really are no easy days to be alone, are there? Some of my dearest friends are limping through the loneliness of grief. Others have spent years longing for a spouse or a family, but those dreams have not yet come true. They are burdened by the loneliness of unfulfilled longings. Some are separated from their families by miles or by unforgiveness, stuck in the loneliness of regret. Brothers and sisters, so many around us are hurting and feeling alone. Even those who aren't lonely may be feeling defeated by problems with health or work or finances or parenting. The truth is, life is hard, isn't it? Job, who knew all about how hard life can be, said that a man's days are few and filled with trouble (Job 14:1). I think most of us would agree.

What kind of trouble are you facing today? If not struggles of your own, you are likely carrying burdens for a loved one. Hardships are a part of life. The question is, what are you going to do in the hard place where you find yourself? What is your goal for this day? Some days it is merely survival. Eventually though, we need to set our goals higher. Rather than waiting for our problems to go away or be resolved, we can achieve victory in the midst of them. Victory means bringing glory to God wherever you happen to be. Your most powerful testimony to those around you may be the peace and hope of God that fill your life in the middle of terrible storms.

No matter what struggle you are facing today, victory is possible in Jesus Christ. "His divine power has given us everything we need for life and godliness through our knowledge of him who called us by his own glory and goodness. Through these he has given us his very great and precious promises, so that through them you may participate in the divine nature and escape the corruption in the world caused by evil desires" (2 Peter 1:3,4). Brothers and sisters, no matter what your circumstances, there is no excuse for second-rate Christianity. Each Christian has been given everything we need for godly living. Everything we need. Therefore, if we are not living in victory, it is because we are not making use of the resources available. Several years ago I heard Pam Thum sing "Life is hard, but God is good."[50] That statement is true all the time, no matter what we may be feeling. If it is possible to rise up out of the pit of despair, to walk in hope and peace, that is what we want. How then, do we experience victory over our feelings and our circumstances? 2 Corinthians 10:5 reminds us to "Take captive every thought to make it obedient to Christ." We start by setting our minds on God rather than on our problems. Choose a song of praise or a verse about how great he is and set that on continuous play cycle in your brain. Lay your burdens at his feet, and communicate with him all throughout the day. Abide in him and bring glory to His Name by your attitude and your outlook. He is the author of hope and nothing is too hard for him (Jeremiah 32:17). As Beth Moore says, "You have never met a situation that can't be changed."[51] Our God is more than able to work in any and every circumstance for our good and his glory. May he be glorified in your life and in mine today.

Put Out to Pasture

Have you ever been so discouraged and empty that you wondered whether it was even worth the effort to keep striving? I guess we all feel that way at times. I know I do. Over the years friends have expressed weariness and a desire to just be done with living and all the pain life brings. Perhaps you too struggle with feelings of futility. This problem is not a new phenomenon of the 21st century.

Numbers tells the story of twelve men, one from each tribe, chosen to go as spies and check out the land God had promised to give to his people. Ten out of twelve men brought back a negative, pessimistic report and convinced the Israelites not to try to enter. The people not only doubted God and refused to enter the land, but also rebelled against Moses and Aaron for bringing them (Numbers 13 and 14). God put those ten spies to death, and sentenced the rest of the people to forty years in the wilderness until that generation passed on. Talk about being put out to pasture. They were basically just wandering around, waiting to die so the next generation could have a chance to go into the Promised Land. Sounds like a death row sentence. No purpose, no reason to try. What were they supposed to do?

Can you relate? Have you reached a point in your life where you don't have a sense of purpose? Maybe it is because of physical limitations. Maybe it is the result of choices – your own or somebody else's. Do you feel like you're sitting on a shelf, or wandering aimlessly, going nowhere? Those feelings can be very strong, but that does not make them truth.

If you are still breathing, God still has a purpose for you, just as he did for those Israelites. Actually, their final assignment turned out to be one of their most important tasks. They were to train up the next generation to know and trust God. Talk about trying to give your children a better life than you had! Those who chose to give their best in a bad situation, rather than collapsing in a pile of self-pity, played a very important role in conquering the Promised Land even though they never set foot in it. They trained and taught and prepared the next generation to know and honor and trust God.

Friend, one of the most important tasks that God has given to all of his followers through all generations is to teach others to know him and to be his disciples. That is just as true today as it was hundreds of generations ago. Whether your own biological offspring or someone else's – you have an opportunity to help change a life for eternity. Don't miss it. Many a person rendered unable to do much of anything has spent a season of his/her life praying for people. I wouldn't be surprised to learn one day that those hours of prayer bore greater spiritual fruit than all of the "useful" busy years of life that preceded those days. Brother, Sister, there is still work to be done. "Let us not become weary in doing good, for at the proper time we will reap a harvest if we do not give up" (Galatians 6:9).

Are You the Gifted or the Gift?

There was a day in my mid-twenties when I clearly heard the Holy Spirit tell me that God was preparing me to be a partner in ministry to the man I would one day marry. I wasn't sure what to do with the information, but I had great peace that it would eventually work out just as God had said. A few years later, after Bart had heard and responded to the call to ministry, God brought the two of us together. Today I am honored to help Bart and help this church in the work of the kingdom.

Scripture makes it very clear that God works out his plans in and through individual lives. In some cases he called leaders like Moses and Noah and Gideon, giving them the strength, and courage, and skills they needed as they needed them. In other cases he gave gifts and abilities to certain people, so that they could be

313

used in his service at a future time. For example, exactly three months after God led them out of Egypt, the Israelites came to Mt. Sinai and Moses went up the mountain to meet with God (Exodus 19). The next eleven chapters record laws and instructions God gave to Moses. In additional to the Ten Commandments and other rules for community living, God also gave Moses detailed directions for building the ark, the altar, the Tabernacle with all its articles, and the priestly garments. At the end of all these complicated instructions, the Lord said to Moses, "See, I have chosen Bezalel son of Uri, the son of Hur, of the tribe of Judah and I have filled him with the Spirit of God, with skill, ability and knowledge in all kinds of crafts – to make artistic designs for work in gold, silver and bronze, to cut and set stones, to work in wood, and to engage in all kinds of craftsmanship. Moreover, I have appointed Oholiab son of Ahisamach, of the tribe of Dan, to help him. Also I have given skill to all the craftsmen to make everything I have commanded you" (Exodus 31:1-6). God had equipped people to do the work even before they knew what God wanted them to do. He is still doing that today, even in your life.

God assigned Moses' brother Aaron to be the high priest and his descendants to be priests for all future generations. He said, "I am giving you the service of the priesthood as a gift" (Numbers 18:7). The opportunity to serve God is a gift. Not only that, but he gave the rest of Aaron's tribe, the Levites, "as a gift" to Aaron, to help him in the work of the Tabernacle (18:6). The help and support of other people was given as a gift, not by the people themselves but by God. It is interesting to note, in the story of Moses and Aaron, that each of them was given as a gift to help others before being given a gift of leadership responsibility. God gave Moses as a gift to the Israelites, even as he was giving him the gift of leadership responsibility. Moses initially resisted this gift (which he didn't see as a gift at all), so God gave Aaron to him as a gift, to help him lead the people. Aaron was given as a gift to assist Moses, before he received from God the gift of priestly leadership responsibility. Could it be that the humility of being willing to be given as a gift to help someone else minister is part of the training process that must precede being gifted for leadership?

Then as now, people rebelled against being told what to do. Leaders and citizens among the Israelites rose up against Moses' leadership several times. They considered themselves just as able to lead, and encouraged people to rebel (see Numbers 16 and 17). God made it very clear that Moses and Aaron were chosen by him. He considered the questioning of their authority as treating him with contempt (Numbers 16:30). Pride led to destruction, and 250 leaders and their families were swallowed alive by the earth.

Friends, we can learn a lot from the recorded history of the Israelites. Each of us is being equipped for the work God wants us to be doing. Some will receive the gift of leading a particular area of ministry (for a season or for a lifetime). Those individuals should respond in willingness even though they do not feel qualified. Those God calls, he equips. In our weakness his power is revealed (2 Corinthians 12:9). The rest of us need to humble ourselves and be willing to be given as gifts to those in leadership, in order to help them in the work of the kingdom. Pride is one of the favorite and most effective tools of the enemy. He will try to convince us that we are more talented, and more qualified to lead in a given area than those who currently occupy those positions. I caution you, if you are entertaining critical thoughts toward those in leadership of various areas of ministry, be very careful. God does not take rebellion lightly. Moses and Aaron were not perfect, but they were chosen by God and he defended them. Leaders today obviously are not perfect either. It is the responsibility of us followers to pray for them, to uphold them and encourage them, rather than tearing them down – even in our own minds (see Hebrews 13:17 and 1 Thessalonians 5:12,13). Let us pray regularly that pride will not gain a foothold in our hearts or in our churches. Be willing to receive the gift of serving or to be given as a gift – whichever will bring God the greatest glory.

God is Always Watching

The writer of Hebrews chapter 11 describes faith as "Being sure of what we hope for and certain of what we do not see." When my children were young we had the opportunity to visit a water park. Five-year-old Sierra was going down a water slide. She wanted me to catch her at the bottom, which I did. After several rides, I started just catching her hand at the bottom and letting her land on her own feet. Soon she had the courage to land on her own, as long as I was nearby. Before long I was able to sit on the closest edge of the pool and watch her slide down and land on her own. As I watched her, I realized that our heavenly Father works just the same way with his children. When a newborn believer lands in deep water, God is right there, revealing himself through Scripture, people, songs, and circumstances. He "catches" the young Christian. As we begin to grow in our faith, the evidences of his presence during trials may be fewer, or delayed, or more subtle than before. Gradually, through experiences and trials, our faith grows stronger. We learn to hold on to what we know to be true about God, even when we cannot feel his presence close by.

These thoughts came to me as I watched my daughter play. Being a psychologist, I naturally had to try a little experiment with this analogy. Each time she turned her back to climb up the steps, I moved a little further away from the slide. Sure enough, each time she landed in the water, she looked immediately to where I was sitting and showed no fear. Soon I was about twenty feet away from her. She continued to play with complete confidence, checking to make sure my gaze was upon her each time she landed. That is how our loving Father wants us to be, confident in deep water because we know his eyes are on us. A mature believer going through severe trials may not feel the Presence of the Savior, yet his faith will hold steadfast because God has taught him that he can always be trusted.

Today, if you are facing a trial and wondering why God does not seem as close as he did in previous trials, take courage. God has been developing your character and your faith. His eyes are on you every moment, and he is involved in every detail of your life. "If the Lord delights in a man's way, he makes his steps firm; though he stumble, he will not fall, for the Lord upholds him with his hand" (Psalm 37:23-24). Hebrews 13:5b tells us that Jesus said, "Never will I leave you, never will I forsake you." And the Psalmist reminds us that God "will neither slumber nor sleep" (Psalm 121:4). Take courage as you seek to draw closer to him.

A Heart For People

I think that those of us who have grown up in the church and participated in many types of ministry, have a tendency to lead based on our training and experience. We plan and organize and try to equip others for the work. That was my approach leading up to a mission trip. I started with what I had to offer. I tried to teach people some Spanish, and I helped to plan Bible story presentations for the children. Once in Guatemala we got to know some of the people of the mountain village, especially the kids. While I was thinking of how to use what we had prepared, someone else was thinking about what those kids needed and wanted, a party with a piñata to make them feel loved and special. That night was the highlight of the trip. I had been trying to lead with my head. A fellow team member led with his heart. I started with what I had to offer. He started with where the people were. His approach reminded me of Christ.

Jesus showed compassion and met needs. Lame people were enabled to walk. Blind people were able to see. The deaf could hear. Lepers and others who were sick received healed from Jesus. Some who had died were brought back to life. In addition, the good news was preached (Luke 7:22). Jesus used the power of God to help people. He expected his followers to use the power God gave them to continue the work Christ had begun. God still works through disciples today to show compassion and to meet needs.

I want to thank John Whitney for showing me what it means to have Christ's heart for people. I also want to encourage each of you to listen to your heart so that God can love others through you. I once heard a speaker say, "God is not nearly as interested in your ability, as he is in your availability." Let us learn to make ourselves available to whatever God is leading us to do in His Name and for his glory. Let us be praying for the kind of passion for lost people that Jesus Christ himself has.

A Hard Gift to Give

"This is how God showed his love among us; he sent his one and only Son into the world that we might live through him. This is love: not that we loved God, but that he loved us and sent His Son as an atoning sacrifice for our sins. Dear friends, since God so loved us, we also ought to love one another. No one has ever seen God; but if we love one another, God lives in us and his love is made complete in us" (1 John 4:9-12). God gave us his Son, opening a pathway to himself. In return, he wants us to love him and love others. "This is love for God: to obey his commands" (1 John 5:3a). Obedience shows love. Jesus said, "If you love me, you will obey what I command" (John 14:15). My friend Jennifer has used two concise reminders in teaching her children to obey. First, "Slow obedience is no obedience" and second, "Disobedience hurts."

Unfortunately, many of us adults need these reminders from our heavenly parent. Rather than just saying we love God, we need to show it by our obedience to his Word. This applies not only to those "big" commands like "Do not kill," but also to warnings against gluttony, lying, complaining, and poor stewardship. The Bible says, if we are not heeding these warnings, we do not truly love God. Furthermore, until we obey the direct commands in his Word, he is not likely to give us more specific instructions regarding his plans for us. I remember my Dad saying, "We have no business asking God to give us more light when we are not yet walking in the light he has already given us." Slow obedience equals disobedience.

Most of us know what God has commanded us to do – seek to reconcile a relationship, end a relationship which is outside of his will, conquer a destructive habit, start using his gifts, etc. I think often we just don't want to put forth the effort and self-sacrifice that true obedience would require. I would like to share with you something I read in a novella by Francine Rivers called *Unafraid*. This is fiction about the life of Mary, the mother of Jesus, using the information found in Scripture, and then filled out based on research of the way things were in Bible times. In Rivers' adaptation of the story, at the point in the life of Jesus when his earthly father was dying, Mary pleaded with him to heal Joseph. Jesus had the power to do so. Instead, he chose obedience to God's will, at the cost of his personal comfort and his mother's broken heart. Talk about total obedience![52]

I urge you to receive God's love in the person of His Son, Jesus. Then, I urge you to give to him the gift of obedience. To call him Lord is to call him Master – deserving of unquestioning obedience. Let us make that our commitment. Let's start today.

References

[1] Stone,Nathan. <u>Names of God</u>. Northfield Pub. 1999. p. 11

[2] Lawrence, Chuck. <u>He Grew the Tree</u>. EMI Christian Music Group, 1982

[3] Watson, Wayne, <u>Walk in the Dark</u>, Word Music,1993

[4] Tozer, A.W. <u>That Incredible Christian</u>. Christian Publicatioins, 1964. p. 124

[5] Gabriel, Charles H. <u>Glory For Me</u>, 1900

[6] O'Martain, Stormie. <u>The Power of a Praying Parent</u>. Eugene, Oregon: Harvest House, 1995. p.21

[7] "Memorial." <u>Webster's New World Dictionary</u>. 2nd College ed. 1986

[8] Hussey, Jenn?e E. <u>Lead Me To Calvary</u>, 1921

[9] Kizziar, Ti?. (as quoted by Francis Chan in <u>Crazy Love</u>, Colorado Springs: David C. Cook, 2008, p. 93)

[10] Tozer, A. W. <u>The Pursuit of God</u>. Harrisburg, PA: Christian Publications, 1948

[11] Mohr, Jon. <u>Find Us Faithful</u>. Recorded by Steve Green. EMI Christian Music Group, 1987

[12] http://watchman-nee.net/watchman_nee/index.html

[13] Ingram,Chip.<u>God: As He Longs For You To See Him</u>. Grand Rapids: Baker Books, 2004. p.20

[14] Ibid. p. 32

[15] Carroll, Andrew. <u>Grace Under Fire: Letters of Faith in Times of War</u>. Waterbrook Press, 2007

[16] Barna, George. <u>Transforming Children Into Spiritual Champions: Why Children Should Be Your Church's #1 Priority</u>. Ventura: Regal Books, Gospel Light, 2003. p. 78

[17] Henry, Carl F.H. http://home.snu.edu/~hculbert/slogans.htm

[18] "Plumb Line." International Standard Bible Encyclopedia, 1939

[19] Martin, W.C. with John Fornof. <u>Small Town Big Miracle: How Love Came to the Least of These</u>. Focus on the Family, 2007

[20] http://www.adoptuskids.org/for-families/state-adoption-and-foster-care-information/michigan#info

[21] Chambers, Oswald. <u>My Utmost For His Highest</u>. Barbour, Classic ed. 1935. p.239

[22] Hoffman, Elisha A. Is Your All On The Altar, 1905

[23] Moen, Don. God Will Make a Way. Provident Music Distribution, 2003

[24] Tozer, A. W. That Incredible Christian, p. 19

[25] Tozer, A.W. The Knowledge of the Holy. New York: HarperCollins, 1961. p. 60-61

[26] Ingram, Chip. GOD: As He Longs For You To See Him. p. 132

[27] MacDonald, Gail. High Call, High Privilege. Peabody Massachusetts: Hendrikson, 1998. p.2

[28] Alger, Pat, Larry Bastian, and Garth Brooks, Unanswered Prayers. No Fences Album. Universal Music Corp. 1989

[29] Kent, Carol. When I Lay My Isaac Down: Unshakable Faith in Unthinkable Circumstances. NAV Press, 2004

[30] Story, Laura. Blessings, Gleaning Publishing, 2011.

[31] Chapman, Gary. The Five Love Languages: How to Express Heartfelt Commitment to Your Mate. Chicago: Northfield Publishing, 1992. p. 150-158

[32] Barna, George. Grow Your Church From the Outside In: Understanding the Unchurched and How to Reach Them. Gospel Light, 2004

[33] Warren, Rick. Better Together: What on Earth Are We Here For? Lake Forest: Purpose Driven Publishing, 2004. p.45

[34] Lossing, Benson J. Lives of the Signers of the Declaration. 1848, reprinted by Wallbuilder Press, 1995

[35] Jamieson, Fausset and Brown. Commentary Critical and Explanatory of the Whole Bible. 1871

[36] Ramsey, Dave. Financial Peace University. Brentwood, TN: Lampo Group, Inc. 2007

[37] Watts, Isaac. Joy To The World, 1719

[38] Giglio, Louie. How Great Is Our God. Six Step Records, 2009

[39] Moore, Beth. Here and Now . . . There and Then: A Lecture Series on Revelation. Houston: Living Proof Ministries, 2009. Workbook p.89

[40] Rees, Erik. SHAPE: Finding and Fulfilling Your Unique Purpose For Life. Zondervan, 2006

[41] Lucado, Max. Next Door Savior, Thomas Nelson, 2006. p. 148

[42] Kingsbury, Karen and Gary Smalley. Reunion. Redemption Series, Book 5. Carol Stream, IL: Tyndale House 2004. p. 231, 232

[43] C.S. Lewis, The Chronicles of Narnia: Prince Caspian. New York: Scholastic, 1951. p. 142

[44] Anonymous, I Have Decided To Follow Jesus, arr. Lillenas Publishing Co. 1993

[45] Keller, Phillip W. A Shepherd Looks at Psalm 23, Zondervan 2008. p.18

[46] http://www.goodreads.com/author/quotes/838305.Mother_Teresa?page=2

[47] Holmen, Mark.Faith Begins At Home: The Family Makeover with Christ at the Center. Ventura: Regal Books, 2005. p. 48

[48] Tozer, A. W. That Incredible Christian. p 62

[49] Green, Keith, The Live Experience (Special Ed.), Sparrow Records, 2008

[50] Thum, Pam. Life Is Hard (God Is Good). 1997

[51] Moore, Beth. Daniel: Lives of Integrity, Words of Prophecy. DVD Lecture Series. LifeWay Press 2010

[52] Rivers, Francine. Unafraid, Lineage of Grace Series, #5. Tyndale House, 2001

Made in the USA
Lexington, KY
09 October 2012